**Books are to be returned on or before
the last date below**

The farm business

L. G
£2.50 net

The farm business

L. Norman, B.Sc.(Reading), M.Sc.(Wales)
Principal, Hampshire College of Agriculture, Sparsholt, Nr. Winchester
formerly Deputy Principal, Plumpton Agricultural College, Sussex

and

R. B. Coote, N.D.A., Dip. Farm Management (Hons.)
(Seale Hayne)
Assistant Manager, Duke of Norfolk's Farms Department, Arundel, Sussex
formerly Senior Lecturer, Plumpton Agricultural College, Sussex

Longman

LONGMAN GROUP LIMITED
London
*Associated companies, branches and representatives
throughout the world*

© Longman Group Limited 1971

First published 1971

ISBN 0 582 42418 6 cased
ISBN 0 582 42419 4 paper

Printed in Great Britain by
T. and A. Constable Ltd, Edinburgh

Contents

Acknowledgements

We are indebted to the following for permission ro reproduce copyright material:

Ministry of Agriculture, Fisheries and Food for quotations from *Great House Review, 1963, 1964, 1965 and 1967;* tables from *Bridgets E.H.F. Farm Guide, 1968 and 1969;* a table from *High Mowthorpe E.H.F. Farm Guide 1965.* V. Baker of the Agricultural Economics Research Unit for a table, 'Rates of Depreciation of Farm Machinery'. The Agricultural Mortgage Corporation Limited for a table from *A.M.C. Booklet.* The Agricultural Research Council for a quotation from *The Nutrient Requirements of Farm Livestock Number 2, Ruminants.* City and Guilds of London Institute, I. G. Reid and A. K. Giles for examination questions (278 Farm Organisation and Management) from *the written paper of this examination over the past nine years.* Author and Crosby Lockwood Limited for a table from *Fertilisers and Profitable Farming* by Dr Cooke. Author and Crosby Lockwood Limited for a table from *Profitable Farm Mechanization* by C. Culpin. Author for an extract from *Potato Production in Yorkshire – An Economic Study* by E. Dawson. The Fertiliser Manufacturers Association Limited for figures from *Fertilizer Statistics 1967.* Her Majesty's Stationery Office for a table and a graph from *Annual Review and Determination of Guarantees 1970* and selected data from *Agricultural Statistics 1942, '52, '62 and '67; Agricultural Statistics 1959-68; Agricultural Statistics 1934-43, 1956-65 and 1968.* Author for a table from *Farm Planning Handbook* by H. T. W. Kerr. I.C.I. Agricultural Division for a quotation from *Modern Beef Production, Autumn 1969 and Henley Manor Farm.* Authors for a quotation from *The Potato Crop in Kent* by A. M. Middleton and J. P. G. Webster. Milk Marketing Board for a table from the *United Kingdom Dairy Facts and Figures 1969:* a table from the *National Milk Records* 1969; a table from *Report of the Breeding and Production Organisation;* a table and a graph from *Low Cost Production Report 1967.* The Potato Marketing Board for statistics from the *Potato Marketing Board Statistics Bulletins 1968 and Annual Report 1969.* Author for figures from *Farm Business Statistics for the South East Supplement for 1969* by I. G. Reid. Author and the Grassland Research Institute for an extract from *Technical Report No. 3 March 1966* by J. C. Taylor.

Foreword

It is exactly ten years since the publication of C. H. Blagburn's book *Farm Planning & Management* and the first edition of Dexter and Barber's well-used paperback *Farming for Profit*. Since that time, farm business management has undergone a mild revolution and there has been a dramatic increase in the number of adult students receiving formal instruction in the subject. Perhaps because of the pace at which the subject has been developing, these students – and their tutors – have often searched in vain for a contemporary and comprehensive text that would meet their particular needs. Now, with the appearance of this volume – *The Farm Business* – many of them will feel that their search is at an end.

Mr Norman and Mr Coote have arranged their book so as to look first at the farm business as a whole, and then at each of the main farm enterprises. Throughout, and in the 'enterprise' section in particular, the authors have provided a blend of the technical and economic aspects of management that is so frequently missing from farm management literature, and which should be welcomed by their readers.

The authors have made it clear that they have aimed their book essentially at the students and teachers of the 'City and Guilds: 278' syllabus and their selection of past questions and worked answers will be particularly helpful to all concerned. It seems likely, however, that a book which has been so painstakingly compiled – it really does cover a lot of ground in a lot of detail, will be used by students and teachers, at all levels as well as by do-it-yourself farmers and managers.

A. K. GILES,
*Dept. of Agricultural Economics,
Reading University.*

*Chief Examiner City & Guilds of
London Institute: 278 (Farm
Organisation and Management)*

Authors' note

Farm business management is essentially concerned with costs and prices in an industry which is continually changing. Since this text was prepared the agricultural industry has seen changes in both levels of prices and in government policy.

Costs and outputs used as illustrations throughout this book were those currently obtaining at the time of writing and it is appreciated that these will not remain appropriate for very long. These are, however, used with the prime objective of illustrating principles to be applied in assessing the productivity of enterprises and the reader will, therefore, need to keep these *constantly* under review.

L. N.
R. B. C.

Preface

During the 1960s the business approach to farming developed considerably; the Farm Management Association was formed and county Farm Management Study Groups were set up, the National Agricultural Advisory Service appointed Regional Farm Management Advisors and also the number of private farm management consultants, farm recording and secretarial agencies increased. The same period saw the Government establish the Farm Business Recording Scheme providing grants to farmers who kept simple physical and financial records that could be analysed to produce efficiency measures relating to their farm business.

With the wider recognition of business management techniques applied in agriculture, farm business management and related subjects gained a more significant place in college syllabuses. In 1961 the City and Guilds of London Institute started a new Stage III examination course in Farm Organisation and Management for adult students of sound practical background. The demand for this course has increased rapidly in the years following 1961 as the general interest in the business approach to farming gathered momentum.

This rapid spread of interest in farm business management meant that many farmers, farm managers, teachers (and even some advisors) sought some source of business management information that was presented in a logical, systematic way that could be applied to farm case studies and practical management problems in the field.

The need for a textbook of this type became obvious to us while we were both members of Staff of the Plumpton Agricultural College in East Sussex, where we were involved in teaching both technical and management subjects. Those seeking business management information often asked for a textbook that could be recommended and in particular one that covered the City and Guilds Farm Organisation and Management syllabus comprehensively. Furthermore, colleagues who were lecturing in other colleges found themselves for various reasons having to teach this examination subject while they themselves were only trained in technical aspects of agriculture. This inevitably led to enormous variations in the interpretation of the City and Guilds syllabus with some courses failing to deal adequately with farm business management techniques and their realistic application to farm case studies.

This textbook was, therefore, written in the hope of meeting this need and at the same time standardising the approach to the subject of analysis of performance of farm businesses and in planning for future changes.

When planning this work, the need for such a book was also confirmed by the then Senior Examiner in the subject for the City and Guilds of London Institute, Mr I. G. Reid of the Department of Economics, Wye College, whose initial guidance we wish to acknowledge as well as permission to use figures from the Wye College Farm Business Statistics Data (Supplement 1969). We would also like to thank Mr J. Nix of the same Department for permission to quote information from his *Farm Management Pocketbook* (3rd Edition 1969), and for his constructive comments on the final manuscript.

Throughout the writing of this book we have received enthusiastic encouragement from the Principal of Plumpton Agricultural College, Mr N. J. D. Nickalls, M.A., Dip.Agric.(Cantab.), to whom we are most grateful. In addition, we would like to thank colleagues on the Staff of Plumpton Agricultural College for their assistance; in particular Mr K. R. S. Wilson, Lecturer in Agriculture, for checking the text, and Mr H. J. S. Jones, Head of the Poultry Department, for his comments on the Poultry Enterprise Study.

We are grateful to Mr A. K. Giles of Reading University (who is present Senior Examiner in Farm Organisation and Management for the City and Guilds Examination No. 278) for writing a foreword to this book, and to the City and Guilds of London Institute for permission to include past examination questions.

Finally, we wish to acknowledge the great efforts of Madeleine Shepherd and Topsy Saxby in typing and correcting the manuscript. Any errors, however, remain our own responsibility.

Hampshire College of Agriculture *Duke of Norfolk's Farms Department*
Sparsholt *Lee Farm*
Nr. Winchester *Nr. Arundel*
Sept. 1970

1 | Analysis of the farm business

Comparative account analysis

The physical and financial records of the farm business will if properly analysed and interpreted provide essential information upon which to make effective management decisions. Analysis will pinpoint weaknesses in the business which can be corrected and will also highlight satisfactory levels of performance which may be more fully exploited. This is a simple diagnostic technique which involves the calculation of a number of 'efficiency factors', which can be compared with similar measures calculated for comparable farms.

When beginning to analyse a farm business the various physical and financial records of the farm should be examined. Some farmers may keep a very comprehensive set of records, while others may keep very few. Whatever the case, all farmers will have a farm trading account relating to each year's trading, since this is necessary for taxation purposes. Inevitably, there is always some delay between the end of the trading year and the actual completion of the trading account. Because of this, it can be argued that the information it contains is out of date. While this cannot be denied, the trading account, if properly presented, does contain useful information which can be analysed to produce a number of meaningful efficiency measures which can be of value to the farmer. In the short term these measures may assist him in the management and running of his farm; in the longer term they will be of value in the planning and organisation of his business.

A farm trading account normally covers a twelve months' period which may be the calendar year from 1 January to 31 December, the financial year from 5 April to 4 April of the following year, or the farming year from 1 October through to 30 September. In fact, any period can be covered and the trading year can begin at any time. In reality though, the starting date is often influenced by the major enterprises on the farm or simply the month of the year the farmer started farming.

Layout of a farm trading account

The basic layout of the farm trading account covers four sections:
(*i*) Opening valuation of livestock, crops and cultivations, and stores on the farm at the beginning of the trading year.

(*ii*) The items of actual expenditure in the farm business during the year.
(*iii*) The sums of revenue (receipts) received by the farm business during the trading year.
(*iv*) The closing valuation at the end of the year of the same items as in the opening valuation.

FARM TRADING ACCOUNT

(*i*) Opening valuation	£	(*iii*) Receipts	£
e.g. Dairy cows		e.g. Sales of milk	
Sheep		Sales of cull cows	
Wheat		Sales of wheat	
Feedingstuffs		Cereal deficiency	
(in store)		payment	
Fuel and oil		etc.	
etc.			
(*ii*) Expenditure		(*iv*) Closing valuation	
e.g. Feedingstuffs		e.g. Dairy cows	
Replacement		Sheep	
heifers		Wheat	
Wages		Feedingstuffs	
Fuel and oil		(in store)	
etc.		Fuel and oil	
		etc.	

Profit _____	Loss _____
£ Balancing total	£ Balancing total

Compiling a farm trading account

The information set out in a farm trading account comes from financial records and an annual valuation. The trading account must reflect a true picture of trading by the farm during the year and, therefore, it may be necessary to adjust items of expenditure and receipts to allow for any debtors and creditors which were outstanding both at the beginning and at the end of the trading year.

When the trading account is made up the items comprising the opening valuation and expenditure (shown on the left-hand side of the account) are totalled, and those items comprising receipts and closing valuation (shown on the right-hand side of the account) are also totalled. The figure at the bottom of each side of the account is made to balance and the balancing figure is called 'profit' if it falls on the left and 'loss' if it falls on the right.

Standardising the farm trading account

The final profit figure shown in a farm trading account will be influenced by a number of factors beside the success or otherwise of the farm itself.

Some farms are saddled with certain charges, e.g. interest on overdrafts or mortgages on capital borrowed to purchase land. Some farms will carry a rent charge while others may be owned with no rent paid. Some farms may be 'staffed' by family labour for which no allowance may be made in the trading account. It can be seen, therefore, that considerable variations in the final 'profit' figure between similar farms may result, depending on the number of these items included in the trading account. This being the case, it is necessary to standardise the farm trading account before valid inter-farm comparisons can be made. The following adjustments should be made when standardising a farm trading account:

1. Remove from the trading account the following items:
   (*a*) interest charges (e.g. interest on bank overdraft),
   (*b*) mortgage payments,
   (*c*) capital repayments (e.g. private lenders),
   (*d*) tithe payments,
   (*e*) expenditure on owner/occupier's repairs.
2. If the farm is owned then impute a rent to the farm – a figure representative of rents actually being paid by similar farms in the area should be used.
3. A sum should be included in the account for any family labour used on the farm, i.e. actual manual effort as opposed to managerial effort. This should be done to ensure that family manual labour, for which no actual payment is made, is set against the 'profit' of the farm business.

The 'profit' figure which now results from the standardised trading account can be compared with the figure in the standardised accounts of similar farms; also any efficiency measures calculated from the standardised accounts can be similarly compared.

Information in the standardised trading account

The standardised trading account itself reveals the following information:
   (*i*) The 'profit' or 'loss' during the trading year which can, genuinely, be compared with that of other similar farms.
   (*ii*) The amount of tenant's capital invested in the farm at the beginning and end of the year (excluding that in farm machinery, car and tenant's fixtures).
   (*iii*) The details, and totals, of actual expenditure and receipts of the farm over the trading year.

The need for analysis of the standardised trading account

The information shown by the farm trading account, even after standardisation, is very limited and reveals little that can be used either by a farmer to correct faults which are present in his farm business or to plan future changes for his farm. The information does not indicate which enterprises are doing well and which ones are not 'pulling their own weight'. In fact, the good enterprises may be 'masking' the poor ones quite unbeknown to the farmer. The expenditure and receipts sections indicate purchases and sales, respectively, but do not indicate actual inputs and outputs of the farm.

It is obvious, therefore, that some further detailed investigation of the standardised trading account will be necessary and efficiency measures must be calculated which can be compared with standards of achievement of similar farms in the same area.

Analysis of a farm business

When beginning the analysis of a farm business it is most important to visit the farm and meet the farmer or manager so as to be familiar with background details of the business. In this case details of a 300-acre farm have been constructed and a detailed analysis of this farm business will be followed through. The background information is as follows:

Littledown Farm is situated in the south-east of England and has some medium loam soil with some clay and some chalk land. The farm grows cereals and potatoes and carries a herd of Friesian dairy cows and followers and a flock of Kerry Hill ewes crossed with a Suffolk ram, which graze leys and permanent pasture. There is also a Large White × Landrace pig enterprise producing weaners for sale. The farm employs three full-time men, plus the farmer with occasional help from his wife. Details of the cropping and stocking of the farm over three years are given in the following tables:

Table 1.1   *Littledown Farm: Acres of crops – years 1, 2 and 3*

	Year 1	Year 2	Year 3
Winter wheat	25	20	30
Spring barley	60	65	65
Maincrop potatoes	15	15	15
Leys	150	150	140
Permanent pasture	50	50	50
Total	300	300	300

Conservation of grass in Year 2:
       Hay: 8 acres
       Silage: 52 acres
Reseeding: 38 acres of ley reseeded in Year 2
Approximately half the barley grain is fed and half sold.
All the wheat is sold off the farm.

Table 1.2   Littledown Farm: Livestock numbers – year 2

Enterprise	Opening number	Purchased	Transferred in	Died	Sold	Closing number	Average No. Year 2
Dairy cows	70	3	16	—	17	72	71
Ewes	148	40	—	3	33	152	150
Rams	4	1	—	—	1	4	4
Sows	20	7	—	1	8	18	19
Boars	1	—	—	—	—	1	1
Dairy young stock							
0–1 year	16	—	—	—	—	16	16
1–2 years	16	—	—	—	—	16	16
2-2½ years	8	—	—	—	—	8	8
Sucking pigs	50	—	—	—	—	48	—

Table 1.3   Littledown Farm: Machinery, car and tenant's fixtures valuations at beginning and end of year 2

	Opening valuation	Purchases (new)	Trade in	Closing valuation	Depreciation
	£	£	£	£	£
Machinery	5500	Tractor 1000	Tractor 450	5260	790
Car	400	—	—	350	50
Tenant's fixtures	1000	150	60	940	150

Trading account for Littledown Farm

A trading account for this farm for Year 2 from 1 January to 31 December is presented in Table 1.4. From the trading account it will be seen that no family labour is included in the expenses section of the account; a rent is included since the farm is a tenant farm and some bank interest charges are also included.

Standardisation of the trading account for Littledown farm – year 2

The trading account must be standardised before efficiency measures can be calculated from it and compared with those for other farms. The adjustments that are necessary are shown in Table 1.5.

Net farm income is the income to the farm as a result of the year's trading. Management and investment income is the reward to the farmer for the management of his farm business and the return on the tenant's capital

Table 1.4   Littledown Farm: Farm Trading Account – Year 2. 1 January – 31 December

OPENING VALUATION	£	£	RECEIPTS	£	£
Dairy cows	6300		Dairy cows	935	
Dairy young stock	2240		Calves	644	
Sheep	1244		Milk	8032	
Breeding pigs	550		Sheep	137	
Other pigs	150		Lambs	1315	
Wheat	1242		Sows	120	
Barley	1200		Pigs	1920	
Straw	90		Wool	200	
Potatoes	2025		Wheat	1127	
Forage	950		Barley	651	
Tillages	960		C.D.P. wheat	276	
F.Y.M.	150		C.D.P. barley	300	
Fertilisers	30		Potatoes	2430	
Seeds	20		Produce to house (milk)	30	
Fuel and oil	25		Private use of car	50	
Concentrate feed	123		Private use of electricity	30	
Sundries	100		Fertiliser subsidy	400	
		17399	Rental value of farmhouse	75	
EXPENDITURE			Sundries	20	
Heifers	390				18692
Sheep	425				
Pigs	245				
Concentrate feed	3429		CLOSING VALUATION		
Hay	120		Dairy cows	6480	
Straw	180		Dairy young stock	2240	
Seed	991		Sheep	1276	
Fertilisers	2405		Breeding pigs	490	
Sprays	174		Other pigs	135	
Wages and Nat. Insurance	2750		Wheat	945	
Casual labour	95		Barley	1440	
Machinery:			Straw	78	
Depreciation	840		Potatoes	2250	
Fuel, oil and electricity	420		Forage	1038	
Repairs, tax and insurance	660		Tillages	1030	
Contract	180		F.Y.M.	150	
Deprec. on tenant's fixtures	150		Fertilisers	60	
Repairs to tenant's fixtures	45		Seed	60	
Vet., med. and livestock sundries	705		Fuel and oil	17	
Haulage	40		Concentrate feed	97	
Water	40		Sundries	90	
Rent	2300				17876
Rates	100				
Office, gen. ins. and prof. chgs.	450				
P.M.B. levy	45				
Bank interest	520	17699			
'Profit'		1470			
		36568			36568

Table 1.5   Adjustments necessary to standardise the trading account

	£
Trading Account 'Profit' (see Table 1.4)	1470
ADJUSTMENTS	
Add back—bank interest	520
∴ Net farm income =	1990
Subtract—value of family manual labour: farmer	700
wife	250
∴ Management and Investment Income	1040

employed in the farm business, since an allowance has been made for the manual labour put into the farm during the year by the farmer and his family.

Systematic analysis of the standardised farm trading account

In analysing the standardised trading account for Littledown Farm a logical sequence should be followed which can be applied to any farm trading account. A set of analysis worksheets has been drawn up and these will be followed through sheet by sheet.

If a number of farm accounts are to be analysed it is suggested that the seven worksheets, which are presented in the following pages, be stencilled and used in each case, since the design of the worksheets is such that they can be used in the analysis of any farm trading account.

Worksheet 1

Description of the farm

On Worksheet 1 (Table 1.6) details of the farm can be set out for reference purposes. The information under 'classification of farm' cannot be filled in at this stage but must be left until enough information has been revealed about the farm to enable it to be classified for comparative purposes with similar farms.

Worksheet 2

Calculation of gross output

The standardised farm trading account can now be taken and various efficiency measures calculated from it. These will be defined as the analysis progresses:

Gross Output. The gross output of an enterprise is the receipts of that enterprise (including value of products consumed) adjusted for valuation changes less purchases of livestock replacements. The total gross output of the farm is the total of the enterprise gross outputs, plus sundry receipts.

When calculating gross output it is not sufficient to take just the sales of a particular enterprise – obviously consideration must also be given

Table 1.6   Worksheet 1

Farm account analysis Work sheet

Farm reference   Littledown Farm

Year ending   31st December, Year 2

Full-time workers (incl. farmer)   4

Acreage   300 acres

Part-time workers   Wife

Tenant/~~Owner-Occupier~~

Date visited

System of farming   Cereals, dairy cows and followers and sheep on leys and permanent pasture.

Maincrop potatoes and sows producing weaners for sale.

Soil types   Medium loam, clay, and chalk land.

Buildings   Yard and parlour.
Farrowing house and Sow yard.
Dutch barn.

Livestock   Friesian cows.
Kerry Hill ewes × Suffolk ram.
Large White sows × Landrace boar.

Cropping		Acres	%
Cereals	W. Wheat	20	6·6
	Sp. Barley	65	21·7
Permanent pasture		50	16·7
Leys		150	50·0
Other crops: Maincrop potatoes		15	5·0
Total		300	100·0

Classification of farm
Farm type   Milk and Arable

Acreage size group   250–450 acres

Comparative data reference   *Farm Business Statistics for S.E. England* (1969 Supplement), pp. 18/19*

Comparative data year   'Average' Group 1967–68
'Premium' Group 1965–68

* Published by Wye College (Dept. of Economics) (University of London), near Ashford, Kent

to products in store (valuations), products consumed and livestock purchases.

A simple formula for calculating gross output is:

gross output = (receipts + closing valuation) −
(opening valuation + expenditure)

For example pig enterprise in Year 2 as shown in the trading account:

$$\text{Gross output of pigs} = \left\{ \begin{array}{l} \text{£120 culls (receipts)} \\ \text{£1 920 weaner sales} \end{array} \right\} + \left\{ \begin{array}{l} \text{£490 closing valuation sows} \\ \text{£135 closing valuation suckling pigs} \end{array} \right.$$

$$\textit{Minus} \qquad \begin{array}{l} \text{£245 gilts purchased} \\ \text{(livestock replacements)} \end{array} + \left\{ \begin{array}{l} \text{£550 opening valuation sows} \\ \text{£150 opening valuation pigs} \end{array} \right.$$

$$= £1 720$$

Worksheet 2 (table 1.7) clearly shows how each enterprise in the farm trading account is taken and its gross output calculated.

The total gross output of the farm is obtained by totalling each enterprise gross output including sundry receipts. The total gross output of this farm in Year 2 was £17 228.

What does gross output measure? The gross output of an enterprise reflects the total output of that enterprise irrespective of the costs of producing that output. The total gross output of the whole farm similarly reflects total output and will be influenced by:

(*i*) Yield of the various enterprises
(*ii*) Price per unit received for products
(*iii*) Scale of the enterprises
(*iv*) Valuation changes.

'Inputs' or cost items

When calculating levels of 'inputs' or costs for the farm business during the trading year, opening and closing valuations of these items which can be stored must not be ignored. It must be remembered that the expenditure section of the trading account indicates actual expenditure during the year; in this analysis the actual amount used in the farm business must be calculated. For instance, a farmer may actually purchase £500 worth of fertiliser in a trading year, but only use £150 worth of it in that trading year, leaving £350 of fertiliser in the closing valuation. Clearly, it follows that only £150 worth of fertiliser 'input' went into the farm business in that particular trading year and not the whole £500 worth which was purchased.

Table 1.7   Worksheet 2

Analysis of financial information for year 2

		1	2	3	4	5	6	7
		Opening val'n	Expenditure	Sub-total (1+2)	Receipts	Closing val'n	Sub-total (4+5)	Gross output (6−3)
		£	£	£	£	£	£	£
OUTPUT—inc. relevant subsidies	D. Cows ⎫	6300	390		935	6480		
1. Cattle(inc.Dairy) DYS ⎭		2240		8930	644	2240	10299	1369
2. Milk (plus milk used in house)					8032 30			8062
3. Sheep and wool		1244	425	1669	sheep 137 lambs 1315 wool 200	1276	2928	1259
4. Poultry and eggs (plus home consumed)								
5. Pigs		550 sows 150 sucklers	245	945	120 sows 1920 weaners	490 sows 135 sucklers	2665	1720
6.								
7.								
Total livestock (1–7)								(12410)
8. Cereals (inc. C.D.P.)	Wheat 1242 Barley 1200		—	2442	1127+276 651+300	945 1440	4739	2297
9. Straw		90	180	270	—	78	78	−192
10. Potatoes		2025	—	2025	2430	2250	4680	2655
11. Forage and tillage	Forage 950 Tillage 960 FYM 150		120	2180		1038 1030 150	2218	+38
Total crops (8–11)								(4798)
12. Misc. subsidies (excl. fertilisers)								
13.								
14.								
15.								
16.								
17. Sundry receipts					20		20	20
18.								
Total miscellaneous (12–18)								(20)
Gross Output								17228

In calculating levels of inputs from the information in the trading account the expenditure on an item is taken and adjusted in the following ways:

(a) for valuation changes;
(b) any subsidies (e.g. fertiliser subsidies) which are deducted from the cost price;
(c) the rental value of the farmhouse should be deducted from the total farm rent because the function of the analysis is to indicate the performance of the farm itself;
(d) a rental value should be imputed to the farm if the farmer is an owner occupier;
(e) manual labour of the farmer and his family should be evaluated and included;
(f) private use of car, fuel and electricity is deducted from the relevant cost items;
(g) sales of resources of purchased commodities, e.g. feedingstuffs, should be credited back to the appropriate item.

A simple formula for calculating levels of inputs is:

$$\text{Input} = \left\{ \begin{array}{l} \text{opening} \\ \text{valuation} \end{array} + \text{expenditure} \right\} - \left\{ \begin{array}{l} \text{closing} \\ \text{valuation} \end{array} + \text{receipts} \right\}$$

For the input of fertiliser on the farm in Year 2 the calculation would be as follows:

Input of fertilizer = (£30 opening valuation + £2405 expenditure)
Minus (£60 closing valuation + £400 receipts i.e. subsidy)
= £1975

Worksheet 3 clearly shows how each input item is calculated from information in the trading account.

Variable costs

Input (cost) items on Worksheet 3 (Table 1.8) have been grouped: those numbered 20 to 28 inclusive are called variable costs. These are the cost items which alter with any change in scale of enterprise and can be easily allocated to particular enterprises, e.g. feed, seed, fertilisers, casual labour, contract work, sprays, vet. and medicine. These costs are also referred to as allocatable or direct costs.

Fixed costs

Those cost items numbered 29 to 42 are referred to as fixed costs. These are the cost items which do not alter very much with small changes in scale of an enterprise and are items which are not easily allocated to particular enterprises, e.g. machinery costs, labour and general overhead costs.

Table 1.8   Worksheet 3

Inputs	1 Opening val'n	2 Expendi- ture	3 Sub- total (1+2)	4 Receipts	5 Closing val'n	6 Sub- total (4+5)	7 Total input (3−6)
	£	£	£	£	£	£	£
20. Bought feed	123	3 429	3 552	—	97	97	3 455
21. Bought seed	20	991	1 011	—	60	60	951
22. Fertilisers (net of subsidies)	30	2 405	2 435	400	60	460	1 975
23. Casual labour		95	95				95
24. Contract work		180	180				180
25. Sprays		174	174				174
26. Vet and medicines		705	705				705
27. Other miscellaneous *Variable* costs	Haulage P.M.B. levy	40 45	85				85
28. Total variable costs							(7 620)
29. Regular labour paid		2 750 Wife 250	3 000				3 000
30. Regular labour unpaid		700	700				700
31. Machinery deprec.*		840	840	20*		20	820
32. Fuel and oil* Electricity and coal	25	420	445	15* 30*	17	62	383
33. Machinery repairs, tax and insurance*		660	660	15*		15	645
34.							
35. Rent (less rental value of farm house)		2 300	2 300	75		75	2 225
36. Rates (less rates on house)		100	100				100
37. Repairs to tenant's fixtures		45	45				45
38. Office expenses and general insurance		450	450				450
39. Depreciation on tenant's fixtures		150	150				150
40. Other miscellaneous overheads	100	Water 40	140		90	90	50
41.							
42. Total fixed costs							(8 568)
Total costs (Variable and fixed)							16 188

Management and Investment Income £	1 040
Family Manual Labour	950
Net Farm Income	1 990

* Less private use, e.g. car, electricity, fuel and oil

It is most important to note that with large changes in scale then fixed costs will alter substantially – for example, if a farmer increases his dairy herd by three cows the relevant variable costs will automatically increase, i.e. feed, veterinary and medicines and forage variable costs, but the fixed cost items of labour, machinery, etc., will not alter. If, however, the farmer increased his dairy herd by 30 cows then the fixed costs' items of labour, machinery, buildings etc., will change as well as the relevant variable costs.

Management and investment income and net farm income

When the total input for the farm has been calculated (the sum of the variable and fixed costs' items) and is subtracted from the total gross output of the farm (as calculated on Worksheet 2 (Table 1.7)), the resulting margin is called Management and Investment Income (M.I.I.). This represents the reward to the farmer for the management of his farm and the income on the tenant's capital invested in the farm business – whether or not borrowed capital is involved. In summary the calculation is:

M.I.I. = gross output − total inputs (variable and fixed costs)
£1040 = £17228   − £16188

In calculating management and investment income the manual work of family labour was evaluated and included in the fixed costs. Sometimes it is difficult to calculate the value of family labour (called unpaid labour), and therefore a useful measure which eliminates this problem is called Net Farm Income (N.F.I.). This is simply the income to the farm for the year's trading, and completely ignores any family labour.

N.F.I. can be calculated as follows:

N.F.I. = gross output − total inputs (excluding unpaid manual labour)
or N.F.I. = M.I.I. *plus* unpaid manual labour.

Points to observe when calculating gross output and inputs

The following suggestions may prove useful when analysing a trading account to produce gross output and inputs:

1. Sundry cost items often appear in a trading account. These should be classified as variable or fixed costs if possible: otherwise regard them as fixed costs.

2. When working through the trading account and extracting data to be entered on the worksheets, tick off each item on the trading account when it has been extracted on to the analysis worksheet. This will help when checking later, especially if an error has been made.

3. If the total inputs (Worksheet 3 (Table 1.8)), when subtracted from the gross output (Worksheet 2), do not give the right answer for the farm's management and investment income, then each column on Worksheets 2 and 3 (Table 1.7, 1.8) can be totalled down the worksheet, thus giving a built-in check – a quick way to spot arithmetical errors.

Worksheet 4

Forage acres

In order to measure and compare the efficiency of stocking density of this farm with that of similar farms it is necessary to calculate the total amount of forage used in the farm business during the trading year in terms of both acres and 'acres equivalent' of grass and forage. Obviously, it would be inadequate to take only acres of grass in any calculation which was to measure efficiency of forage used on the farm. Three basic terms are commonly used:

1. *Farm forage acres*. These are the total acreage of crops grown for feeding to livestock (excluding cereals).
2. *Forage acres*. These are the farm forage acres after allowing the acreage equivalents for hay sales, forage valuation changes and let and rented keep.
3. *Adjusted forage acres*. These are forage acres plus an acreage allowance for bought hay and other bulk feeds. The average output per acre of forage is taken as £30 and can be assessed as follows:

   Average yield per acre of hay – say three tons at £10 per ton = £30.

   Average yield per acre of silage – say eight tons at £3·75 per ton = £30.

In the calculation of adjusted forage acres for the 300-acre farm on Worksheet 4 the acreages of grass (leys 150, permanent pasture 50) are taken and the 'acreage equivalents' of purchased forage as well as those of the opening and closing valuation of forage are calculated taking £30 equal to one acre.

The resulting adjusted forage acres for the farm in Year 2 is 201·1 acres.

Tenant's capital

This is the amount of capital invested in the farm by the farmer as a tenant and embraces his investments in livestock, crops, cultivations, stores, machinery, car and tenant's fixtures. By definition, items of landlord's capital – land, buildings, etc. – are not included, even if the farmer is an owner/occupier.

In the analysis of the farm business and the subsequent calculation of efficiency measures relating to the business, the average level of investment in tenant's capital during the trading year must be known. To get this the average of the opening and closing valuations of tenant's capital items is taken as shown in Table 1.9. The livestock, crops and cultivations and stores items are taken from the opening and closing valuations of the trading account. The level of investment in machinery, car and tenant's fixtures are extracted from the farmer's capital account – details are given in Table 1.3.

In Worksheet 4 (Table 1.10) the average level of investment in tenant's

Table 1.9   Littledown Farm: details of tenant's capital items

Tenant's capital items	Opening valuation £	Closing valuation £
Livestock:		
Dairy cows	6300	6480
Dairy young stock	2240	2240
Sheep	1244	1276
Breeding pigs	550	490
Other pigs	150	135
Total	10484	10621
Crops and cultivations:		
Wheat	1242	945
Barley	1200	1440
Straw	90	78
Potatoes	2025	2250
Forage	950	1038
Tillage	960	1030
FYM	150	150
Total	6617	6931
Stores:		
Fertilisers	30	60
Seeds	20	60
Fuel and oil	25	17
Concentrate feed	123	97
Sundry stores	100	90
Total	298	324
Machinery	5500	5260
Car	400	350
Tenant's fixtures	1000	940
Total	6900	6550
Total Tenant's capital	24299	24426

Table 1.10   *Worksheet* 4

Adjusted forage acreage

		£	Acres or 'Acres equivalent'
Grass	Leys		150·0
	Permanent pasture		50·0
Kale			—
Rape			—
Feed roots			—
Rented keep			—
Purchased forage $\frac{£}{30}$		£120 ÷ 30	4·0
Opening valuation of forage, i.e., hay, silage, etc. $\frac{£}{30}$		£950 ÷ 30	31·7
Total Available			235·7
Less			
Let keep			
Closing valuation of forage, i.e., hay, silage, etc. $\frac{£}{30}$		£1038 ÷ 30	[34·6
Forage sold $\frac{£}{30}$			
Adjusted forage acres			201·1

Tenant's capital

	Opening Valuation	Closing Valuation	Average of O.V. & C.V.	£/acre avg. valn.	Comparative data £/acre	
					Avg.	Premium
Livestock	10484	10621	10553	35·2	19·7	19·8
Crops and cultivations	6617	6931	6774	22·6	13·1	12·0
Stores	298	324	311	1·0	2·6	2·1
Machinery	5500	5260	5380	17·9⎫	⎫	⎫
Car	400	350	375	1·3⎬22·4	17·6	17·1
Tenant's fixtures	1000	940	970	3·2⎭	⎭	⎭
Total	24299	24426	24363	81·2	53·0	50·9

capital per acre for each item is given and this can be compared with the levels of investment on similar farms. The information for the comparative farm groups cannot be entered on Worksheet 4 until this farm has been classified for comparative purposes, and this will be done on Worksheet 5 (Table 1.11).

Worksheet 5

Calculations of comparative data

Worksheet 5 (Table 1.11) is designed for the calculation of certain standards for the acres of crops and head of livestock on the farm; these standards will be compared later with similar ones for comparable farms. The number of acres for each crop enterprise and the average number of head of livestock for the year is taken. If a weighted monthly average of livestock numbers is available then this should be used.

Calculation of standard output

Standard output is in fact the gross output that the farm would have obtained during the trading year if average levels of yields and prices had been realised. Data is available from University Departments of Agricultural Economics indicating levels of standard output for farm enterprises in their respective areas. In calculating standard output only sale crops are included; the output of feed crops is accounted for in the value of livestock products derived from them.

When standard outputs have been calculated for each enterprise, these can be totalled to give the total farm standard output and this will be used as a basis for calculating certain efficiency factors which will be discussed later.

Grazing livestock units

Most farms will carry various types of grazing livestock which need to be reduced to a common denominator for comparison purposes with other farms, since head of cows, ewes and dairy young stock, as such, cannot be added together. The measure used is the grazing livestock unit which permits a comparison of like with like. In the calculation of grazing livestock units all types of grazing animals are equated to the cow which is equal to 1·0 grazing livestock unit. The ratios used are based on the estimated annual starch equivalent requirement of each class of stock, e.g. 1 cow = 1·0 g.l.u., 1 ewe = 0·2 g.l.u. (i.e. 5 ewes = 1 cow). Grazing livestock units will be used to calculate certain efficiency measures later in the analysis.

Standard man-days

A standard man-day represents eight hours of work by an adult male worker. Standards are available indicating the 'average' amount of labour required for particular farm enterprises, e.g. one cow (parlour milked) requires 9·0 standard man-days per year.

Table 1.11 Worksheet 5

Calculations of standard output, livestock units, standard man-days and tractor hours

	Opening number	Closing number	Av. no.	Standard output		Grazing livestock units		Standard man days		Tractor units	
Bulls				—		1·0		4		5	
Dairy cows:											
(a) parlour milked	70	72	71	125	8875	1·0	71·0	9	639	8	568
(b) cowshed milked				125		1·0		12		8	
Beef cows				—		1·0		2		5	
Calves to weaning (no. produced)											
(a) single suckled				40		—		—		—	
(b) multiple suckled				25		—		1		1	
Other calves under 6 months	8	8	8	25	200	0·1	0·8	2	16	1	8
Other cattle:											
½–1 year (no. produced)	8	8	8	12	96	0·2	1·6	1	8	3	24
1–2 years	16	16	16	25	400	0·6	9·6	2	32	4	64
Over 2 years	8	8	8	25	200	0·8	6·4	2·5	20	5	40
Barley beef				70		—		3		5	
15/18 month beef (6–18 mths)				45		0·7		3		5	
Rams	4	4	4	—		0·2	0·8	0·75	3	1	4
Ewes	148	152	150	8	1200	0·2	30·0	0·75	112	1	150
Other sheep over 6 months				5		0·2		0·5		1	
Sows	20	18	19	75	1425	—		5	95	2·5	47
Boars	1	1	1	—		—		2	2	0·5	1
Other pigs over 2 months				28		—		0·75		1·3	
Laying birds (intensive) per 100				200		—		10		4	
Pullets per 100 no. produced				70		—		5		1	
Broilers per 100 no. produced				20		—		1		—	
Turkeys per 100 no. produced				120		—		10		2	
Standard L/S output					12396						

	Acres		Standard output		man-days		Tractor work units
Wheat for sale	20·0	40	800	2	40	10	200
Barley for sale	32·5	35	1138	2	65	10	325
Oats for sale		33		2		10	
Feed and seed corn	32·5			2	65	10	325
Potatoes	15·0	130	1950	15	225	28	420
Feed roots (cut)				12		30	
Feed roots (folded)				3		10	
Kale (grazed)				1		8	
Beans and Peas	30			2·5	90	7	
Oilseed rape	25			3		10	
Fallow				1		8	
Hay and silage 1 cut	60·0			1·5	90	10	600
Hay and silage 2 cut				2·0		15	
Total grass acreage	200·0			0·5	100	3	600
Direct reseeding	38·0			1·0	38	8	304

Standard crop output		3888
Total standard output		16284
Total grazing L/S units	120·2	
Total standard man days	Total 1550 +15% 233	1783
Total tractor work units		3680

Standard output		%
Milk	8875	54·5
Sheep/cattle	2096	12·9
Pigs and poultry	1425	8·7
Arable	3888	23·9
Total S.O.	16284	100·0

Classification – Milk and arable farms group

Using these standard man-day figures it is possible to calculate the total theoretical labour requirement of a farm in standard man-days. Normally 15 per cent is added to this total to cover general farm work which is not allocated to particular enterprises, e.g. hedging, ditching, general farm maintenance and holidays.

When the total theoretical labour requirement for the farm has been calculated this can be compared with the number of man-days actually available on the farm and can also be used to calculate other efficiency measures relating to the utilisation of labour. This concept of standard man-days was also used in helping to determine size of business in the Small Farm (Business Management) Scheme, 1965, the Small Farm Scheme, 1959, and for grants for amalgamations.

Tractor units

A tractor unit represents one hour of tractor work (note no additional 15 per cent is added). As in the case of standard man-days, standards are available indicating the average number of tractor hours required per year by each farm enterprise – see Worksheet 5 (Table 1.11).

When the total farm requirement of tractor units has been calculated this figure is later used as a basis upon which certain efficiency measures relating to machinery are calculated.

Classification of Littledown Farm for comparison purposes

If inter-farm comparisons are to be valid, then it is important to ensure that like is compared with like. The farm in question must be compared with farms in the same area having similar enterprises and a similar acreage. The basis of classification of farms for comparative purposes is the percentage standard output from the main enterprises. Now that standard output has been calculated for each enterprise on Littledown Farm it is a simple exercise to calculate the percentages from the main enterprises.

The comparative data that will be used in this exercise is that published by Wye College (University of London) for farms in the south-east of England.[1] This data will have been collected from a large number of farms in the south-east and has been grouped according to farm type.

In the case of Littledown Farm 54·5 per cent of its standard output came from milk and 23·9 per cent from arable crops, therefore, this farm is best compared with those grouped as milk and arable farms, since the percentage of the total standard output arising from milk and arable is greater than 75 per cent (it is in fact 78·4 per cent on this farm).

Now that the farm has been classified a reference for the group can be completed at the bottom of Worksheet 1 (Table 1.6). (This was left unexplained

[1] *Farm Business Statistics for South-East England* (1969 Supplement), Wye College (University of London), Department of Economics

when Worksheet 1 was referred to since it is only at this stage of the analysis that the section can be completed.) Obviously this is useful when checking through various case studies where a set of worksheets similar to these are being used.

It is now possible to enter the levels of investment of tenant's capital items for 'average' and 'premium' farms in the table of tenant's capital in Worksheet 4.

Worksheet 6

Comparative analysis of financial information

Now that the farm trading account has been standardised and the farm classified on a basis of standard output, it is possible to compare the farm's achievements (both physical and financial) with the group of comparative farms from the Wye College data. Worksheet 6 (Table 1.13) brings together, in summary form, the financial efficiency measures for this farm and the comparative data for 'average' and 'premium' farms is also presented. The grouping of farms as 'average' and 'premium' refers to their profitability (as measured by their return on tenant's capital); the 'premium' farms being the top 50 per cent in each group.

In Worksheet 6, two new measures appear – these are:

1. *Net output.* If comparison between farms is limited to gross output it would be impossible to compare farms which grow their own feedingstuffs with those that buy in feedingstuffs. Also it would not be possible to compare farms which buy in seed with those that save their own seed. Therefore, net output is used since it permits a more effective comparison.

Net output is gross output minus purchased feed and seed.

A simple example will illustrate this point – see Table 1.12.

Table 1.12   Calculation of gross and net output for two similar farms

	Farm A	Farm B
Number of cows	50	50
Output per cow (£)	120	120
Total gross output from cows (£)	6000	6000
Acres – cereals	50	50
Output per acre	30	30
Total cereal sales (£)	1500	nil
Total farm gross output (£)	7500	6000
Purchased feedingstuffs (£)	2000	500
Net output (£)	5500	5500

B

Table 1.13   *Worksheet* 6

Summary of financial information

| | Total | Results £ per acre | | |
	This farm	This farm	Group* Average	Group* Premium
Cattle	1369	4·6	6·8	7·4
Sheep and wool	1259	4·2	0·6	0·7
Pigs	1720	5·7	—	—
Poultry and eggs				
Milk	8062	26·9	24·7	24·4
Total livestock	(12410)	(41·4)	(33·4)	(34·7)
Cereals (inc. straw)	2105	7·0	12·7	12·4
Fruit and hops				
Other crops—potatoes	2655	8·8	1·2	0·9
Total crops	(4760)	15·9	(13·9)	(13·3)
Forage and tillage valn. changes	38	0·1	0·2	−0·5
Other receipts	20	0·1	0·5	0·7
Gross Output	17228	57·4	48·0	48·2
Net output	12822	42·7	38·1	38·8
Expenditure Bought feed	3455	11·5	8·3	8·0
Bought seed	951	3·2	1·6	1·3
Total (Bought feed and seed)	4406	14·7	(9·9)	(9·3)
Fertilisers	1975	6·6	3·9	3·5
Casual labour	95	0·3	0·5	0·5
Contract work	180	0·6	0·6	0·5
Misc. variable costs	964	3·2	2·0	1·7
(28) p. 3. *Total variable costs*	7620	25·4	16·9	15·5
Total Gross Margin	9608	32·0	31·1	32·7
Regular labour (paid)	3000	10·0	9·1	9·7
Regular labour (unpaid)	700	2·3	1·7	1·1
Machinery depreciation	820	2·7	2·8	2·8
Fuel and oil	383	1·3	1·4	1·6
Mach. repairs, tax and insurance	645	2·2	2·2	2·8
Rent and rates	2325	7·8	4·8	3·5
General overhead costs	695	2·3	3·4	2·9
(42) p. 3. *Total fixed costs*	8568	28·6	25·4	24·4
Total inputs (fixed plus variable costs	16188	54·0	42·3	39·9
Management and investment income	1040	3·4	5·7	8·3
Net farm income	1990	6·6	7·2	9·4

* The comparative data for this farm is taken from the group 'milk and arable farms' pp. 18/19, *Farm Business Statistics for South East England* (1969 Supplement), Wye College (University of London).

Both Farms A and B are similar; they are the same size; they have the same combination of livestock and crops and the same levels of yields are obtained. Farm A sells all his cereals and buys in his feedingstuffs. Farm B feeds all his own cereals.

It is quite clear that it would be very unfair to compare these two farms on the basis of gross output since although each farm is producing the same value of produce, one sells his cereals and the other feeds his cereals and buys in a little protein supplement.

If a comparison between these two farms is limited to gross output, then Farm A looks far more efficient than Farm B, but when feed costs are deducted to give net output then the real output of these two farms is found to be the same. Therefore, net output is a more realistic and reliable measure of output than gross output.

2. *Total gross margin.* Total gross margin is simply the total gross output of the farm less the total variable costs. Gross margins will be covered thoroughly later when gross margins will be calculated for each of the farm enterprises.

Worksheet 7

Further measures of efficiency for the farm business

As a result of the calculations made earlier in the analysis further measures of efficiency can now be calculated for the farm business relating to intensity of the business and yields, livestock performance and forage productivity, efficiency of labour and machinery and finally level of investment and return on that investment.

A. MEASURES OF YIELD AND INTENSITY

1. *Standard output (S.O.) per acre*

This efficiency measure indicates the expected level of Gross Output (G.O.) for the farm at average levels of yields and prices.

2. *System index*

This index provides a guide to the general level of intensity of the farm compared with similar farms. It is calculated by expressing the standard output per acre over the group average standard output per acre as an index:

$$\text{System index} = \frac{\text{Farm S.O. per acre}}{\text{Group S.O. per acre}} \times 100.$$

Table 1.14 Worksheet 7		This farm per acre	Group Reference	
			Average per acre	Premium per acre
A. Measures of yields and intensity				
1. *Standard Output per acre*				
$\dfrac{\text{Total Standard Output}}{\text{Acreage}}$		$\dfrac{16\,284}{\div 300}$ 54·3	46	46
2. *System index*				
$\dfrac{\text{S.O.} \times 100}{\text{Group avg. Standard Output}}$		$\dfrac{54\cdot3 \times 100}{\div 46}$ 118	—	—
3. *Yield index*				
$\dfrac{\text{G.O.} \times 100}{\text{S.O.}}$		$\dfrac{1\,722\,800}{\div 16\,284}$ 106	104	104
B. Measures of livestock performance and forage production				
1. *Grazing L/S output per adj. forage acre*	Cattle £1369			
$\dfrac{\text{G.O. from Milk+Cattle+Sheep}}{\text{Adjusted forage acres}}$	Sheep £1259 Milk £8062	53·2	72	72
	£10690 ÷ 201			
2. *Adjusted forage acres/G.L.U.*				
$\dfrac{\text{Adjusted Forage Acres}}{\text{Av. G.L.U.'s}}$		$\dfrac{201\cdot1}{\div 120\cdot2}$ 1·67	1·9	1·85
3. *Milk yield per cow*		53450 ÷ 71 753	829	871
4. *Milk sales per cow*		8062 ÷ 71 113·5	146	144
5. *Margin of milk sales over concentrates*	Milk 8062			
$\dfrac{\text{Total Milk Sales-Value Concs. to cows}}{\text{Av. no. Cows}}$	2402* 5660 ÷ 71	80	102	122
C. Measures of labour and machinery efficiency				
1. *Labour cost/100 std. man days*	Labour Paid 3795 £3000			
$\dfrac{\text{Labour cost} \times 100}{\text{Total S.M.D.}}$	Unpaid £700 Casual £95 £3795	$\div 1783$ 213	272	263

2. *Machinery costs × 1 000 tract. hrs.*		Total	per 1000 tractor hours		
$\dfrac{\text{Machy. costs} \times 1\,000}{\text{Total tractor hrs.}}$					
Repairs, tax+Ins.		645	175	211	269
Fuel and electricity		383	104	140	158
Contract		180	49	62	54
Depreciation		820	223	272	267
Total mach. cost		2028	551	685	748

3. *N.O./£100 labour*		This farm	Average	Premium
$\dfrac{\text{N.O.} \times 100}{\text{Labour cost (inc. unpaid)}}$		$\dfrac{12822}{\div 3795}$ 338	351	352
4. *N.O./£100 machinery costs*				
$\dfrac{\text{N.O.} \times 100}{\text{Machinery cost}}$		$\dfrac{12822}{\div 2028}$ 632	555	515
5. *N.O./£100 Lab. & machy. costs*	Machinery £2028	12822 ÷ 5823		
$\dfrac{\text{N.O.} \times 100}{\text{L \& M costs}}$	Labour £3795 £5823	220	210	206
D. Measures of investment and return				
1. *Tenant's capital per acre*		$\dfrac{24363}{\div 300}$ 81·2	53·0	50·9
2. *Return on tenant's capital*				
$\dfrac{\text{M.I.I.} \times 100}{\text{Tenant's capital}}$		$\dfrac{104000}{\div 24363}$ 4·3%	10%	16%

[* See Table 1.20]

In effect, it is what this farm would produce per acre at standard yields and prices compared with the comparative group farms' output per acre at standard yields and prices. If the farm standard output per acre is greater than the group standard output per acre then the system index will be greater than 100 (and vice versa).

3. *Yield index*

This index gives a guide to the actual farm's yields and prices compared with average 'standard' levels of yields and prices for the area.

$$\text{Yield index} = \frac{\text{Gross Output}}{\text{Standard Output}} \times 100.$$

The index can be split into a crop and livestock yield index:

$$\text{Crop index} = \frac{\text{Gross Output (crops)}}{\text{Standard Output (crops)}} \times 100$$

$$= \frac{4760}{3888} \times 100$$

$$= 122$$

$$\text{Livestock yield index} = \frac{\text{Gross Output (livestock)}}{\text{Standard Output (livestock)}} \times 100.$$

$$= \frac{12410}{12396} \times 100$$

$$= 100$$

B. MEASURES OF LIVESTOCK PERFORMANCE AND FORAGE PRODUCTION

1. *Grazing livestock output per adjusted forage acre*

This measure indicates the actual gross output from livestock utilising forage and, therefore, indicates the production from adjusted forage acres.

2. *Adjusted forage acres per grazing livestock unit*

This measure shows the stocking rate on the adjusted forage acres of the farm.

3. and 4. *Milk yield per cow and milk sales per cow*

The total milk yield in Year 2 was 53450 gallons and, therefore, the average yield and average value of milk sold per cow over the year can be calculated as shown.

5. Margin of milk sales over concentrates

This measure is easily calculated and is a quick guide to the efficiency of concentrate usage in milk production.

Note: When interpreting these results all the measures relating to livestock performance should be considered together, since checking one measure in isolation can be very misleading.

C. MEASURES OF LABOUR AND MACHINERY EFFICIENCY

Labour and machinery costs per acre (see Worksheet 6 (Table 1.13))

When assessing labour and machinery efficiency in a farm business, the levels of labour and machinery costs per acre can be examined and compared with those for similar farms.

Any such comparisons must be interpreted with great care since labour costs are affected by intensity of enterprises.

1. Labour cost per 100 standard man-days

2. Machinery cost per 1000 tractor hours

These measures of labour and machinery efficiency, based on the theoretical requirement of the farm for each resource, overcome the weakness of the per acre measures. The theoretical requirements for labour and machinery were calculated in Worksheet 5 as standard man-days for labour and tractor units for machinery. Although it may be argued that the 'standard' figures used in these calculations do not suit all farms, the calculation does provide, nevertheless, a useful comparison between similar farms.

3. Net output per £100 labour

4. Net output per £100 machinery

5. Net output per £100 labour and machinery

So far labour and machinery have been assessed only on a physical basis in relation to costs. The most important consideration will be their financial productivity in terms of real and net output per unit cost. Although these measures, based on net output, are easy to calculate it must be remembered that many factors combine together to influence the net output of a farm. If net output is high enough, poor physical use of labour and machinery may be justified. If, however, there is a poor level of net output these measures will be low when compared with similar farms, yet the physical efficiency of the labour and machinery on the farm may be satisfactory. The reason for calculating net output per £100 labour and machinery together is that these resources can, to some extent, replace one another, i.e. machines can replace men and costs of one may be high if costs of the other are low.

From the above measures of labour and machinery efficiency it is apparent that each measure has its limitations and deals with separate aspects of labour and machinery efficiency within the business. It is essential, therefore, that any conclusions made on the labour and machinery efficiency on a farm should not be drawn until all the measures have been considered together. Any conclusions drawn from just one or two measures in isolation may give a false impression of the facts.

D. MEASURES OF LEVEL OF INVESTMENT AND RETURN ON CAPITAL

1. *Tenant's capital per acre* (*see also Worksheet 4* (*Table 1.10*))

This is the measure of the tenant's level of investment in the farm business. The details of the average levels of investment in 'productive' items, e.g. livestock, and 'non-productive' items, e.g. machinery, were calculated in Worksheet 4, where the average of the opening and closing valuations were taken from the trading account and the details of machinery, car and tenant's equipment were extracted from the farm's capital account.

2. *Return on tenant's capital*

This is calculated by expressing the management and investment income as a percentage of the tenant's capital. The percentage return on tenant's capital is the yield obtained from the tenant's capital invested in the farm business. Since an allowance was made for family manual labour, this is a measure which can be fairly compared with likely returns from investments in any form of business, whether in farming or otherwise.

Trading account analysis: Conclusions

Now that the farm trading account has been systematically analysed, it is very apparent that all the efficiency measures that have been calculated relate to the farm business as a whole and not to individual enterprises. It is necessary, therefore, to examine each enterprise on the farm individually since the good ones may be 'masking' the poor ones – a fact that would not have been identified in the trading account analysis. The analytical technique that will be used for the examination of individual enterprises is that of gross margin analysis, and when the gross margins for each of the farm enterprises have been calculated, then the results of both the trading account analysis and the gross margins' analysis will be interpreted giving a complete picture of the strengths and weaknesses of the farm business.

Gross margin analysis

The gross output for each individual enterprise is calculated and its variable costs deducted, leaving a margin which is called the 'gross margin'. Fixed costs items are completely ignored in this form of analysis and do not enter into it.

For each individual enterprise on Littledown Farm gross margins are to be calculated. For the livestock enterprises gross margins are usually calculated for the same 12 months' period as is covered by the trading account. The information required to calculate gross margins for the livestock enterprises will, therefore, be found in a particular year's trading account, and by examining the physical and financial records relating to that year's trading.

The crops enterprise gross margins will need to be calculated for a particular *crop year* so that the gross margins of each particular crop is found. The information that will be required for crop gross margins may well bridge two, or even three years' trading accounts. Figure 1.a for the winter wheat crop on Littledown Farm illustrates this point.

Figure 1.a clearly shows how some variable costs items fall into Year 1 as well as Year 2, and the receipts items for grain fall into Year 3. It will be necessary then to have information from different years' trading accounts before the final gross margin figures can be calculated for the winter wheat

Figure 1.a Information needed to calculate gross margin for winter wheat crop harvest harvested in Year 2

Trading account year	Technical operations for winter wheat	Variable cost incurred	Receipts received
Year 1 October	Winter wheat sown	seed Seedbed fertilizer	
Year 2 April	Top dressing of fertilizer	Nitrogen fertilizer	
May	Spray with herbicide	Herbicide	
August/ September	Harvest and store		
Year 3 April			Grain sales
June/July			Storage incentive and cereal deficiency payments
September			Final deficiency payment

and spring barley crops harvested in Year 2. The same is true of the potatoes which were not sold until Year 3. It should be noted that farms whose trading account ends in the summer may encounter a further complication with Cereal Deficiency Payments (C.D.P.) for barley and oats, since part is paid in January following the crop harvest, and the final payment is made the following autumn.

It follows, then, that information will probably be needed from two or even three years' trading accounts when calculating crop gross margins. If gross margin calculations are being done for a crop at a time when the product is still in store, then the valuation of the crop in store should be taken, together with an estimate of any other likely receipts, e.g. Cereal Deficiency Payment, that may be payable.

Crops enterprise gross margins

A breakdown of the variable costs for crops and forage on Littledown Farm is given in Table 1.15. The winter wheat crop is the only crop where information on variable costs has had to be extracted from the Year 1 trading account. Some of the variable costs in the Year 2 trading account do, however, relate to the winter wheat crop which will be harvested in Year 3 – see Table 1.15; this crop will, of course, have been sown in the autumn of Year 2.

The fact that variable costs items have been extracted from the previous year's trading account for gross margin analysis does not alter the final profit figure for the Year 2 trading account. This is so, because these items will have been included in the tenant right (forage and tillage) valuation made at the end of Year 1, and appear, therefore, in the opening valuation of the Year 2 trading account.

It should be noted that the totals' column in Table 1.15 provides a check against the total inputs of each of these variable costs items which were calculated in Worksheet 3.

In calculating the gross margins for the crop enterprises on Littledown Farm it is assumed that the calculations are being done fairly soon after the end of Year 2 (which ended on 31 December). At the end of Year 2 all of the wheat harvested in Year 2 was still in store (valued in the closing valuation, see Table 1.16); some of the barley harvested in Year 2 had already been fed by 31 December of Year 2, but the remainder was in store (valued in the closing valuation, see Table 1.16). Of this amount of barley in store at the end of Year 2, some will be fed and the rest sold in Year 3. All the potatoes lifted in Year 2 were in store at the end of Year 2 and appear in the closing valuation.

Since some of these crop products were still in store at the end of Year 2 it will be necessary to estimate the Cereal Deficiency Payment which will not be received until later for the wheat and barley; similarly, the storage incentive payment for the wheat and barley to be sold and the Home Grown

Table 1.15 Littledown Farm: Allocation of all variable cost items from the Year 2 trading account, and other relevant variable costs for crops' enterprises harvested in Year 2

Harvest year			Year 2 harvest			Year 3 harvest	Total
Crop enterprise	Winter wheat	Spring barley	Main Crop potatoes	Forage	Unallocated variable costs	Winter wheat	Variable costs from year 2 tr. a/c
	£	£	£	£	£	£	£
Variable costs from year 2 trading account							
Seeds	—	146	525	190	—	90	951
Fertiliser (seedbed)	—	260	225	—	—	90	⎫
Fertiliser (top dressing)	50	—	—	1350	—	—	⎬ 1975
							⎭
Sprays	20	49	105	—	—	—	174
Casual labour	—	—	95	—	—	—	95
Contractor	—	—	80	—	100	—	180
P.M.B. levy	—	—	45	—	—	—	45
Haulage	—	—	—	—	40	—	40
Relevant variable costs from year 1 trading account							
Seed	60	—	—	—	—	—	—
Fertiliser (seedbed)	60	—	—	—	—	—	—

Table 1.16 Littledown Farm: The spring barley and winter wheat crop harvested in Year 2

Spring barley

Acres grown	65 acres
Yield per acre	32 cwts
Total yield	104 tons
Amount fed by 31 Dec.–end of Year 2	32 tons at £20/ton = £640
Remainder in closing valuation–Year 2 trading account	72 tons at £20/ton = £1440
Total	104 tons at £20/ton = £2080
Amount to be fed in Year 3:	35 tons
Amount to be sold in Year 3:	37 tons
Total (= Amount in Closing Valuation)	72 tons

Winter wheat

Acres grown	20 acres
Yield per acre	35 cwts
Total yield	35 tons
All in closing valuation of Year 2 trading account	£945 (35 tons at £27/ton)

Cereals Authority's (H.G.C.A.) bonus payment for the forward contracting of the wheat and barley to be sold in Year 3 must be estimated at this stage and details are given in Table 1.17.

Table 1.17 Littledown Farm: Estimates necessary to calculate Gross Output for crops enterprises harvested in Year 2

	Winter wheat	Spring barley
Acres (Year 2 harvest)	20	65
C.D.P. (inc. storage incentive)	£227 (35 tons at £6·5/ton)	£357 (65 acres at £5·5/acre)
H.G.C.A. – forward contract bonus	£14 (35 tons at £0·4/ton)	£15 (37 tons at £0·4/ton)
Grain from Year 2 harvest fed before 31 December of Year 2	—	£640* (32 tons at £20/ton)

* See also Table 1.19

The details of the calculations of the crop enterprise gross margins for crops harvested in Year 2 are shown in Table 1.18.

Table 1.18 Littledown Farm: Gross margins for crops harvested in Year 2

Crop enterprise acres grown (Year 2)	Winter wheat 20	Spring barley 65	Main crop potatoes 15
	£	£	£
Gross output			
Sales	—	—	—
Fed on farm	—	640	—
Closing valuation			
(Year 2 tr. a/c.)	945	1 440	2 250
*C.D.P. (estimated)	227	357	—
*H.G.C.A. bonus (estimated)	14	15	—
Total	1 186	2 452	2 250
Variable costs†			
Seed	60	146	525
Fertilisers	110	260	225
Sprays	20	49	105
Casual labour	—	—	95
Contractor	—	—	80
P.M.B. levy	—	—	45
Total	190	455	1 075
Gross margin	996	1 997	1 175
Gross margin per acre	49·8	30·7	78·3

* See Table 1.17   † See Table 1.15

Livestock enterprise gross margins

Firstly, the forage variable costs should be allocated between the various grazing livestock enterprises. Unless very detailed records are kept so that forage seed, fertiliser and spray costs can be allocated to each grazing enterprise, the allocation should be done on a basis of livestock units (details of which were given on Worksheet 5 (Table 1.11)). The details of the forage costs for Littledown Farm were given in Table 1.15 – seed £190, fertilisers £1350 = £1540. To allocate this on a basis of grazing livestock units, the number of grazing livestock units in each enterprise should be calculated (these were calculated in Worksheet 5 (Table 1.11)).

$$
\begin{aligned}
&\text{Dairy cows – Average no. } 71 \times 1\cdot0 && = 71\cdot0 \text{ g.l.u.}\\
&\text{Dairy young stock – Average no:}\\
&\qquad\text{under six months } 8 \times 0\cdot1 = 0\cdot8\\
&\qquad\quad\tfrac{1}{2}\text{–1 year } 8 \times 0\cdot2 = 1\cdot6\\
&\qquad\quad 1\text{–2 years } 16 \times 0\cdot6 = 9\cdot6 \quad\Big\}\ 18\cdot4\\
&\qquad\quad 2\text{–}2\tfrac{1}{2}\text{ years } 8 \times 0\cdot8 = 6\cdot4\\
&\text{Sheep} \qquad\qquad\qquad\qquad 154 \times 0\cdot2 = 30\cdot8\\
&\qquad\qquad\qquad\qquad\qquad\qquad\qquad\quad \overline{120\cdot2}
\end{aligned}
$$

The forage variable cost of £1540 can now be allocated using the following formula:

$$
\frac{\text{Total forage cost}}{\text{Total no. of g.l.u. on farm}} \times \text{No. of g.l.u. in an enterprise}
$$

		£
1. Dairy cows	$\dfrac{£1540}{120\cdot2 \text{ g.l.u.}} \times 71$ g.l.u. (cows)	= 910
2. Dairy young stock	$\dfrac{£1540}{120\cdot2 \text{ g.l.u.}} \times 18\cdot4$ g.l.u. (D.Y.S.)	= 236
3. Sheep	$\dfrac{£1540}{120\cdot2 \text{ g.l.u.}} \times 30\cdot8$ g.l.u. (sheep)	= 394
		$\overline{£1540}$

In addition to the allocation of forage variable costs to the various grazing livestock enterprises the following information – see Tables 1.19 and 1.20 – is also required, in addition to that in the trading account for Year 2 (Table 1.4).

The gross margin calculations for the livestock enterprises on Littledown Farm are presented in Table 1.21.

For comparison with the crops enterprises the gross margin per forage acre should be calculated for the grazing livestock enterprises. Details of these calculations for each of the grazing livestock enterprises on Littledown Farm are given in Table 1.22.

Table 1.19   Littledown Farm: Details of transfers between enterprises

(*i*) *Livestock*
   (*a*) Sixteen heifer calves transferred from the dairy herd to the dairy young stock enterprise, valued at £10 each = £160.
   (*b*) Sixteen down-calving heifers transferred from the dairy young stock enterprise back to the dairy herd, valued at £80 each = £1 280.

(*ii*) *Barley fed to livestock*
   The following amounts of barley were fed to livestock:

	Dairy cows		Sheep		Pigs		Total	
	tons	£	tons	£	tons	£	tons	£
Barley (harvested Year 2) (valued at £20/ton)	19	380	3·25	65	9·75	195	32	640
Barley (harvested Year 1) (valued at £20/ton)	16	320	2·75	55	8·25	165	27	540
Total	35	700	6·0	120	18·0	360	59	1 180

Table 1.20   Littledown   Farm: Allocation   of   variable   costs   to   livestock enterprises

Enterprise	Dairy cows £	Dairy young stock £	Sheep £	Pigs £	Total £
Purchased feed	2402	408	57	588	3455
Vet. and medicines	497	50	48	110	705

Note on calculating livestock gross margins
The opening and closing valuations of all livestock enterprises should be included as shown in the calculations in Table 1.21, since changes in these valuations will influence gross output and consequently gross margin.

Reconciliation of the enterprise gross margins with the total farm gross margin
The total of the individual enterprise gross margins will not necessarily balance with the total farm gross margin shown on Worksheet 6 (Table 1.13), which comprises total gross output less total variable costs.
   Enterprise gross margins must, however, be reconciled with the total farm gross margin and a balance drawn up to prove that the enterprise gross margins have been correctly calculated, and that nothing has been overlooked.
   A table should be drawn up – see Table 1.23 – to show that all items included in calculating farm gross output can be accounted for, and a further table – see Table 1.24 – can be used to balance the variable costs items between the enterprises.

Table 1.21   Littledown Farm: Livestock enterprise gross margins

	Dairy cows	Dairy young stock	Sheep	Pigs
	£	£	£	£
Gross output				
Closing valuation	6480	2240	1276	625
Sales: culls	935	—	137	120
progeny	644	—	1315	1920
products	milk 8062	—	wool 200	—
Transfers out	160	1280	—	—
Sub-total	16281	3520	2928	2665
Less Opening valuation	6300	2240	1244	700
Livestock purchases	390	—	425	245
Transfers in	1280	160	—	—
Sub-total	7970	2400	1669	945
Gross output	8311	1120	1259	1720
Variable costs				
Purchased feed	2402	408	57	588
Homegrown grain	700	—	120	360
Vet. and medicines	497	50	48	110
Total	3599	458	225	1058
Gross margin (excluding forage costs)	4712	662	1034	662
Less Forage costs	910	236	394	—
Gross margin after forage	3802	426	640	662
Avg. stock number per Enterprise	71 cows	18·4/livestock units	150 ewes	19 sows
Gross margin per head (excluding forage costs)	£66·4/cow	£36/livestock unit	£6·9/ewe	£34·8/sow
Final gross margin per head (after deducting forage costs)	£53·5/cow	£23·1/livestock unit	£4·3/ewe	£34·8/sow

Table 1.22 Littledown Farm: Gross margin calculations per forage acre for grazing livestock

$$\frac{\text{Gross margin}}{\text{per forage acre}} = \frac{\left\{\begin{matrix}\text{Enterprise} & -\text{allocated}\\ \text{gross margin} & \text{forage costs}\end{matrix}\right\} \times \begin{matrix}\text{Total no. of}\\ \text{g.l.u's. on farm}\end{matrix}}{\begin{matrix}\text{No. of g.l.u's.}\\ \text{in enterprise}\end{matrix} \times \begin{matrix}\text{Total no. of forage}\\ \text{acres on farm}\end{matrix}}$$

$$\text{Dairy cows} = \frac{(£4712 - £910) \times 120\cdot2 \text{ g.l.u's.}}{71\cdot0 \text{ g.l.u's.} \quad \times 201\cdot1 \text{ fge. acres}}$$

$$= £32\cdot0/\text{acre}$$

$$\begin{matrix}\text{Dairy young}\\ \text{stock}\end{matrix} = \frac{(£662 - £236) \times 120\cdot2 \text{ g.l.u's.}}{18\cdot4 \text{ g.l.u's.} \quad \times 201\cdot1 \text{ fge. acres}}$$

$$= £13\cdot84/\text{acre}$$

$$\text{Sheep} = \frac{(£1034 - £394) \times 120\cdot2 \text{ g.l.u's.}}{30\cdot8 \text{ g.l.u's.} \quad \times 201\cdot1 \text{ fge acres}}$$

$$= £12\cdot4/\text{acre}$$

Total farm gross margin = Total farm gross output − Total variable costs

£9 608 = £17 228 − £7 620

The next stage in reconciling the gross margins is to total the individual gross margins for all the enterprises costed. This will give the total enterprise gross margin which must now be adjusted in order to balance with the total farm gross margin.

The necessary adjustments have been made in Table 1.25 and are enumerated as follows:

1. Sundry receipts must be added since they do not occur in the enterprise gross margins.

2. Any crops' costs which have occurred in the previous year's trading account and have been used in calculating enterprise gross margins must be added back.

3. Crops from the previous year which were in store at the beginning of the trading year may have been sold. Any gains above the opening valuation figure should be added back, and any losses subtracted. C.D.P.'s and bonuses relating to the previous year's crops should be included in this calculation.

4. Forage and tillage valuation changes must be added if positive or deducted if negative.

5. Not all the variable costs shown on the trading account can be directly allocated amongst the enterprises. Any unallocated variable costs should, therefore, be deducted.

Table 1.23 Littledown Farm: Allocation between enterprises of farm gross output from Year 2 trading account

	Year 1 crops	Year 2 crops — Barley	Year 2 crops — Wheat	Year 2 crops — Potatoes	Dairy cows	Dairy Y.S.	Sheep	Pigs	Unallocated	Transfers	Total
	£	£	£	£	£	£	£	£	£	£	£
1. Cattle	—	—	—	—	249	1120	—	—	—	—	1369
2. Milk	—	—	—	—	8062	—	—	—	—	—	8062
3. Sheep and wool	—	—	—	—	—	—	1259	—	—	—	1259
4. Poultry and eggs	—	—	—	—	—	—	—	—	—	—	—
5. Pigs	—	—	—	—	—	—	—	1720	—	—	1720
6.											
7.											
Total livestock					8311	1120	1259	1720			12410
8. Cereals	Wheat * 161 / Barley * 291	2080	945	—	—	—	—	—	—	−540 † / −640 ‡	2297
9. Straw	—	—	—	—	—	—	—	—	−192	—	−192
10. Potatoes	405 *	—	—	2250	—	—	—	—	—	—	2655
11. Forage tillage	—	—	—	—	—	—	—	—	38	—	38
Total crops	857	2080	945	2250					−154	−1180	4798
12.–16.											
17. Sundry receipts	—	—	—	—	—	—	—	—	20	—	20
Total misc.	—	—	—	—	—	—	—	—	20	—	20
Gross output	857	2080	945	2250	8311	1120	1259	1720	−134	−1180	17228

* Gains upon realisation of o.v.—see page 39.
† Barley from Year 1.
‡ Barley from Year 2.

Table 1.24 Littledown Farm: Allocation of variable costs from Year 2 trading account

	Year 2 crops			Year 3 crops wheat	Dairy cows	Dairy Y.S.	Sheep	Pigs	Forage	Unallocated	Total
	Barley	Wheat	Potatoes								
	£	£	£	£	£	£	£	£	£	£	£
20. Pchsd. feeds	—	—	—	—	2402	408	57	588	—	—	3455
21. Pchsd. seeds	146	50	525	90	—	—	—	—	190	—	951
22. Fertilisers	260	—	225	90	—	—	—	—	1350	—	1975
23. Casual labour	—	—	95	—	—	—	—	—	—	—	95
24. Contract	—	—	80	—	—	—	—	—	—	100	180
25. Sprays	49	20	105	—	—	—	—	—	—	—	174
26. Vet and med.	—	—	—	—	497	50	48	110	—	—	705
27. Miscellaneous P.M.B. levy	—	—	45	—	—	—	—	—	—	—	45
haulage	—	—	—	—	—	—	—	—	—	40	40
Total *v.* costs	455	70	1075	180	2899	458	105	698	1540	140	7620

Table 1.25 Littledown Farm: Reconciliation of enterprise gross margins with total farm gross margin

ENTERPRISE GROSS MARGINS	£	£	£	TOTAL FARM GROSS MARGIN From Worksheet 6 (*Table 1.13*)	£
Wheat			996		9 608
Barley			1 997		
M/c. potatoes			1 175		
Dairy cows			3 802		
Dairy young stock			426		
Sheep			640		
Pigs			662		
Total enterprise gross margins			9 698		
Plus:					
1. *Sundry receipts*		20			
2. *Crops costs occurring in Year 1 account*					
Wheat seed	60				
Wheat ferts.	60				
		120			
3. *Gains on o.v. relating to Year 1 crops**					
Wheat	161				
Barley	291				
Potatoes	405				
		857			
4. *Forage and tillage valuation change*		38			
			1 035		
			10 733		
Less:					
5. *Unallocated* v. *costs*					
Contract	100				
Haulage	40				
		140			
6. *Estimated C.D.P.*					
Wheat	227				
Barley	357				
		589			
Estimated H.G.C.A. Bonus		29			
7. *Crop costs relating to Year 3*					
Wheat seed	90				
Wheat ferts.	90				
		180			
8. *Valuation change straw*		192			
			1 125		
			9 608		9 608

* See facing page.

6. Deduct any subsidies, deficiency payments or bonuses which have been estimated for the purpose of calculating enterprise gross margins but which have not actually occurred in the trading account.
7. Any crop costs which have occurred in the trading account, but which relate to crops sown for the following harvest year, should be deducted.
8. Valuation changes occurring in stores or produce, e.g. straw, which are not included in the enterprise gross margins should be added if positive and deducted if negative.

Table 1.25 clearly shows how the reconciliation of enterprise gross margins should be presented and made to balance mathematically with the total farm gross margin figure. In the analysis of other farm businesses other items might appear which must not be ignored in striking this balance, e.g. receipts for keeper sheep (agistment receipt); it follows, therefore, that each farm business must be examined carefully to ensure that all items are considered, otherwise reconciliation will be impossible.

Interpretation of the trading account analysis, comparative data and gross margin analysis

Now that the trading account for Year 2 has been analysed and efficiency measures are available, together with comparative data from similar farms and gross margins for each of the enterprises on the farm, an interpretation of all these measures should be made. The analytical work so far has really been routine – a job which a competent clerk can easily do, but now the more interesting aspects of farm business analysis come to light in the interpretation of these results.

It is recommended that a logical sequence be followed when undertaking an interpretation of data from a farm business analysis. The sequence shown in Figure 1.b has been drawn up for this purpose.

Interpretation of the results of the analysis of Littledown Farm business

Following the suggested scheme of interpretation of the analysis results (see Figure 1.b), the first measure to examine is the return on tenant's capital.

---

* *Gains upon realisation of Year 1 crops in store at 1 January*

	Wheat		Barley		Potatoes	
	£	£	£	£	£	£
o.v.	1242	—	1200	—	2025	—
C.D.P.	—	276	—	300	—	—
Value fed	—	—	—	540	—	—
Sales	—	1127	—	651	—	2430
Gain	161	—	291	—	405	—
Total	1403	1403	1491	1491	2430	2430

Figure 1.b   Suggested   scheme   for   systematic   interpretation   of   efficiency measures

Standardise account and compare results with those achieved by similar farms, i.e. Group Comparison.

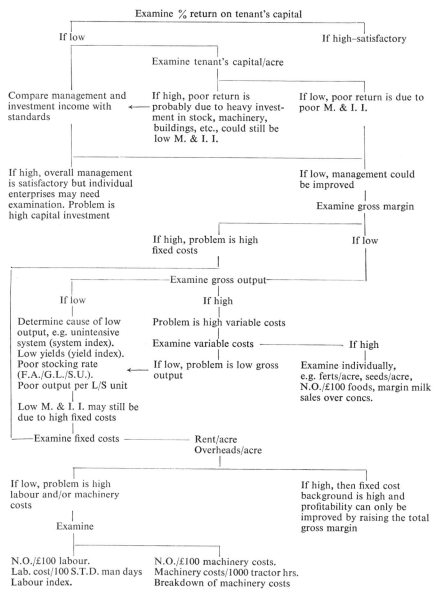

Examine % return on tenant's capital

If low   If high–satisfactory

Examine tenant's capital/acre

Compare management and investment income with ← probably due to heavy invest- poor M. & I. I. standards

If high, poor return is probably due to heavy investment in stock, machinery, buildings, etc., could still be low M. & I. I.

If low, poor return is due to poor M. & I. I.

If high, overall management is satisfactory but individual enterprises may need examination. Problem is high capital investment

If low, management could be improved

Examine gross margin

If high, problem is high fixed costs   If low

——Examine gross output——

If low

Determine cause of low output, e.g. unintensive system (system index). Low yields (yield index). Poor stocking rate (F.A./G.L./S.U.). Poor output per L/S unit

Low M. & I. I. may still be due to high fixed costs

If high

Problem is high variable costs

Examine variable costs ————— If high

If low, problem is low gross ← output

Examine individually, e.g. ferts/acre, seeds/acre, N.O./£100 foods, margin milk sales over concs.

——Examine fixed costs ————— Rent/acre
Overheads/acre

If low, problem is high labour and/or machinery costs

Examine

If high, then fixed cost background is high and profitability can only be improved by raising the total gross margin

N.O./£100 labour.
Lab. cost/100 S.T.D. man days
Labour index.

N.O./£100 machinery costs.
Machinery costs/1000 tractor hrs.
Breakdown of machinery costs

Return on tenant's capital. At 4·3 per cent this is unsatisfactory compared with the return of 10 per cent obtained by the group of 'average' farms and 16 per cent by the group of 'premium' farms.

This low percentage return is due to two main factors:

1. The management and investment income achieved by the farm of £1040 (= £3·4 per acre) is low compared with the 'average' farms at £5·7 per acre and 'premium' farms at £8·3 per acre.
2. A high level of investment in tenant's capital of £81·2 per acre compared with £53·0 per acre on 'average' farms and £50·9 per acre on 'premium' farms.

Both the low M.I.I. and the high level of investment in tenant's capital auger together to give the poor percentage return on tenant's capital.

Total gross margin. The total gross margin per acre is £32·0 which is just above that of the 'average' group figure of £31·1 per acre and just below the 'premium' group figure of £32·7 per acre. Gross margin is the result of a high gross output per acre (£57·4 per acre) and very high variable costs, £25·4 per acre compared with £16·9 per acre on 'average' farms and £15·5 per acre on 'premium' farms.

Fixed costs. While the total gross margin is just above average, the level of total fixed costs is £3·2 per acre above the 'average' group of farms and, therefore, the low management and investment income is primarily due to the high fixed costs which will therefore need further investigation.

Total gross output. The high gross output is due to a very intensive combination of enterprises; this is indicated by the system index of 118, showing that if average levels of prices and yields had been obtained then a gross output of £54·3 per acre would have resulted. However, the actual gross output of the farm was £57·4 per acre indicating that the overall level of performance was slightly above average – as shown by the yield index of 106 compared with the figure of 104 on both 'average' and 'premium' farms. But, if the crops and livestock enterprise outputs are examined separately and a yield index calculated for each, then the livestock yield index is 90·9 and the crops yield index is 122 – indicating a fundamental weakness in the livestock enterprise.

Further investigations into the main weaknesses of the business

Although the net farm income of £1990 (= £6·6 per acre) would appear high enough to give a reasonable living for the farmer and his wife, the percentage return on the tenant's capital which he has invested in the farm business is less than he could obtain by secure investment outside the farm. It is essential now that a fuller examination be made of the apparent weaknesses of this farm business with a view to rectifying them.

Level of fixed costs. In making a more detailed investigation of fixed costs it can be seen that machinery costs are below average both on an acreage basis and also on the basis of the farm's theoretical machinery requirements in tractor hours. Both net output per £100 machinery and net output per £100 labour and machinery are better than the comparative group figure and although this is partly due to a marginally superior net output, it may safely be concluded that machinery costs are not excessive.

General overhead costs are also below average, leaving rent and rates at £3 per acre above average as the main fixed costs' offender, followed by labour costs which are £1·5 per acre higher than the figure for the comparative group of farms.

Rent and rates are unlikely to be controllable by management, so labour costs are now examined more closely for any signs of excess which could be trimmed back.

Labour costs on a per-acre basis are £1·5 per acre higher than those on the 'average' and 'premium' groups of farms. Labour costs in relation to theoretical labour requirements expressed as standard man-days, are below average while the net output per £100 labour cost is slightly poorer than the figure for the comparative group farms.

These measures indicate that while labour costs are justified on a physical basis, the efforts involved are not producing a sufficiently high financial output.

It appears, therefore, that this farm has a high fixed costs background, which is unlikely to be reduced without drastic re-organisation. Any improvement in profitability is more likely to result from increasing the total gross margin of the farm against this high fixed costs' background rather than by concentrating on the reduction of the fixed costs themselves.

If there is any scope for increasing the total gross margin of the farm this will be indicated by closer examination of the individual enterprise gross margins of the farm.

Crop enterprise gross margins. Gross margins for each of the farm's crop enterprises confirm that these enterprises are making a satisfactory contribution to the farm business – see Table 1.26.

The gross margin per acre for the winter wheat crop is above the premium figure, the spring barley gross margin per acre is above average and the gross margin for the potato crop is a bit below average due, to some extent, to a large amount of casual labour and contract having been included in the variable costs – see Table 1.18. From Table 1.26 it can be seen that levels of variable costs are about average for each enterprise; the average gross margins for barley and potatoes result from only average levels of gross output.

Table 1.26   Littledown Farm: Gross margins of crop enterprises for Year 2 with comparative figures

Enterprise	Winter wheat			Spring barley			Main crop potatoes		
	This farm	Aver- age	Pre- mium	This farm	Aver- age	Pre- mium	This farm	Aver- age	Pre- mium
	£	£	£	£	£	£	£	£	£
Gross output per acre	59·3	47·8	55·1	37·7	37·5	42·7	150·0	158	195
Variable costs per acre	9·5	9·5	9·5	7·0	8·0	8·0	71·6	70	70
Gross margin per acre	49·8	38·3	45·6	30·7	29·5	34·7	78·3	88	125

Livestock enterprise gross margins. The gross margins for livestock enter-prises were calculated in Table 1.21. In Table 1.27 they are presented on a per unit basis, in summary form.

From the information given in Table 1.27 it is clear that the sow unit shows a satisfactory performance when compared with average standards. The grazing livestock enterprises are the weaker section. The grazing livestock output per adjusted forage acre of £53·2 per acre is well below the group comparative figure of £72 per acre (see Worksheet 7 (Table 1.14)). This is in spite of the fact that the stocking density, as measured by adjusted forage acres per grazing livestock unit, is heavier than on comparative groups. This can only indicate that grazing livestock output per animal unit of grazing stock is at fault and the figures in Table 1.27 substantiate this. Each of the grazing livestock enterprises has a poor level of gross output per animal; the gross margin figures are unsatisfactory due to a poor gross margin per head and not to stocking density which is good.

Looking more closely at each grazing livestock enterprise it appears that the gross margin per cow of £66·4 compares very badly with the standards. Gross outputs are low due to low milk yield per cow per year. Concentrate costs, by comparison, are very high leaving an extremely poor margin of milk sales over concentrate costs.

Dairy young stock show a poor gross margin of £13·84 per acre. This is due, primarily, to the rather low transfer value of £80 per head credited to the down calving heifers joining the dairy herd. Variable costs to replace-ments are average at £24·9 per livestock unit.

The gross margin from sheep is only moderate at £6·89 per ewe. This is due to a low gross output per ewe which comes from a low effective lambing percentage since only 130 lambs are sold per 100 ewes in the flock.

44 | *The farm business*

Table 1.27 Littledown Farm: Gross margins for livestock enterprises for Year 2 with comparative figures

Enterprise	Sows			Dairy cows			Dairy young stock		Sheep		
	This farm	Aver-age	Pre-mium	This farm	Aver-age	Pre-mium	This farm	Aver-age	This farm	Aver-age	Pre-mium
	£	£	£	£	£	£	£	£	£	£	£
Gross output	90·5 (Per sow)	89	113	117·0 (Per cow)	138	158	60·9 (Per livestock unit)	70	8·39 (Per ewe)	10·0	11·1
Variable costs (exc. forage)	55·7 (Per sow)	58	61	50·6 (Per cow)	40	40	24·9 (Per livestock unit)	23	1·50 (Per ewe)	1·8	1·8
Gross margin (exc. forage)	34·8 (Per sow)	31	52	66·4 (Per cow)	98	118	36·0 (Per livestock unit)	47	6·89 (Per ewe)	8·2	9·3
Gross margin after deducting forage costs	—	—	—	32·0 (Per forage acre)	52	64	13·84 (Per forage acre)	22	12·4 (Per forage acre)	19·0	29·0

Conclusions

This farm is producing an inadequate return on capital because a heavy investment is producing a poor level of management and investment income.

This is due primarily to the high level of fixed costs with which the business is saddled and which are unlikely to be reduced. Variable costs are also well above average.

An increase in gross margin must, therefore, be sought.

Crop production is already efficient and although there is some scope for improvement of the pigs enterprise, the grazing livestock enterprises, particularly the dairy herd, need more immediate attention and effective remedial action.

Costing systems for the farm business

Comparative farm account analysis

In the analysis of the Littledown Farm business the technique of comparative farm account analysis was thoroughly covered. Unfortunately, like all analysis techniques, this has its limitations and shortcomings.

Limitations of comparative farm account analysis

Comparative farm account analysis only shows the levels of outputs and inputs per acre over the whole farm acreage. There is no attempt to divide costs and outputs between enterprises and, therefore, the relative profitability between different enterprises is not shown. It follows, therefore, that one very profitable enterprise may be 'covering up' for an unprofitable one.

Cost accounting or enterprise costing

There is, however, an analysis technique which is used in farm business analysis, which does allocate both outputs and inputs to particular enterprises. This technique is called cost accounting or enterprise costing. This particular analysis technique was not applied to the enterprises on Littledown Farm, but if it had been, a profit figure for each enterprise on the farm could have been calculated as well as for each item of output, e.g. profit per ton of potatoes, profit per acre of wheat and profit per cow or per gallon of milk.

Limitations of cost accounting

First impressions suggest that cost accounting is a useful technique for analysing farm enterprises, since all cost and output items are allocated to particular enterprises overcoming the 'weakness' of comparative farm account analysis. Unfortunately, this apparent advantage of costs allocation involves the problem of allocating fixed costs and since this cannot be done accurately the final profit figure is not reliable.

It would be easy to allocate wages if time sheets were kept of time spent on each enterprise but there would still remain the problem of allocating holidays, national insurance, and time spent on maintenance and non-productive work. At first sight it would seem that rent and rates would present no problems since they could be allocated on a per acre basis. Unfortunately, this system would not be acceptable to pig and poultry 'concrete' enterprises which use a very limited area. Similar problems arise when trying to allocate other fixed cost items. Some machinery costs can be allocated by keeping hourly records, but the problem arises of un-productive work and its allocation to particular enterprises. It may be argued that electricity and water can be easily allocated by installing meters, but a very real problem will be encountered when trying to allocate general overhead costs viz.:

all miscellaneous costs, fees, subscriptions, office expenses;
telephone and other sundry items.

What basis of allocation should be adopted? A number could be used:

(*i*) percentage gross output of each enterprise;
(*ii*) percentage net output of each enterprise;
(*iii*) percentage standard output of each enterprise;
(*iv*) percentage of allocated costs to each enterprise;
(*v*) percentage acreages of each enterprise;
(*vi*) percentage labour requirements of each enterprise;

all of these are acceptable by accounting standards, but none are reliable.

The outcome of cost accounting is, therefore, a profit figure for each enterprise which is very largely affected by the proportion of the farm's fixed costs that it carries depending upon the method of allocation or apportionment of fixed costs that was employed.

Gross margin analysis

Since the early 1960s the gross margin has become recognised as a useful comparative measure between enterprises. Originally the gross margin was intended as a measure of productivity for cash crops but it has since been extended to almost every agricultural (and horticultural) enterprise.

It is possible, therefore, to calculate gross margins for individual enterprises and total these to give the total farm gross margin. The difference between this and the fixed costs gives the farm's management and investment income. The level of fixed costs which exist on a farm will, to a large extent, dictate the type of enterprise which will be carried since a high level of fixed costs will necessitate a high gross margin if a margin is to be left as a trading profit. Conversely, where the overall level of fixed costs is low, a margin will still be achieved from enterprises producing a relatively low gross margin.

Limitations of gross margin analysis

There are a number of restraints which must be considered when applying gross margin analysis to a farm business. These are:

1. The gross margin is confined to strictly defined cost areas. It does not take into account any changes that may occur in fixed cost structure of the business and therefore must be used with care in farm planning. This caution is necessary since fixed costs are, of course, not fully fixed. Some fixed cost items do not change except over a period of time, e.g. rent, while others do alter, e.g. labour and machinery costs. It is dangerous in farm planning to assume that all fixed costs will remain constant, since some of these will undoubtedly alter, particularly when major changes of policy are being considered.
2. The gross margin of an enterprise is not necessarily an indication of its profitability. This is only one aspect of an enterprise; many other items and factors are involved before the ultimate profitability is known.
3. Confusion and misinterpretation can easily occur unless the full gross margin calculation can be examined, i.e. an insight into exactly how the figures were calculated:

   Example: *Potato enterprise*
   Contract harvesting   = variable cost
   Using own harvester = fixed cost
   Casual labour   = variable cost
   Regular labour   = fixed cost

   If gross margins were calculated for two farmers A and B, both of whom had the same acreage of potatoes, same yield, same sale price, same percentage ware, same seed, fertiliser and spray costs, but:

   Farmer A harvests by contract and uses casual labour, while
   Farmer B uses his own harvester and uses his regular labour force,

   obviously, Farmer B's gross margin for his potato enterprise will be much higher than that of Farmer A.

   Similarly with cereal enterprises; crops harvested by contractor will, other factors being equal, show a lower gross margin than crops harvested with farm-owned machinery. The profitability may be in reverse.
4. Increasing the intensity of enterprises on a farm may well increase the total farm gross margin but it will not necessarily increase the total farm profit, since the fixed costs may also rise in greater proportion, i.e. profit is not proportional to gross margin. In fact, a higher gross margin may be achieved on a farm, but this could easily lead to a lower farm profit if the resultant increase in fixed costs were greater than the increase in gross margin.

5. Gross margin makes no allowance for the complementarity and inter-relationships which often exist between enterprises, for example:
   pigs and market garden enterprises;
   stock and arable crops;
   dairy cows and sugar beet;
   sheep and grass seed production.

6. Outputs and costs alter with scale of enterprises. It follows, therefore, that if an enterprise is increased it may not necessarily maintain its gross margin per acre or per animal unit.

7. Outputs and costs alter with seasons; to allow for this gross margins ought to be normalised over at least a three-year period, if using them as a basis for farm planning.

8. Gross margins should always be interpreted in relation to the total farm business rather than in terms of allocated gross margin per acre: see Figure 1.c.

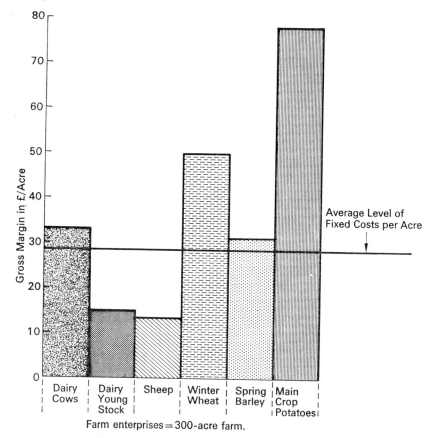

Figure 1.c   Littledown Farm: Gross margins and average levels of fixed costs per acre for Year 2

The gross margins per acre and average level of fixed costs per acre figures in Figure 1.c are those for enterprises on Littledown Farm in Year 2. When this information is presented in such a way it might be assumed that neither the sheep nor the dairy young stock were profitable and, therefore, they should be discontinued. This would be a completely incorrect interpretation of the situation and a disastrous action to effect since the sheep contribute to the total farm gross margin and also help to maintain fertility and yield levels of other crops. Furthermore, the proportion of fixed costs incurred by the sheep enterprise is unfairly represented in the average level of fixed costs per acre figure.

This form of misinterpretation of gross margin calculation is frequently applied to sheep and break crop enterprises since neither of these generate a very high gross margin in themselves, but they do help to maintain the level of gross margin achieved by other enterprises. The overall objective, therefore, should be to maximise total farm gross margin.

General conclusions

None of the analysis techniques or costing systems which have been described are perfect. Each system has its strong points and each one has its limitations. Nevertheless, each system is useful and the results of more than one analysis technique are very valuable when drawing conclusions about a farm business and its performance, provided that the interpreter of the results remains aware of the limitations of the analysis systems employed.

2 | Budgeting for the future of the business

The really successful and efficient farm business is seldom the result of chance. The successful business venture whether in farming or in industry is usually the product of careful and determined planning – of decisions carefully made and of the right action taken at the right time.

Farm management techniques need to be just as concerned with helping farmers to make decisions about the future as they are with examining and analysing the results of the past.

Accounts and records show what has occurred in the past and where and why the business has succeeded or failed, but unless this information is used constructively in planning for future policy, there is little point in going to all the fuss and bother involved in its collection and analysis.

In this chapter, techniques are discussed by which a farmer can look at the future of his farm business and plan his policies constructively.

When talking to farmers, one is frequently amazed and sometimes quite alarmed at the way in which important decisions affecting policy are often made.

Decisions which may ultimately affect the whole future of the farm business and even the solvency of the farmer and the future livelihood of both himself and his family are often made upon the most flimsy evidence and as a result of the most illogical reasoning.

How often one hears farmers stating categorically that 'sheep don't pay', or 'there's a lot of money in beef', or 'there's nothing in poultry nowadays', or even 'rearing dairy replacements doesn't pay'; worse still 'old so and so's making a lot of money out of his pigs, so let's go in for more pigs'.

How many farmers, sick to death of the drudgery of milking cows and the endless toil involved by a dairy herd, have cursed themselves bitterly for giving up their cows in favour of the apparent easy money to be made in some other enterprise such as beef or sheep? They now find that it was infinitely preferable to be tied up by an old cow's tail than to be shackled by a bank overdraft which becomes steadily heavier since ends no longer quite seem to meet. Such tragedies are all too common in farming and many could well have been avoided by a little careful thought and logical financial planning.

The truth of the matter is, of course, that no two sets of circumstances are quite the same and that what is sauce for the goose is not necessarily sauce for the gander. Just because Farmer A finds that it does not pay him to rear his replacement dairy heifers, there is no reason for Farmer B to assume that the same conclusions can automatically be drawn about his own business.

In short, every case has to be judged on its own merits.

The right decision about any particular farm business can only be made after a careful examination of all the facts and by studying the likely implications of future policy upon farm income and the balance sheet.

This technique of estimating future income and expenditure is called **Budgeting** and is an essential aspect of farm planning. The technique of budgeting can be broadly considered in two forms:

1. Complete budgeting
2. Partial budgeting.

In the complete budget the whole farm business is considered. This is a technique by which estimates are made of future income and expenditure in order to ascertain the future position of the total farm business with regard to capital requirements and expected profitability.

The partial budget on the other hand considers the likely effects of future policies or changes in future policy upon a given section or *part* of the farm business. This can be used as a logical approach towards deciding which will be the most profitable of possible alternative enterprises or alternative methods of using resources.

The two forms of budget are now considered in more detail.

The complete budget

The complete budget, involving the whole farm business, can be used in the following ways:

1. To obtain as accurately as possible an estimate of the future profit level of the business. This involves making up an estimated trading account for some period in the future.

All cash income and expenditure will be included and provision must also be made for the 'paper' changes, i.e. changes in valuations of stock and crops and the depreciation incurred by machinery and fixed assets.

If the estimates of income and expenditure (Example I (Table 2.1)) are accurate the farmer can expect to make a net farm income of £490 in the next trading year.

2. To obtain an estimate of future capital requirements of the business. This type of budget is termed the 'Capital Budget' or 'Cash Flow Budget', and examines future receipts and expenses in the light of the actual transactions which will be made either in cash or through the bank account.

This is not the same as a future trading account and it is not intended to show a future measure of profit, since it makes no provision for either

Example I

Table 2.1   Estimated profit and loss account for the next year's trading on a 50-acre dairy farm

Opening valuation	£	£	Estimated sales and receipts	£	£
30 dairy cows at £80	2400		29000 gallons of milk	4350	
Stores	500		7 cull cows	350	
		2900	30 calves	210	
					4910
Estimated expenses			*Closing valuation*		
10 replacement heifers	1000		33 dairy cows at £80	2640	
Feedingstuffs:			Sundry stores	500	
32 tons cake at £30	960				3140
Seeds:					
12 acres at £4/acre	48				
Fertilisers at £6/acre	300				
Vet. medicines and dairy sundries	210				
Wages and Nat. Insurance	800				
Fuel and oil	150				
Repairs and machinery insurance	150				
Rent and rates	400				
Sundry overheads	300				
		4318			
Provision for depreciation on machinery and tenant's fixtures	342				
Estimated Net Farm Income	490				
		8050			8050

Table 2.2   Machinery account to show depreciation on machinery and tenant's fixtures

	Opening valuation	Purchases	Sales	Closing valuation	Depn.	Profit
	£	£	£	£	£	£
Tractor A	320	—	410	—	—	90
Tractor B	—	1000	—	718	282	—
Sundry machinery	1000	—	—	850	150	—
	1320	1000	410	1568	432	90
Less profit					90	
					342	

depreciation or valuation changes. The capital budget is designed to show the likely cash position in the future and will indicate the periods when capital must be borrowed and also when there is likely to be a surplus of available capital.

Such a budget can be calculated for any given period of time; it may be annual, quarterly, monthly or even weekly. The results of such budgets, in terms of surplus or deficiency of working capital, can be plotted to show the 'Capital Profile' of the farm business.

Example II

Simple capital budget

A very simple illustration of a capital budget is as follows. It is assumed that a suitable building containing fattening space for 20 pigs is available, and that weaners are bought and fattened for pork. It takes three months to fatten a batch of pigs and as soon as one lot is sold another is bought in. One pig is lost out of each batch, and the feed requirements increase as the pigs grow.

Purchase price per weaner £5·50
Price of feed   £100 per batch
Sale price per pig   £12 after levy and marketing expenses.

The capital profile for this very simple business is calculated in Table 2.3 and illustrated in Figure 2.a.

The graph (Figure 2.a) shows the capital position of this little business throughout the year. Starting with nothing, £110 has to be borrowed to buy in the first 20 weaners. By the end of the first month these pigs have eaten £20 worth of food. As they grow, they consume more food, the cost of which is added to the capital deficit so that by the end of the second month the business has an overdraft of £160. The fat pigs are sold by the end of the third month and the receipts from this sale more than balance the accumulated cost of the weaners and their feed, leaving a surplus of £18.

This profit is immediately ploughed back and a further batch of pigs bought in. The same capital pattern follows in the next three 3-month periods so that by the end of the year a surplus or profit of £72 has been built up, and the initial capital has been turned over approximately four times.

Additional items to be included in the capital budget

The cash flow sheet needs to go deeper than the farm account alone. Almost invariably the farmer's personal requirements need to be drawn from the same cash reservoir, so the cash flow sheet also needs to provide for:

1. Personal drawings
2. Personal taxation (usually payable on the previous year's profits)
3. Repayment of borrowed capital.

A complete budget for Littledown Farm is included in Appendix A.

c

Table 2.3 Capital budget for a pig fattening enterprise

Month:	Jan.	Feb.	Mar.	Apl.	May	June	July	Aug.	Sept.	Oct.	Nov.	Dec.
	£	£	£	£	£	£	£	£	£	£	£	£
Expenses												
Weaner pigs	110	—	—	110	—	—	110	—	—	110	—	—
Foodstuffs	20	30	50	20	30	50	20	30	50	20	30	50
Total expenses	130	30	50	130	30	50	130	30	50	130	30	50
Receipts												
Sale of porkers	—	—	228	—	—	228	—	—	228	—	—	228
Monthly balance	−130	−30	+178	−130	−30	+178	−130	−30	+178	−130	−30	+178
Cumulative balance	−130	−160	+18	−112	−142	+36	−94	−124	+54	−76	−106	+72

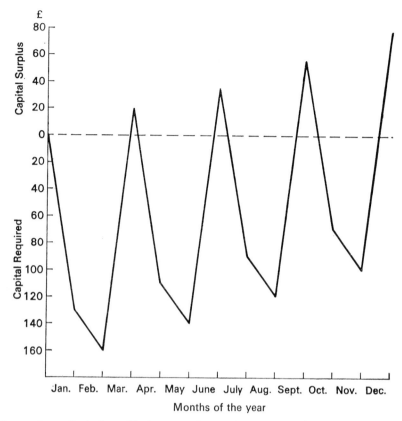

Figure 2.a   Capital profile for a pig fattening enterprise (see Table 2.3)

When to use the complete budget

The technique of complete budgeting can be of value to the farmer in the following circumstances:

(*a*) in estimating future profitability and capital requirements for the purpose of obtaining credit;
(*b*) when submitting a tender for a farm tenancy;
(*c*) in setting up and operating a system of budgetary control;
(*d*) in planning future tax commitments.

Estimating capital requirements when arranging loans

It is particularly important to be able to estimate the likely movement of cash in and out of the bank account when arranging short-term loans. Some banks now require farmers applying for overdrafts to fill up a form designed to indicate the future cash flow of their businesses.

Such an estimate of cash flow is of value both to the borrower and to the lender (in this case the bank manager) since (*a*) it sets a limit to the loan and serves as a danger warning should this be exceeded; (*b*) it shows the purpose for which the loan is required; (*c*) it indicates the length of time for which the loan is required.

This exercise also serves to make the farmer look more closely at his business and helps to indicate to both the borrower and the lender the likely viability of the loan.

(b) *Submitting a tender for the tenancy of a farm*

A prospective tenant will be well advised to carry out a careful examination of his likely expenditure and income in the first years of his tenancy, in order to determine (*a*) whether he can raise sufficient capital to take on the farm and run it properly; (*b*) how much rent he can afford to pay, and at the same time meet all his expenses, pay his interest charges, repay his loans and still have enough to live on and pay his income tax.

Many land agents now require such a budget to be drawn up by prospective tenants when tendering for a farm.

(c) *In setting up a system of budgetary control*

The purpose of budgetary control is to provide a measure of current levels of performance and efficiency within the farm business.

Future receipts and expenses are estimated on a monthly or quarterly basis. The actual result for each item is then recorded alongside the budgeted figure.

In this way any deviations from the expected levels of output and expenditure can be spotted as they occur and can be investigated. Thus mistakes and inefficiencies are noticed at the right time and action can be taken before it is too late. Analysed accounts tend to be historical in nature, and while they may eventually show the weaknesses in the business, the information is obtained too late for effective remedial action to be taken.

(d) *In planning income tax commitments*

This is rapidly becoming an important consideration in farm business planning. If profit is very high one year and very low the next, it tends to be more heavily taxed than if the same total profit is spread evenly over the years, also the burden of tax payment tends to be delayed, so that the tax deducted from income earned in a good year has to be paid in a bad year, when the cash may not be available.

The budgetary control system can thus be extended and used not only as a yardstick with which to compare current performance, but also as an indicator of anticipated high profits before the end of the accounting year.

If the profit looks like being too high, then there is still time before the end of the trading year to change a tractor or combine or start on buildings' repairs, so that the maximum deductions can be claimed and the taxable income minimised.

Budgetary control has long been accepted as a necessary method of financial control in industry and is rapidly gaining recognition as an advanced technique of farm management.

The partial budget

This is a method for estimating the likely effects that changes in policy or prices may have upon the future profitability of the farm business.

It is a means by which a farmer may test the financial implications of proposed improvements and alterations to the farm business.

If one looks objectively at a farm business, one is frequently faced with such problems as – whether to carry dairy cows or beef cattle on a given acreage of grass and forage crops; whether to keep pigs or poultry in a given set of buildings that have become available; whether to invest capital in a machine and thereby reduce labour costs or whether to use the money to intensify a given section of the business and increase profitability by increasing turnover.

Whenever a change is considered or suggested the first question is always 'will it pay?' 'Will it pay', for example, to get rid of the cows and grow more corn?

The situation is frequently more complicated since there is usually more than one alternative way of changing the farm business, in which case the question becomes 'Which will pay best?'

The technique of partial budgeting is a method of solving such problems by applying logic to the situation so that the likely effects of a proposed change in farming policy can be examined dispassionately in the light of expected farm profit. The partial budget looks forward to a future trading account to determine what effects any changes in policy are likely to have upon the final profit.

The technique is basically very simple, and provided one is familiar with the workings of a trading or profit and loss account, the rules which follow are not difficult to apply.

The rules of partial budgeting

Rule 1

The budget should only include items which will actually appear or alter in the future trading account.

For any proposed change in policy or for any pair of alternatives being considered, the changes can be examined under:

(*a*) extra costs incurred;
(*b*) costs saved;
(*c*) revenue foregone;
(*d*) extra revenue obtained.

This means that the budget is primarily concerned with outputs and variable costs. However, the partial budget differs from the gross margin calculation in that it recognises that some items previously broadly defined as 'fixed costs', e.g. machinery, buildings and labour, will change with changing policy.

Gross margin figures can be used as an extremely crude form of partial budget, but these are restricted to rigidly defined groups of costs and unless fixed costs are given due consideration they may give misleading results. To be sure of finding the right answer, a deeper examination should be made and the partial budgeting techniques should be used. However, in carrying out such budgets, one needs to be extremely careful when dealing with such items as buildings, machinery and labour costs, to stick to the basic rule and remember only to include those items that will actually change in the trading account.

With buildings, the basic capital cost is not permitted in the budget. Only the annual charges resulting from such an investment should be included. These are:

(1) depreciation on extra buildings;
(2) repairs on extra buildings;
(3) interest on capital invested in extra buildings.

These are the annual or running costs of the buildings and will occur in the trading account whereas the initial investment in the buildings is a capital cost and will not.

Similarly with machinery, if a change in policy involves the purchase of a machine then the budget should include the annual costs of such a machine i.e. depreciation, repairs and interest on the capital invested – not the original cost of the machine. Where a change in policy does not involve investing in extra buildings or machinery, the annual charges on existing machinery and buildings will not be included in the budget, since they remain unaltered by the change of policy, i.e. they do not come into any of the four categories mentioned.

Labour costs are also fairly easy to deal with in partial budgeting. The annual cost of the basic regular labour force is considered as a constant and will remain the same irrespective of small changes in policy. It is permissible, however, to include as extra costs or costs saved any changes in the requirements for casual labour or overtime labour since these are costs that will actually change in the annual trading account. The inclusion of regular labour charges is only permissible where a change in policy involves a change in the labour force, i.e. since men are indivisible, getting rid of one or more men or employing one or more extra men.

A basic mistake frequently made in partial budgeting (and often by people who should know better) is to assume that a theoretical saving in man hours will result in a saving on cash. It will not, of course, unless it involves getting rid of a man altogether or making a saving in expenditure on casual labour or overtime. (Some of the early promoters of agricultural work study were past masters at this sort of wool-pulling.)

Rule 2

A budget should always be calculated on the basis of a common denominator to the alternatives being considered.

The common denominator used will always be one of the basic factors of production – those items with which students who have suffered the dreary early lectures on agricultural economics will be familiar – land, labour and capital. The most important limiting factor which is common to both alternatives is always the basis upon which alternative policies are compared.

For example, if one were comparing the likely profitability of sheep or dairy cows one would be most likely to base the budget on the land requirement, e.g. 120 breeding ewes on 30 acres *v.* 20 dairy cows.

If one were budgeting the likely profitability of pigs or poultry one would base the budget on either the capital or labour requirements, since land is a minor consideration in such circumstances, for example:

(*a*) on the basis of labour:
Forty sows and their progeny fattened to pork *v.* 5000 laying hens per man
(*b*) on the basis of capital in the form of an existing building – say 1000 sq. ft.
Pork pigs at 10 sq. ft. per pig = 100 per batch
Poultry at 2 sq. ft. per bird = 500.

It will be possible to put 3–4 batches of pork pigs through the house in a year so the final comparison will be:

350 porkers *v.* 500 laying hens per year.

If one were to budget the likely profitability of extending the business by increasing either the pigs or the dairy cows, the budget would have to be calculated on the basis of either their common capital or labour requirement since land is only an important factor of production in the case of the cows.

Rule 3

Always be very conservative in making estimates of future levels of production and prices. It is always safer to err on the pessimistic side. A mistake made frequently in budgeting is that of seeing the future through rose-tinted spectacles and of flavouring budgets with that happy – almost political – optimism which invariably leads to downfall in the cold reality of business.

Rule 4

Be impartial. Avoid prejudice and trying to weigh one alternative more favourably than the other.

Stick to the cold facts at this stage. Obtain an answer in terms of hard cash and then consider personal preference in making the final decision.

Never let personal preferences interfere with the budget itself.

Setting out a partial budget

The partial budget is a forward-looking trading account for a section of the farm business and can be used to examine the effect of either:

(*a*) increasing the business by the expansion of one or more of its enterprises, or introducing new enterprises.

 or

(*b*) Increasing the margin of the business by effecting a reduction in costs.

 or

(*c*) Finding the most profitable of two or more alternative policies.

The basic layout of the budget is always as follows:

Extra costs Revenue Foregone		Costs Saved Extra Revenue	
	A		B
Total		Total	

The two sides of this forward-looking trading account must balance. If the balancing figure comes on the left-hand side, i.e. at A, then the budget indicates that extra income is likely to be achieved. If on the other hand the budget balances on the right-hand side, i.e. at B, then the budget indicates a loss of income for the projected policy.

Always be careful, particularly when compiling a business report or when answering examination questions, to make a clear heading to the budget and to state clearly at the outset any assumptions that it is necessary to make.

Example of a partial budget

A farmer has accommodation for 60 cows, he can easily handle this number and he has sufficient grazing for them but he only has 56 cows in his herd.

What will be the effect on his annual profit if he increases his herd by four cows in order to bring it up to full production? Certain assumptions have to be made. He will have to buy in all the extra concentrates they require, he will incur extra charges for A.I. and sundries and he will have to save more bedding straw which he could otherwise have sold. He will have to borrow the money to buy the extra cows and pay interest – say 8 per cent on the money. He will also have to buy in the replacement heifers required to maintain the four extra cows.

His fixed costs, i.e. rent, labour, machinery, buildings, will be the same for 60 cows as for 56 cows.

The layout of the partial budget then looks like this:

Table 2.4 Budget: 60 cows v. 56 cows on same acreage

Extra costs	£	*Costs saved*	£
1 replacement heifer/year	100		
Concentrates:			
4 cows at 1 ton/cow at £30/ton	120		
Vet., medicines and sundries at £7/cow	28		
Interest on 4 cows at £100 at 8%	32		Nil
Revenue foregone		*Extra revenue*	
4 tons straw at £5/ton	20	Milk:	
		4 cows × 800 galls at £0·15/gallon	480
		4 calves at £7	28
Extra income	258	1 cull cow/year	50
	558		558

Thus under such oversimplified circumstances an increase in income of £258 is likely to result from increasing the herd by four cows.

Suppose now that the circumstances are a little more complicated (or perhaps a bit more realistic): the problem remains basically the same, i.e. to increase the herd from 56 cows to 60 cows, but in this case, in order to increase his cow numbers, the farmer will have to reduce his cash cropping acreage (which is assumed to be wheat) to provide the extra grazing and grass for conservation for the extra cows. In order to keep four extra cows at 1·5 forage acres per cow, the wheat must be reduced by six acres, with corresponding loss of output, but on the other hand the variable costs of growing it will be saved. Machinery costs and other fixed costs will remain the same if the farmer already has his own harvesting and grain-handling equipment. (The only possible cost to alter here will be the fuel costs, but it is unlikely that the fuel costs of grassland husbandry and conservation will differ very significantly from the fuel costs of growing a cereal crop – it is too small an item to worry much about anyway.)

The budget now looks like this:

Table 2.5 Budget: Four extra cows v. wheat on six acres

Extra costs	£	Costs saved	£
1 replacement heifer/year	100	*Variable costs of 6 acres wheat:*	
Concentrates:		Fertilisers at £3/acre	18
4 cows at 1 ton/cow at £30/ton	120	Seeds at £3/acre	18
Vet., medicines and sundries at		Sprays at £0·5/acre	3
£7/cow	28	Twine and sundries at £0·5/acre	3
Interest on 4 cows at £100 at 8%	32		
Fertilisers to grassland at £6/acre	36		
Annual share of grass seeds:			
6 acres £4 ÷ 4 years	6		
Revenue foregone		*Extra revenue*	
4 tons straw at £5/ton	20	Milk:	
		4 cows × 800 galls at £0·15/gall.	480
		4 calves at £7	28
		1 cull cow/year	50
Output from 6 acres wheat:			
6 × 1·5 tons at £24/ton	216		
6 tons straw at £5/ton	30		
Extra income	12		
	600		600

Thus when the loss of gross margin from the wheat is taken into consideration, the extra cows are not as profitable as they were previously and the final farm profit is only increased by £12 a year as a result of keeping an extra four cows in place of six acres of wheat.

To progress with this same problem a stage further and to bring the theoretical budget into an even more realistic light, let us now consider the effect on final profit if new accommodation had to be provided for the extra cows. Without indulging in anything very elaborate, extra loose housing might be provided at a capital cost of £50 per cow. This will appear in the budget as:

1. Depreciation on the building
2. Interest on the capital involved in the building
3. Repairs (if any).

The budget now reads as follows:

Table 2.6   Modified budget: Four extra cows v. *wheat on six acres*

Extra costs	£	Costs saved	£
1 replacement heifer/year	100	Fertilisers at £3/acre	18
		Seeds at £3/acre	18
Concentrates:		Sprays at £0·5/acre	3
4 cows at 1 ton/cow at £30/ton	120	Twine and sundries at £0·5/acre	3
Vet., medicines and sundries at £7/cow	28		
Fertilisers to 6 acres grass	36		
Interest on 4 cows at £100 at 8%	32		
Share of grass seed	6		
Depreciation on extra buildings 10% of 4 × £50	20		
Interest on capital in buildings 8% of $\frac{200}{2}$	8		
		Extra revenue	
Revenue foregone		Milk:	
4 tons straw at £5/ton	20	4 cows × 800 galls at £0·15/gall.	480
		4 calves at £7	28
		1 cull cow/year	50
Output from 6 acres wheat:			
6 × 1·5 ton × £24/ton	216		
6 tons straw at £5/ton	30	*Income lost*	16
	616		616

Now that all the extra costs are fully accounted for, the wheat looks a better proposition than the extra cows.

How misleading the result would have been had we relied on the gross margin calculation as a means of budgeting between the two alternatives. The results would have been as shown in table 2.7:

The gross margin *only* deals with outputs and variable costs; no consideration is given to fixed costs at all and so it cannot tell the whole story or represent the situation clearly enough to enable the right decisions to be made. Since additional buildings costs, including interest charges, have been incurred and, therefore, included in the budget, the balance is consequently weighted in favour of continuing the wheat crop rather than increasing cow numbers.

The 'break-even' budget

It is obvious, however, that if the yield of wheat was lower *or* if the yield of milk was higher, then milk production could be as profitable as wheat if not more so.

Table 2.7   Partial budget using gross margin only

			£	£	£
Cows –	*Sales:*	Milk	480		
		Calves	28		
		Cull cow	50		
				558	
	Less 1 replacement heifer			100	
	Gross output				458
	Less variable costs:				
		Concentrates		120	
		Vet., medicines and sundries		28	
		Straw		20	
		Fertilisers to grass		36	
		Share of grass seeds		6	
				210	
	Gross margin				248

i.e. £62/cow or £41·33 *per acre* (at 1·5 acres/cow)

		£	£
Wheat –	*Sales:*		
	Wheat – 9 tons at £24	216	
	Straw – 6 tons at £5	30	
	Gross output		246
	Less variable costs:		
	Fertilisers	18	
	Seed	18	
	Sprays	3	
	Twine	3	
			42
	Gross margin		204

i.e. £35·33 *per acre*

This is the basis of a calculation known as a 'break-even budget' by which it is possible in any given set of circumstances to determine the necessary level of price or performance which must be achieved by any given factors so that the profitability of the alternatives in question will be the same.

Let us firstly consider the factor of milk yield in the last budget. Income lost – £16

This represents $16 \times \dfrac{20}{3}$ gallons of milk (at £0·15 per gallon)

or $16 \times \dfrac{20}{3} \times \dfrac{1}{4}$ gallons of milk per cow.

i.e. 27 gallons of milk per cow.

Therefore the 'break-even' yield of milk is $800 + 27 = 827$ gallons per cow. Below this yield wheat is more profitable than milk; above this yield milk is more profitable than wheat.

A similar calculation can be made to find the 'break-even' yield of wheat. Extra income of £16 for wheat represents

$$16 \times \frac{20}{24} \text{ cwts. of wheat (at £24 per ton)}$$

$$\text{or } 16 \times \frac{20}{24} \times \frac{1}{6} \text{ cwts of wheat per acre}$$

i.e. 2·2 cwt wheat per acre.

Therefore the 'break-even' yield of wheat is $(30 - 2 \cdot 2) = 27 \cdot 8$ cwt per acre. Below 27·8 cwt per acre milk is more profitable than wheat. Above 27·8 cwt per acre wheat is more profitable than milk.

This could be carried a stage further and for any given yield of wheat per acre, a corresponding yield of milk per cow can be calculated so that the budget breaks even.

Example III

In the following examples it is assumed that the factors of milk yield and wheat yield are variable but that all other factors, e.g. concentrates use, fertiliser use, prices, stocking rates, etc., remain at the levels in the budget.

Table 2.8 summarises the budgetary margins for varying levels of wheat yield achieved for three possible levels of milk yield. By showing these results on a graph (see Figure 2.b) it is possible to plot the corresponding 'break-even' point in milk yield for any given yield of wheat and vice versa.

This technique of assessing the 'break-even' point can be of immense value where it is not possible to quote a definite price or yield for a particular commodity. It is thus possible to plot the 'break-even' price or yield in any given circumstances and to plot the likely profitability of a whole range of possible yields and prices.

These calculations may not be 100 per cent accurate – they never claim to be, but in this way one at least puts the problem into proper perspective. Having done this one is in a far better position to make a rational decision and is far less likely to make wildcat – spur-of-the-moment – decisions that one might spend the rest of one's life regretting (like giving up those cows!).

The limitations of budgeting

All budgets suffer from one serious shortcoming in that they are basically guesswork. Since most items of future income and expenditure have to be estimated, there is always an element of uncertainty involved where future yields, levels of fertiliser, food and fuel use, as well as prices are concerned.

Table 2.8 *'Break-even' budget: Four cows* v. *six acres wheat*

To find budgetary margin in favour of wheat at varying levels of wheat yield and at different milk yields

	Yield of wheat (cwt./acre)					
	20		30		40	
	£	£	£	£	£	£
1. At 700 galls/cow:						
Extra costs	350		350		350	
Revenue foregone						
Straw	50		50		50	
Wheat	144		216		288	
		544		616		688
Costs saved	42		42		42	
Extra revenue						
Milk	420		420		420	
Calves and culls	78		78		78	
		540		540		540
Margin		4		76		148
2. At 800 galls/cow:						
Extra costs	350		350		350	
Revenue foregone						
Straw	50		50		50	
Wheat	144		216		288	
		544		616		688
Costs saved	42		42		42	
Extra revenue						
Milk	480		480		480	
Culls and calves	78		78		78	
		600		600		600
Margin		−56		16		88
3. At 900 galls/cow:						
Extra costs	350		350		350	
Revenue foregone						
Straw	50		50		50	
Wheat	144		216		288	
		544		616		688
Costs saved	42		42		42	
Extra revenue						
Milk	540		540		540	
Calves and culls	78		78		78	
		660		660		660
Margin		−116		−44		28

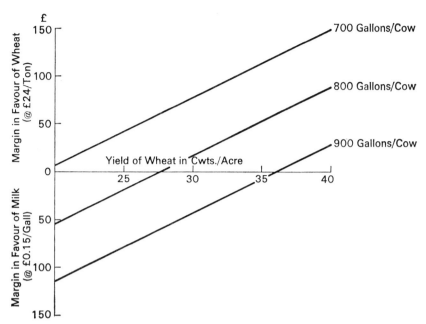

Figure 2.b   Graph to show budgetary margins at varying levels of wheat yield and at different milk yields

When preparing a budget one must aim to minimise this degree of uncertainty.

Under the 1957 Agriculture Act the Industry is guaranteed minimum prices for certain products for a number of years ahead.

Costs of basic raw materials are usually known for a short period ahead and for the purpose of long-term planning can generally be expected to rise slowly.

Information which needs to be estimated with a fair degree of accuracy is that usually referred to as 'input–output' data, i.e. the physical ratios of production in terms of liveweight gain, milk yields and yields of crops in relation to levels of feeding, manuring, stocking densities, etc. It is impossible to standardise such material and the most successful budgeter is the person who can make the shrewdest estimate of the future requirements of raw material in relation to production under any given set of individual farm conditions.

This requires great skill and intimate knowledge of the potential of the land and stock on the particular farm. In other words the more intimately the budget can be tailored to suit the conditions prevailing on the farm, the more reliable it will be as a basis upon which to make a management decision.

If personal knowledge of input–output responses for the particular farm is not available, then the planner has to resort to more general standards. It may be possible to discover the levels of yields achieved locally under similar conditions. If reliable information of this sort is not available from local farmers then the results achieved on research stations or Government experimental husbandry farms under similar conditions may prove a useful guide.

On a broader field one can use county, regional or even national average figures or use standards, such as those published by University departments of agricultural economics.

A further limitation to the partial budget is that it cannot always allow adequately for the interdependence which often exists between enterprises on a farm. Enterprises must be considered as separate entities in the budget whereas in practice they are often complementary to one another, e.g. a market garden enterprise may depend upon a pig enterprise for its muck; grass seeds production may be dependent upon sheep at certain stages (e.g. to help to establish the young plants and to remove flag); cattle and sugar beet may be interdependent, the one supplying the dung and the other beet tops and beet pulp fodder; in fact most arable rotations are at some stage dependent upon livestock to maintain fertility and to utilise grass breaks which are essential to the health of arable crops.

Budgeting, however, is not alone in this limitation for no method of accounting has yet been devised which will accurately accommodate the financial effects of this interdependence. This is a common failing of the comparative farm account analysis, the gross margin calculation and even the full blown and highly complicated cost account.

A final point, never underestimate the importance of the human factor. Always make sure that the standards of performance that you have assumed in your budget can be achieved by the farmer or the person responsible for carrying out the plan. This is tremendously important for individual ability may well be the most important limiting factor, and no matter how well a particular policy may be planned, it can never succeed unless it has the right man in charge.

3 | Farm overheads or fixed costs

Fixed costs are defined as those farm cost items which are not easily allocated to particular farm enterprises and which do not vary very much with small changes in the scale (size) of an enterprise. These costs are also referred to as **Overhead costs, Common costs** and **Unallocatable costs.** Examples are: labour; machinery; buildings; rent and rates and miscellaneous overheads, e.g. office expenses.

It is much more difficult to allocate fixed costs to particular enterprises than it is to allocate variable costs, as has been explained. Allocation is only possible if detailed records are kept involving a large amount of time, effort and paper!

While small-scale changes may not affect the level of fixed costs, there will be a point at which an increase or decrease in the scale of an enterprise will begin to affect one or more of the fixed costs. If substantial alterations in the size of enterprises are being considered, then the consequent changes in fixed costs will occur.

Principles governing fixed costs

The level of fixed costs on a farm vary with the average level of intensity of the farm enterprises. If there is an enterprise on the farm with high labour demands, e.g. sugar beet, or one which requires a special type of machine, e.g. a hop-picking machine, then these items will tend to make the total level of fixed costs higher. Similarly large areas of concrete, de luxe farm buildings, tower silos and other items of high capital investment will lead to a high average level of fixed costs per acre. On the other hand, on a hill farm with a very extensive system, e.g. hill sheep looked after by the farmer himself, then the level of fixed costs per acre will be low, since he has no hired labour, little machinery, few buildings and probably pays a low rent.

Often savings can be made in farm businesses by reducing fixed costs, thereby improving profits. A high level of fixed costs means that a high gross margin must be obtained to cover them, calling for an intensive system with high yields to produce such a gross margin. Therefore, in view of the importance of fixed cost items, an examination of each single one; machinery, labour, buildings and general farm overheads, will now be made.

Farm machinery costs

There are a number of reasons why a farmer should carefully examine his machinery costs. These are summarised below.

1. *Increase in mechanisation of farming operations*

The increase in mechanisation in this country is clearly reflected in numbers of machines on farms during recent years, and consequently the annual expenditure on machinery has continued to increase.

A large proportion of the farmer's expenditure goes on machinery: the trend in recent years, as reflected by numbers of machines, is given in Table 3.1.

Table 3.1 Numbers of some agricultural machines on farms in England and Wales

Machine	Numbers in England and Wales			
	1942	*1952*	*1962*	*1966*
Tractors (wheeled) over 10 h.p.	101 505*	267 385	355 140	336 830†
Forage harvesters	n.a.	3 163‡	15 260	19 680
Sprayers	1 100	9 326	51 120	57 540
Combine harvesters	940	16 470	52 350	60 220§
Combine drills	5 610	28 625	46 730	46 830

* Includes track-laying tractors – later figures do not   † 1967
‡ Includes green-crop loaders – later figures do not   § 1968
n.a. = Not available
(*Source:* Agricultural Statistics, H.M.S.O.)

During the twenty-five years after 1942 the number of farm tractors increased nearly three and a half times; the number of forage harvesters increased tremendously and the number of combine harvesters has increased from only a very small number at the end of the Second World War.

2. *Machinery costs as a proportion of total farm costs*

Machinery costs embracing contract charges, machinery depreciation, fuel and oil, repairs, vehicle tax and insurance, account for some 10–20 per cent of total farm costs on most farms. Considering machinery costs as a percentage of total *fixed costs*, then this input accounts for 25–30 per cent on many farms which is about £7–9 per acre in arable areas – see Table 3.2.

Table 3.2 Machinery and labour costs (£ per acre) on six groups of farms in the South-East of England
(average group figures for 1967–68)

Group:	Predominantly milk farms		Milk and arable		Predominantly arable farms	
	Under 125 acres	Over 200 acres	Under 250 acres	Over 450 acres	Under 250 acres	Over 450 acres
Average acreage	88	288	175	596	169	704
No. of farms in group	12	12	13	8	14	14
Input: Labour paid	8·5	13·1	10·2	11·8	5·6	7·6
£/acre: Labour unpaid	9·8	1·0	3·9	0·3	3·8	0·6
Labour Total	18·3 25·8%	14·1 27·6%	14·1 25·8%	12·1 27·1%	9·4 22·5%	8·2 22·2%
Machinery: Depreciation	2·7	3·3	3·1	2·9	3·5	2·7
Fuel and oil	2·0	1·8	1·9	1·6	1·8	1·5
£/acre: Repairs, tax and insurance	2·6	3·0	2·9	2·9	3·3	2·8
Machinery Total	7·3 10·3%	8·1 15·9%	7·9 14·5%	7·4 16·6%	8·6 20·6%	7·0 19·0%
Total Labour and Machinery	25·6 36·1%	22·2 43·5%	22·0 40·3%	19·5 43·7%	18·0 43·1%	15·2 41·2%
All inputs	70·8	51·1	54·6	44·6	41·7	36·9

(Extracted from *Farm Business Statistics for* South-East England (Supplement for 1969), Wye College, Department of Agricultural Economics)

3. The Danger of Overmechanisation

Overmechanisation is where too great a proportion of the total farm capital is invested in machinery. This is most likely to occur on the smaller acreage farms, where machines are bought but not used to anything like their full capacity. If a small farm of say 50 acres requires a minimum capital investment in machinery of £2000 (this sum soon mounts up even on the small farm where tractor, trailer, plough, fertiliser spreader, forage harvester, etc., are necessary), this is £40 per acre. If, on the other hand, the maximum investment for such a farm is considered to be £5000, then that is equivalent to £100 per acre. The annual cost in the latter case will be much higher and will consequently influence the farm profit margin.

4. The complementary effect of labour and machinery

Machinery costs should be critically examined from time to time, but not only in isolation, since the skilled labour required to operate farm machinery is an ever increasing item of cost. Labour and machinery are complementary to each other and together comprise some 36–44 per cent of all farm costs, on farms in the South-East of England – see Table 3.2.

5. Labour and machinery as a proportion of fixed costs

As the scale of an enterprise is increased, higher variable costs are inevitably incurred. Economies can often be made amongst the items comprising total fixed costs. Since labour and machinery together account for about 66–75 per cent of all fixed costs, a proportionately small saving on these items can significantly increase profits.

Benefits of mechanisation

In addition to the above reasons for critically examining machinery costs it must be remembered that investment in machinery will lead to many benefits. Certain intangible benefits will accrue; for example, reduction in drudgery as experienced in spreading farmyard manure by machine rather than by hand or loading bales by means of a bale-loader rather than a pitchfork.

Buying machines may result in an increase in returns to the farmer. He may obtain a higher price for his product as a result of using a grain cleaner, potato riddler or apple grader. Storage facilities for holding a product may mean that a better market price will be realised, e.g. fruit, potatoes and grain. Having the right machine at the right time may mean more timely and efficient cultivations giving a better return than poorly timed ones. Yields may be increased or at least maintained by possessing one's own sprayer or combine harvester rather than depending on a contractor, and by installing irrigation equipment.

In addition to increasing revenue, investment in machinery can often lead to a reduction in the farm labour bill. If a man's wages are considered to be £1000 per annum and if that man can be completely replaced by a machine, then the capital that can be spent on this machine can be nearly three and a half times that spent on the man's yearly wage (i.e. £3450).[1]

Obviously a large number of factors must be considered before investment in extra machinery is made. In weighing these up, the financial effect of the machine upon the farm business must be foremost in the farmer's mind – what will be the increase in returns, what will be the extra annual cost in addition to the initial capital outlay? In attempting to answer these questions with accuracy, it is essential to know how annual machinery cost items are calculated. The terms fixed (or overhead) costs and running costs are commonly used as explained below.

Machinery fixed costs (overheads)

These are costs which apply to all items of farm machinery and are incurred whether the machine is used a lot or only a little. Machinery overheads consist of 1. depreciation; 2. interest charge on the capital invested when the machine was purchased; 3. tax and insurance for vehicles used on the road; 4. housing for the machine. If the machine is used a lot, then the cost of these items per working hour of the machine will be low; if the machine is used only a little, then their cost per working hour will be much higher.

1. Depreciation

The depreciation of a machine is an annual charge levied against a machine to recoup the original expenditure on that machine. Depreciation covers the deterioration of the machine with age, its obsolescence and its wear and tear. The latter is influenced by the hours of work done by the machine, while the other two items are affected by time.

The period over which a machine is depreciated should resemble the anticipated life of the machine. This is very important: even simple equipment, with only light use, should not be depreciated over more than about 12 years, whereas large machinery intensively used should be depreciated over a much shorter period – say three to four years. Suitable rates of depreciation for machines used under average conditions are given in Table 3.3.

[1] Depreciate machine over 5 years
Repairs, fuel, oil, etc. – 5 per cent of purchase price
Interest on capital, $\frac{1}{2}$ capital × 8 per cent
Worker's wage – £1000 per annum
Let maximum capital required to replace one man be £x
then $x/5 + x/20 + (x/100 \times 8/2) = 1000$
∴ $20x + 5x + 4x = 100000$
∴ $29x = 100000$
∴ $= £3450$

Table 3.3   Rates of depreciation for farm machinery
(Percentage of new price)

Frequency of renewal (Years)	Complex. high depreciation rate, e.g. potato harvesters, mobile pea viners, etc.	Established machines with many moving parts, e.g. tractors, combines, balers, forage harvesters	Simple equipment with few moving parts, e.g. ploughs, trailers
	%	%	%
1	34	26	19
2	24½	19½	14½
3	20*	16½*	12½
4	17½†	14½	11½
5	15‡	13†	10½*
6	13½	12	9½
7	12	11	9
8	11	10‡	8½†
9	(10)	9½	8
10	(9½)	8½	7½‡

* Typical frequency of renewal with heavy use
† Typical frequency of renewal with average use
‡ Typical frequency of renewal with light use
(*Source:* V. Baker, Bristol University)

Methods of calculating machinery depreciation

The diminishing balance method. This is a method of calculating depreciation by taking a constant percentage each year over the 'life' of the machine. For example, if a combine harvester costs £2000 new and is depreciated at 20 per cent per annum, by this method the following results are obtained:

Table 3.4   Annual depreciation – diminishing balance method
(Combine harvester, £2000 new)

End of year	Amount depreciated during year (at 20% per annum)	Written down value
	£	£
1	400	1 600
2	320	1 280
3	256	1 024
4	205	819
5	164	655
6	131	524
7	105	419
8	84	335
9	67	268
10	54	214

This is the method used in calculating the annual wear-and-tear allowance on farm machinery for income taxation purposes, where specific percentage figures are stipulated for different types of machines. These taxation calculation rates are higher than would be recommended for the depreciation of farm machinery for farm management purposes.

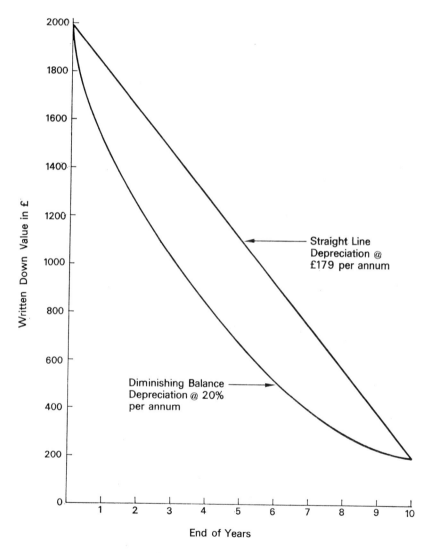

Figure 3.a *Depreciation of combine by diminishing balance and straight line methods*

(Purchase price £2000)

Straight-line method. This is a simple method where the value of a machine is written off over a reasonable period of life. The calculation is

$$\frac{\text{Capital cost of machine} - \text{Sale (scrap) value}}{\text{Life in years}}$$

If the £2000 combine harvester given in the previous example (Table 3.4) is sold after ten years for £214, then the annual depreciation cost will be:

$$\frac{£2000 - £214}{10} = £179 \text{ per annum}$$

A useful guide to the likely 'life' of machines is given in Table 3.5.

Table 3.5 *Estimated useful life of power-operated machinery in relation to annual use*

Equipment	Annual use (hours)				
	25	50	100	200	300
Group 1 Ploughs, cultivators, toothed harrows, hoes, rolls, ridgers, simple potato planting attachments, grain cleaners	12+	12+	12+	12	10
Group 2 Disc. harrows, corn drills, binders, grain drying machines, food grinders and mixers	12+	12+	12	10	8
Group 3 Combine harvesters, pick-up balers, rotary cultivators, hydraulic loaders	12+	12+	12	9	7
Group 4 Mowers, forage harvesters, swath turners, side-delivery rakes, tedders, hedge cutting machines, semi-automatic potato planters and transplanters, unit root drills, mechanical root thinners	12+	12	11	8	6
Group 5 Fertiliser distributors, combine drills, FYM spreaders, elevator potato diggers, spraying machines, pea cutter-windrowers	10	10	9	8	7
Miscellaneous Beet harvesters	11	10	9	6	5
Potato harvesters	—	8	7	5	—
Milking machinery	—	—	—	12	10

	Annual use (hours)					
	500	750	1000	1500	2000	2500
Tractors	12+	12	10	7	6	5
Electric motors	12+	12+	12+	12+	12	12

(*Source:* Culpin, C., *Profitable Farm Mechanisation*, Crosby Lockwood. T .A 2 (1), p. 297)

2. Interest charge

Interest on the capital invested in machinery should be charged and included in comparative calculations, since a farmer could invest that money in some other way which would yield him a return. Interest is normally charged on half the capital invested in the machine. Clearly, since the capital cost of the machine is written off regularly in the form of depreciation charges, the amount falls from that of the purchased price in the first year, to nothing when the machine is completely written off, i.e. interest is paid on the average of the outstanding loan.

3. *Vehicle taxation and insurance*

Annual taxation must be paid on tractors, combines and other self-propelled farm vehicles that regularly use the public highway. All vehicles should be insured and both these cost items are incurred, whether the machines are used a little or a lot.

4. *Housing*

The annual cost of housing for farm machinery is not easy to calculate but obviously if a new machine is being purchased, some consideration must be given to storage, and if this involves a new building additional costs will be incurred.

Machinery running costs

These are costs which are only incurred when a machine is actually being used. These items include fuel and oil, repairs and maintenance and broadly speaking the cost of each item per working hour for a machine doing a particular job is fairly constant.

Fuel and oil

Consumption of fuel and oil will vary somewhat with the particular job being done. Obviously a tractor ploughing all day with a four-furrow plough will consume more fuel than one that spends its time mainly idling. A useful average figure for budgeting purposes is about £0·125 per tractor hour and this is normally used in management calculations for average fuel and oil consumption for medium sized tractors.

Repairs and maintenance

Repairs to farm machinery are necessary to keep the other running costs as low as possible and also to prolong the life of the machine when annual depreciation costs will be small. Considering the lifetime of any machine, the repair cost graph is generally considered to be 'lumpy', i.e. not steady, but with these items occurring unpredictably and usually in fairly large sums. Many farmers believe there is a strong correlation between the 'ability' of the person who operates the machine and the bill for repairs. It follows, therefore, that the calculation of accurate machinery repair costs per annum is impossible, however, estimates can be made which provide a useful guide.

Methods of calculating repair costs

Estimated method. An annual fixed charge for repairs can be calculated by taking 5 per cent of the original purchase price of the machine, depending on the age of the machine. In cases where a machine is older or doing a lot of work in a year a higher figure should be used. This is a very approximate method; the same figure being used for all types of machines. The obvious fact that some machines are more expensive to repair than others is ignored. Nevertheless, it is a useful guide for management calculations.

Detailed estimated method. In this method a percentage of the original purchase price is taken and this varies with the anticipated hours of use of the machine. A series of figures are given in Table 3.6.

Calculating the operating costs of farm machinery

Now that each item composing the overheads (fixed costs) and running costs of machinery have been closely examined, it is possible to make detailed calculations of the actual operational costs of machines, being made up of partly fixed costs and partly variable costs. Two examples are given: firstly that of a potato harvesting machine purchased new at £800 and used to harvest 70 acres of potatoes per annum. The calculation of the operation cost for this machine doing this work has been done by calculating the depreciation of the machine on a 'straight line' basis and repair costs at 5 per cent of purchase price of the machine.

The second example is the calculation of the hourly operating cost of a tractor costing £1000 when new, used at three different levels of use in its third year of life – see Table 3.8.

From Tables 3.8 and 3.9 it can be seen that although the total fixed cost *per annum* increases slightly as the tractor is used more, the fixed cost per hour falls rapidly from £0·47 per hour at the 300 hours per annum level to £0·12 per hour at the 1500 hours per annum level. The running costs per hour do fall slightly with greater use but the fall is nowhere near as great as that of the fixed costs.

Table 3.6 Estimated annual cost of spares and repairs as a percentage of purchase price* at various levels of use

	Lower levels of use per 100 hours Subtract	Approximate annual use (hours)				Additional use per 100 hours Add
		500	750	1 000	1 500	
Tractors	0·5%	5%	6·7%	8·0%	10·5%	0·5%

		Approximate annual use (hours)				Additional use per 100 hour Add
		50	100	150	200	
		%	%	%	%	%
Harvesting machinery						
Combine harvesters, self-propelled and engine driven		1·5	2·5	3·5	4·5	2·0
Combine harvesters, p.t.o. driven, metered-chop forage harvesters, pick-up balers, potato harvesters, sugar beet harvesters		3·0	5·0	6·0	7·0	2·0
Other implements and machines						
Group 1 Ploughs, cultivators, toothed harrows, hoes, elevator potato diggers } Normal soils		4·5	8·0	11·0	14·0	6·0
Group 2 Rotary cultivators, mowers, binders, pea cutter-windrowers		4·0	7·0	9·5	12·0	5·0
Group 3 Disc harrows, fertiliser distributors, farmyard manure spreaders, combine drills, potato planters with fertiliser attachment, sprayers, hedge-cutting machines		3·0	5·5	7·5	9·5	4·0
Group 4 Swath turners, tedders, side-delivery rakes, unit drills, flail forage harvesters, semi-automatic potato planters and transplanters, down-the-row thinners		2·5	4·5	6·5	8·5	4·0
Group 5 Corn drills, milking machines, hydraulic loaders, simple potato planting attachments		2·0	4·0	5·5	7·0	3·0
Group 6 Grain dryers, grain cleaners, rolls, hammer mills, feed mixers, threshers		1·5	2·0	2·5	3·0	0·5

* When it is known that a high purchase price is due to high quality and durability or a low price corresponds to a high rate of wear and tear, adjustments to the figures should be made

(*Source:* Culpin, C., *Profitable Farm Mechanisation,* 2nd Edition, T. A 3, p. 299)

Table 3.7   Operating cost of potato harvester costing £800

	£
Fixed costs	
1. Depreciation over 8 years (straight-line method)	
$= \dfrac{£800}{8 \text{ years}}$	100·0
2. Interest on capital	
$\dfrac{£800}{2} \times 10\%$	40·0
3. Vehicle tax, insurance and housing	—
Total fixed costs	140·0
Running costs	
1. Repairs	
5% of purchase price $= \dfrac{£800}{100} \times 5$	40·0
2. Fuel and oil (for tractor)	
70 acres ÷ 0·25 acre per hour*	
= 280 hours at £0·125 per tractor hour	35·0
Total running costs	75·0
Operating cost	215·0
Operating cost per acre (70 acres)	3·07 per acre

* Average rate of working in acres per hour

When the fixed and running costs are added together to give the operating cost of the tractor, it is important to note that the operating cost per hour falls rapidly between 300 and 800 hours per annum; the fall is not so great at the higher rate of use of 1 500 hours per annum; this is due largely to the spreading of the fixed costs and the higher running costs per hour, due largely to higher repairs. The calculations in Tables 3.8 and 3.9 illustrate the fact that fixed costs are incurred irrespective of whether the tractor is used a lot or a little.

Electricity and contractor's charges

In completing a survey of all the components of machinery costs it must be mentioned that the items of electricity and fuel consumed on the farm are normally grouped in the machinery bracket. Also, strictly speaking, contractors' charges for work done on the farm by an outside contractor are machinery costs and are similarly included. Note, however, for the purposes of gross margin calculations some contract costs are allocatable, e.g. contract combining cereals, and such items are grouped as variable costs.

Table 3.8 *Calculations of hourly fixed and running costs for a tractor at three levels of use*

Tractor costing £1 000 new – *Tractor in its third year of life*

Fixed costs	Light use 300 hours/annum			Average use 800 hours/annum			Very heavy use 1 500 hours/annum		
1. *Depreciation:*	Depreciation at 10%			Depreciation at 13%			Depreciation at 19%		
Diminishing balance calculation (see Table 3.3 for depreciation rates)	New £1 000		WDV	New £1 000		WDV	New £1 000		WDV
	Yr 1	100	900	Yr 1	130	870	Yr 1	190	810
	2	90	810	2	113	757	2	154	656
	3	81	729	3	98	659	3	125	531
∴ Depreciation		81			98			125	
2. *Interest* $\frac{1\,000}{2} \times 10\%$		50			50			50	
3. *Vehicle tax and insurance*		10			10			10	
Total fixed costs		£141			£158			£185	
Fixed costs £/hr		0·47			0·19			0·12	
Running costs 1. Fuel and oil at £0·125/Tr.hr		37·5			100			187·5	
2. Repairs and spares (see Table 3.6 for percentage rates)	at 4%	40·0		at 7%	70·0		at 10·5%	105·0	
Total running costs		77·5			170·0			292·5	
Running costs: £/hour		0·258			0·212			0·195	

Table 3.9 *Calculation of the hourly operating cost of tractor at three levels of use (based on Table 3.8)*

Use Hr/annum	Light 300	Average 800	Heavy 1 500
Fixed cost £/hr	0·47	0·197	0·123
Running cost £/hr	0·258	0·212	0·195
Operational cost £/hr	0·728	0·410	0·318

Conclusions

The need for an appreciation of the economics involved in the use of farm machinery continues to increase. Although it is easy for the farmer to clearly recognise certain machinery cost items – he can hardly fail to notice the cheques made out for fuel, oil and repairs – he must not overlook the fact that the major costs of operating machinery are depreciation and interest on the capital invested.

Farm labour costs

'The general farm worker' of today is a person who needs to have a wide range of ability and skills. On some farms there are a number of workers, while on other farms there is only the farmer's family or possibly just the farmer himself. In fact, over 50 per cent of the 300000 or so holdings in England and Wales employ no paid labour at all. Whether the size of the farm is large or small, whether the farm system is extensive or intensive, the work involved in the running of that farm ranges from the dull monotonous routine tasks to the highly skilled operations. Often a farm worker must be capable of undertaking all these jobs proficiently since where crops and livestock are concerned, a great deal depends on attention to detail and jobs being done properly.

Reasons for examining farm labour costs

The number of workers in the industry continues to fall as is shown in the figures in Table 3.10.

A graph indicating the situation in the United Kingdom during recent years is given in Figure 3.*b*. This clearly shows a rapid decline in the number of whole-time, especially male, workers and a less severe fall in the numbers of part-time workers.

Two major factors have contributed to this decline. Increased mechanisation has meant fewer workers are needed, particularly on arable farms, and at the same time, competition from other employment has drawn many from the land. Invariably industry in rural areas and in towns situated near farming regions is able to offer considerably higher wages than can be generally obtained in farming. Farmers who are faced with such competition for labour must be prepared to pay the higher rates comparable with the competing industries and, therefore, the need for efficient use of this costly resource on farms is all the more important.

Even farmers in areas where competition from other forms of employment is not so great are faced with the continually increasing cost of wages and National Insurance. In February 1970, for example, the statutory minimum wage for male farm workers over twenty years of age was set at £13·75 per week, being the 23rd increase in statutory minimum wage rates made by the Agricultural Wages Board since the war.

Table 3.10   Numbers of agricultural workers at June in the United Kingdom – ('000 workers)

| | Full-time* | | Part-time† | | |
	Males	Females	Males	Females	Total
1946	599	96	197	84	976
1947	611	91	201	77	980
1948	625	90	139	78	932
1949	645	85	135	69	934
1950	639	79	136	64	918
1951	621	70	129	62	882
1952	594	70	132	73	869
1953	578	68	128	68	842
1954	563	64	121	67	815
1955	535	60	119	74	788
1956	510	56	113	75	754
1957	502	55	116	77	750
1958	488	50	114	78	730
1959	480	47	112	80	719
1960	462	43	111	77	693
1961	439	41	107	75	662
1962	420	39	103	71	633
1963	407	37	98	69	611
1964	381	34	97	72	584
1965	355	33	94	69	551
1966	332	31	91	68	522
1967	315	31	76	63	485
1968	296	28	68	58	450
1969	281	27	69	56	433

* Comprises regular whole-time workers and includes members of the Women's Land Army and prisoners-of-war in earlier years
† Comprises workers returned in the agricultural censuses as regular part-time and seasonal or casual workers
(*Source: Annual Review and Determination of Guarantees*, 1970. H.M.S.O. Table J, p. 34. Cmnd. 4321).

Many employers of farm labour pay rates above the minimum wage but even this leaves the farm worker with a low income compared with workers in other industries. Many employers pay more than the minimum because they recognise the ability possessed by their workers; others concerned about the decreasing availability of farm workers wish to retain good men in the face of outside competition.

The weekly pay-packet, however, may not be the sole reflection of a farm worker's earnings. Some employers operate bonus schemes of various types, e.g. a share in profits made, a payment per animal reared, or per gallon of milk produced. In some instances such bonus schemes provide good incentives but in many cases they are subject to abuse and therefore many employees and employers are against them. Some farmers supply their

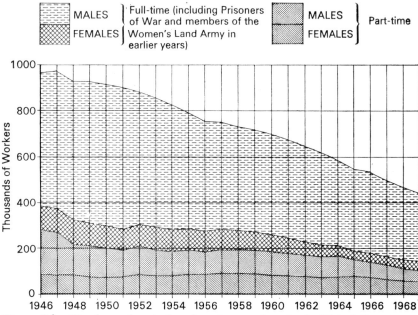

Figure 3.b   Numbers of agricultural workers at June in the United Kingdom
(*Source: Annual Review and Determination of Guarantees*, 1970. H.M.S.O., Figure VI, p. 34. Cmnd 4321)

workers with certain perquisites, e.g. free cottage, milk, potatoes, eggs, etc. These items, though useful to the worker, do little to raise his earnings to the level of his counterpart in industry.

Regular labour is a 'continuous flow resource', i.e. from 'clocking-on' until 'knocking-off' time the worker is available. As the time of day passes, this resource must be employed efficiently otherwise workers lose interest, and relationships between employee and employer are more likely to degenerate. Therefore, use of farm labour must be carefully planned both on a seasonal and day-to-day basis if it is to be put to best use.

As well as being a continuous flow resource it is an indivisible one – namely, half a man cannot be employed (except in the sense of part-time employment). This often leads to overstaffing, especially on arable farms, so that the regular farm labour force can cope with peak labour demands. The decreasing availability of casual labour has undoubtedly encouraged this. Where overstaffing does occur it is all the more important that the deployment of such labour be carefully organised throughout the slacker periods of the year.

Labour is an important 'fixed cost' item: it accounts for some 40 per cent of all fixed costs on farms in the South-East of England (see Table 3.2). In addition to the economics of farm labour and its utilisation, it must be remembered that a human factor is involved here. Workers need careful management and handling – this is most important on all farms, particularly the ones employing large numbers of workers. The principles of 'man management' or 'human relations' are not easy to write about, since rigid formulae cannot be applied. Either a manager has this 'gift' or he does not: if he has not, then the chances are that he will find it difficult to keep good workers for any length of time.

Farm labour is a human resource, and good workers continue to be more difficult to obtain. Labour is a major item of farm expenditure and, therefore, utilisation of it must be carefully planned and certain helpful techniques will be described later.

Before embarking upon methods that can be used to plan farm labour utilisation, it is necessary for the farm manager to examine the present use of the labour he already employs on his farm – whether paid employees or members of the family. Various techniques are used for such an examination and these are presented below.

Examining the efficiency of utilisation of farm labour

Technical efficiency

This is often considered to be the speed and thoroughness with which a worker does a particular job. Such criteria are rather intangible and, therefore, the calculation of a labour efficiency index is recommended. In Chapter 1, Worksheet 7 (Table 1.14) labour cost per 100 standard man-days was calculated.

The standards used to calculate standard man-days are based on average annual hours of labour required for particular enterprises. It must be emphasized that these are only average figures and these standards themselves will vary with the size of enterprise, size and location of the farm, degree of mechanisation, etc., on the farm. They do, however, give a comparative guide between farms of the same type in the same locality and also permit comparisons from year to year.

In addition to calculating labour cost in relation to the theoretical labour requirement of a farm, a labour efficiency index can be calculated when the total standard labour requirement (in man-days) for the enterprises on a farm is obtained. This is then compared with the actual number of man-days available on the farm.

$$\text{Labour efficiency index} = \frac{\text{Number of standard man-days required}}{\text{Actual number of man-days available}} \times 100$$

The meaning of the labour efficiency index is fairly obvious. If the index is high, then the labour is being efficiently used compared with average achievements. If the index is low, the efficiency of utilisation is poor compared with the average. It must be stressed again that the comparison is with an average and, therefore, subject to a number of limitations and any replanning of labour use should be based on other efficiency measures as well as this one.

D

Economic efficiency

Measures of the economic efficiency of labour use were introduced and discussed fully in Chapter 1. Measures of economic efficiency together with the labour efficiency index should lead to a fairly sound analysis of the efficiency with which labour is being employed on a farm.

Work study

Work study involves a detailed analysis of the way in which individual tasks are carried out on farms and the time taken to do them. Obviously it is impossible to go into the details of the techniques employed in a book of this type and the reader should consult specialist books on this subject – see Appendix E.

Work study analysis is a logical investigation of work, and the procedure to follow is: select the problem, record the present methods, examine these methods, develop improved methods, install the better methods and maintain them.

In essence, work study techniques either analyse farm jobs with a view to improving methods of work (method study) or measure the time taken to carry out specific jobs which can be compared with average times (work measurement). This latter method is very specialised and of limited use to the average farmer.

Method study is of immediate value to many farmers who can easily make use of it provided they understand the basic principles involved. A number of logical steps have been put forward and method study is simply a logical approach to a particular problem.

When a problem has been selected, it may involve a complete enterprise or part of an operation, e.g. collecting eggs, when the actual work under examination is recorded. A standard chart together with a series of conventional symbols as abbreviations is used to record what actually happens. The types of charts commonly used are (i) flow process charts, and (ii) multiple activity charts.

Flow process charts. These record either the movement of a man or material and aim at improving the way in which a job is done. The symbols used are as follows:

○ – operation: where something is done or somebody does something, e.g. picking up potatoes.

▢ – inspection: where something is inspected for quality or quantity, e.g. checking bags of potatoes on a trailer.

▷ – transport: where something is moved from one place to another or somebody moves from one place to another, e.g. carrying potatoes in a basket to empty into a sack

– storage: where something is stored, e.g. potatoes put in a clamp.

 – delay: where something or somebody is temporarily taken out of circulation, e.g. waiting for the potato spinner to come round again.

A flow process chart for either man or materials can then be compiled.

Multiple activity charts. These record the activities of more than one person, machine or material. A time-scale is included showing both the sequence of events and the relationship between them as they take place. The standard markings used are:

Man or machine working

Man or machine idle

Man moving from one place to another

Man holding material or equipment

Man inspecting

Using the symbols given, a series of columns can be constructed for each man or machine and thus it can be seen from the multiple activity chart what each is doing at any given time; and obviously to see what each is doing in performing an integrated job, e.g. a team of men making silage or milking in a parlour.

When the information is recorded it should be carefully examined and the following sequence of questions posed: What is achieved? Where is it done? When is it done? Who does it? How is it done?

This progressive system of examination will usually indicate the inefficient items and the improved ways of doing jobs can be applied and put to work. Once a new routine is introduced, it must be maintained and a reversion to old ways prevented.

Work study can lead to better use of farm labour and results achieved, such as a man handling more cows through a parlour, are now well known.

Planning the utilisation of farm labour

In planning the utilisation of the farm labour force over a season, a labour profile can be constructed. Such a profile shows graphically the seasonal labour requirements of each enterprise on the farm and illustrates the total demand of all enterprises on the farm labour in each month of the year. The procedure for constructing a labour profile for a farm is as follows:

(*i*) Calculate the *Standard man-hours* required for each enterprise on the farm, using the figures given in Table 3.11. (These *standard man-hours* are *Standard man-day* figures given in Worksheet 5 (Table 1.11), multiplied by 8.)

(*ii*) Calculate the *Monthly* requirements in *Standard man-hours* for each enterprise by reference to Table 3.11, which gives the percentage distribution month by month.

(*iii*) Then construct a labour profile as shown in Figure 3.c, clearly hatching (or colouring) to indicate each enterprise.

(*iv*) The troughs, or slacker periods, can be used for allocating general farm maintenance work, estate work, repairs to buildings, holidays, etc. Fifteen per cent of the total number of man-hours required on the farm is considered adequate to cover this. Thus, calculate this 15 per cent and distribute it in the 'trough' months on the profile, bringing the slacker months up to the same level.

Constructing a labour profile for Littledown Farm

Cropping and stocking – Year 2

	acres		
Spring barley	65	Sheep (ewes and rams)	154
Winter wheat	20	Dairy followers (replacement	
Main crop potatoes	15	units)	16
Reseeded grass	38	Dairy cows	71
Hay	8	Pigs (sows and boar)	20
Silage	52		
Total grass acreage	200		

The monthly *Standard man-hours* calculated using Table 3.11 are given in Table 3.12. For example, the calculation for spring barley in May is as follows:

(*a*) Standard man-hours per annum for barley:

$$65 \text{ acres} \times 16 \text{ std. man-hrs.} = 1040 \text{ std. man-hrs}$$
(from Table 3.11)

(*b*) In the month of May the requirement for barley is 3 per cent of the annual amount from Table 3.11, therefore:

3 per cent of 1040 std. man-hours = 31 std. man-hours

The labour profile for Littledown Farm, given in Figure 3.c, clearly indicates the times when labour peaks will occur and the slacker periods when estate work, etc., can be carried out. If the number of man-hours available on the farm are plotted, the times of the year when extra-man hours will be needed are easily seen. This may be satisfied by either employing casual labour or paying overtime rates to the regular workers, or a combination of both.

The labour profile is also useful in planning the effects of changes in the scale of enterprises on the seasonal labour demands as well as the effects on the farm labour of introducing new enterprises and eliminating old ones.

Table 3.11 Standard man-hours per annum required by various farm enterprises and the percentage distribution of these requirements on a monthly basis

Enterprise	Man-hours per acre or head	Jan.	Feb.	Mar.	Apl.	May	June	July	Aug.	Sept.	Oct.	Nov.	Dec.
Winter wheat	16·0	—	—	3·3	6·7	—	—	—	23·1	30·6	30·8	5·5	—
Winter barley	16·0	—	—	3·3	6·7	—	—	23·1	30·6	20·0	10·8	5·5	—
Winter oats	16·0	—	—	3·3	6·7	—	—	23·1	30·6	25·0	5·8	5·5	—
Spring wheat	16·0	—	—	30·7	—	3·0	—	—	24·4	25·0	4·0	8·9	4·0
Spring barley	16·0	—	—	27·7	3·0	3·0	—	—	36·6	12·8	4·0	8·9	4·0
Spring oats	16·0	—	—	30·7	—	—	—	—	30·0	22·4	4·0	8·9	4·0
Main crop potatoes	120·0	—	—	9·0	18·2	2·4	4·6	4·6	1·1	9·8	37·5	11·4	1·4
Kale*	8·0	—	—	10·0	28·0	30·0	4·0	—	—	14·0	14·0	—	—
Silage (1st cut)†	12·0	—	—	5·0	—	75·0	15·0	—	—	—	—	—	—
Dairy cows (parlour milked)	72·0	9·3	9·3	9·3	8·2	7·4	7·4	7·4	7·4	7·4	8·3	9·3	9·3
Dairy cows (cowshed milked)	96·0	9·3	9·3	9·3	8·2	7·4	7·4	7·4	7·4	7·4	8·3	9·3	9·3
Dairy followers (per replacement unit)	40·0	12·0	12·0	11·0	5·0	5·0	5·0	5·0	5·0	5·0	11·0	12·0	12·0
Ewes and rams	6·0	8·0	8·0	24·0	10·0	8·0	10·0	5·0	5·0	5·0	6·0	6·0	5·0
Sows and boars	40·0	←					8·34% per month						→
Direct seeding grass‡	4·0	—	—	—	—	—	—	—	40·0	60·0	—	—	—
Total grass acres	8·0	—	—	19·0	19·0	12·0	19·0	19·0	8·0	4·0	—	—	—
Hay (1st cut)§	12·0	—	—	5·0	—	15·0	75·0	2·5	2·5	—	—	—	—

These figures relate to percentage distribution per month

* Kale – sown in May † Silage – mostly made in May ‡ Late summer reseeding § Hay – mostly made in June

Table 3.12 Monthly labour requirements of enterprises, in standard man-hours, for Littledown Farm in Year 2

Enterprise	Acres or head	Standard man-hours per acre or head	Total man-hours required	Jan.	Feb.	Mar.	Apl.	May	June	July	Aug.	Sept.	Oct.	Nov.	Dec.
Spring barley	65	16·0	1040	—	—	288	31	31	—	—	381	133	42	92	42
Winter wheat	20	16·0	320	—	—	11	21	—	—	—	74	98	98	18	—
Main crop potatoes	15	120·0	1800	—	—	162	328	43	83	83	20	176	675	205	25
Reseeding grass	38	4·0	152	—	—	—	—	—	—	—	61	91	—	—	—
Hay	8	12·0	96	—	—	5	—	15	72	2	2	—	—	—	—
Silage	52	12·0	624	—	—	32	—	468	94	15	15	—	—	—	—
Total grass acreage	200	8·0	1600	—	—	304	304	192	304	304	128	64	—	—	—
Sheep (ewes and rams)	154	6·0	924	74	74	222	92	74	92	46	46	46	56	56	46
Dairy followers (per replacement unit)	16	40·0	640	77	77	70	32	32	32	32	32	32	70	77	77
Dairy cows (parlour milked)	71	72·0	5112	475	475	475	421	378	378	378	378	378	426	475	475
Pigs (sows and boar)	20	40·0	800	67	67	67	67	67	65	65	67	67	67	67	67
			13108	693	693	1636	1296	1300	1120	925	1204	1085	1434	990	732
General farm work at 15%			1966	479	479	—	—	—	52	247	—	87	—	182	440
			15074	1172	1172	1636	1296	1300	1172	1172	1204	1172	1434	1172	1172

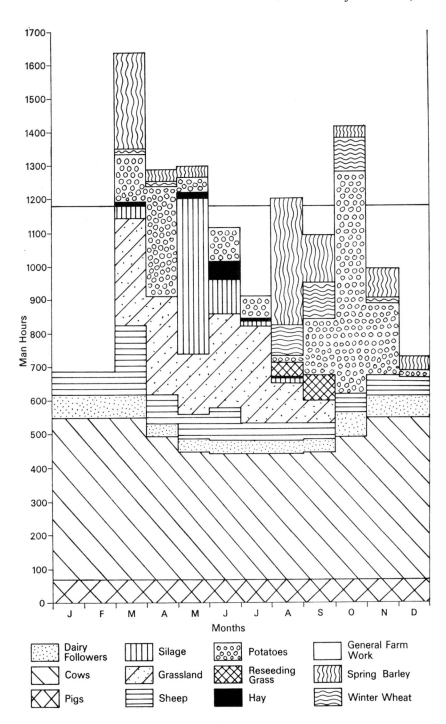

Figure 3.c Labour profile for Littledown Farm

Labour profiles can also aid the selection of combinations of farm enterprises which will minimise peaks and create a more even demand for labour throughout the year.

It may be felt that a lot of calculations are involved in preparing a labour profile, but the outcome can often prove to be very enlightening and the effort expended more than worth while.

Farm buildings and fixed equipment

Once a decision has been made to invest in fixed equipment, then an annual cost will automatically result. It comprises depreciation of the building (or fixed equipment), interest on the capital invested in the building, regular maintenance of the building and insurance on the building.

When considering the depreciation of farm buildings they should not be considered as long term investments like some commercial buildings. The 'life' of farm buildings should be taken as 10–15 years, depending upon the function and type of construction of the building. It is generally agreed that it is wrong to regard farm buildings as long term constructions. 'Shorter life' farm buildings are becoming more common, e.g. pole barns, cow kennels, and timber and alloy rather than concrete and asbestos structures. Like movable machinery, buildings depreciate due to obsolescence, and general deterioration as well as wear and tear.

In any calculations involving farm buildings an interest charge should be included on the capital invested in them. As for farm machinery, a reasonable percentage (say the current bank borrowing rate) is charged on half the capital invested, since the building is written off over this period during which the loan is completely repaid.

Estimating a figure for the maintenance of farming buildings is rather involved. Obviously, maintenance on a building such as a parlour will be greater than for a straw barn. A figure of 1·25 per cent of the capital cost is a useful guide.

The premium for the insurance of farm buildings will vary with the uses and purposes of the building. A general charge is £0·15 per £100 of capital per annum. Obviously the insurance premium will be higher where the risk is greater, e.g. buildings near a source of heat.

No mention has been made so far of payment of rates on farm buildings. The position is that rates do not have to be paid on farm buildings that are situated on agricultural holdings when the enterprise in the building is connected to, or supported by, the farm. Exemption from rates may not be the case, however, for certain intensive enterprises housed in buildings, e.g. intensive poultry units, supplied by purchased feed and possibly situated on only a small area af land.

Although investment in farm buildings may often be regarded as a Cinderella in farming, something resembling a fairy god-mother has appeared since the Second World War, namely government grants to assist farmers financially in putting up buildings. The Farm Improvement Scheme (1957–67) and the modified scheme since 1967 has done a great deal to assist farmers financially in erecting farm buildings and other fixed equipment. The broader terms of the revised scheme (1967) have, no doubt, further encouraged such investment, and the increase in the rate of grant to 40 per cent announced in the 1970 Price Review should help further. Even with a grant of 40 per cent on the likely cost of a building, farmers must look upon this as an investment and make sure that money put up by them is made to pay or 'earn its keep'.

Rent

Rent is the charge made by a landowner to a tenant for the 'hire' of the farm, buildings, farmhouse and cottages. Farm rents in England and Wales have always been regarded as 'low' and returns on landlords' capital are generally of the order of 1–2 per cent excluding capital gains and amenity values. There are many reasons for this, but probably one of the more important is that landowners have invested money in farms and farm land as a long term, secure investment.

Rents are normally payable at half-yearly intervals at the end of each period. In farm management work a rent is imputed to owner occupiers' farms so that their financial results can be compared with those obtained by tenant farmers.

General farm overheads

In all farm accounts there will be a number of fixed cost items which are of a general nature. These may include tithe, the farm water rate, general farm insurances, office expenses including telephone, stationery and postage, and professional charges. Although these items as a group may seem to be small, they must not be overlooked.

General conclusions

The cost items classified as fixed costs are frequently the major proportion of farm costs. Generally speaking, farmers have not paid enough attention to these items in the past and have tended to concentrate on reducing variable costs such as feed consumed or fertilisers spread being items that are more easily controlled.

However, if these so called fixed costs are not carefully controlled, they alter imperceptibly and thus become anything but fixed. The likely consequence is too well known: a smaller profit margin.

4 | The economics of agriculture

The importance of regarding farming as a business has already been stressed in earlier chapters. Anyone who sets out to make a profit from farming must recognise his farm as a business in exactly the same way as other entrepreneurs regard their businesses. Whatever the business, farming or otherwise, certain basic economic principles underlie that business, and these are, in essence, common sense applied according to the rules of logical thought. A knowledge of these principles may, however, help to maintain the success of a business or help to avert its failure.

Farmers, like all businessmen, are continually confronted with the problem of choice relating mostly to the best use of their resources – land, labour and capital. How should each be deployed in the farm business so that the objective for running that business can be achieved? An understanding of the basic economic principles which underlie farming can help a farmer, or farm manager, to make his business successful. However, the farmer must remember that it is only by the application of these principles that he will be able to make better use of his resources.

Some of the basic principles of economics relating to agriculture will be considered in this chapter.

Supply and demand in agriculture

An understanding of the interrelationships between supply, demand and price is important in any business including farming. Stated in the simplest of terms, price will be influenced by the demand for a product and its availability. In a situation of perfect competition (i.e. no guaranteed prices, subsidies, etc.), if the supply of a commodity rises with the demand for it, then price will remain fairly even. If the demand for a commodity increases but supply remains fairly even, then the price of that commodity will rise. When supply of a product rises but demand remains fairly even, then the price of the product will fall; conversely if the supply of a product falls then the price of the product will rise when demand remains constant. In the days of 'free competition' in British Agriculture, when farmers were directly subject to the forces of supply and demand, most farmers were painfully aware of the consequences of supplies exceeding demand. Low milk prices, clamps of rotting potatoes in the early summer and the smell of rotting onions at the roadside were clear evidence of supply having exceeded demand. On the other hand, high prices for potatoes and pigs, where demand exceeded supply, and rock-bottom prices, when supply exceeded demand, gave rise to fluctuations in quantities produced over the years.

Nowadays, with guaranteed prices and assured markets for most agricultural products, producers are no longer left completely exposed to the laws of supply and demand. The 1947 Agricultural Act, together with the 1957 Agricultural Act, provides guaranteed prices for cereals, milk, cattle, sheep, pigs, wool, potatoes, sugar beet and eggs, and these are reviewed each year in the annual price review. Although guaranteed prices exist for a number of agricultural products, the laws of supply and demand still influence farming today. For instance, certain products, e.g. horticultural crops and seed crops, are not covered by the annual price review. Furthermore, some of the products for which there is a guaranteed price have been subject to standard quantities over the years, meaning that national production above a certain level (i.e. the standard quantity) would result in an automatic reduction in the guaranteed price for that product.

Broadly speaking, most farmers nowadays are fairly well insulated from the direct impact of the laws of supply and demand and therefore need not live in fear of 'the bottom dropping out of the market', as was often the fear of their forefathers.

Although farmers' prices may be guaranteed irrespective of quantities of products produced, some attempts have been made to regulate supplies of products. In contrast with some other industries, control of the quantities of output from agriculture is very difficult. Variations in levels of output are inevitable since so many factors are involved which are outside man's control. However, the Potato Marketing Board attempts to limit potato supply by restricting acres planted by means of a quota acreage system and the British Sugar Corporation operates a system of contract acres for sugar beet. Even though there are these attempts to regulate supply the national output of these two products varies considerably from year to year depending on the seasons, etc.

In conclusion, it is fair to say that although the present system of guaranteed prices and assured markets does provide a cushion for the farmer against the direct impact of supply and demand forces, fluctuation in supply and demand, experienced since man first started to farm, are still very evident.

The law of diminishing returns

The Law of Diminishing Returns is essentially very simple. It states that yields of crops and stock do not increase in direct proportion to increases in inputs, but rather, after a certain level of yield, as levels of an input are increased the rate of increase in yields diminishes.

The effect of the law of diminishing returns is clearly shown by the theoretical figures given in Table 4.1, indicating the response of winter wheat to various levels of nitrogen fertiliser applied as a top dressing in the spring.

Table 4.1   Response by winter wheat to different levels of nitrogen applied in the spring

Rate of nitrogen applied (units/acre) (a)	Yield of grain (cwt/acre) (b)	Marginal increase in yield (cwt/acre) (c)
0	21·2	—
10	22·2	1·0 ⎫ increasing returns
20	23·8	1·6 ⎭
30	25·1	1·3 ⎫
40	26·1	1·0 ⎪
50	26·9	0·8 ⎪
60	27·5	0·6 ⎪ diminishing
70	28·0	0·5 ⎬ (decreasing) returns
80	28·3	0·3 ⎪
90	28·5	0·2 ⎪
100	28·6	0·1 ⎭
120	28·5	−0·1 negative return

From Table 4.1 it can be seen that the response of the winter wheat to the nitrogen fertiliser varies at different levels of its application. The response of the wheat at lower levels of nitrogen application is high; at the higher levels of nitrogen application the response decreases and by the time 120 units of nitrogen per acre are applied, the result is, in fact, a depression of yield because the technical limit of the crop has been exceeded and lodging has probably occurred. The response increments are shown in Table 4.1, column (c). In the early stages increasing returns occur; then diminishing returns result and finally the negative response occurs at the 120 unit per acre level.

The figures in Table 4.1 clearly show that after an initial phase of increasing returns, diminishing returns result. The responses are plotted as a graph – see Figure 4.a.

It is important for farmers to remember that diminishing returns will apply to all production processes in agriculture – feeding dairy cows as well as applying nitrogen to grass and cereals. Having established the fact that diminishing returns will occur in a production process, the next obvious question is how much of a particular input should be employed in any production process. To answer this question marginal analysis must be explained.

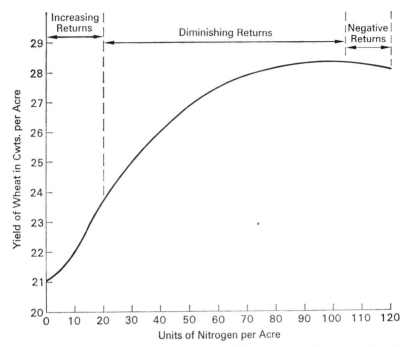

Figure 4a. Response of winter wheat to different levels of nitrogen fertilizer applied in the spring – showing diminishing returns

Marginal analysis

Marginal analysis is concerned with the changes that occur in a production process when further increments of an input are employed. If the figures given in Table 4.1 are taken and the nitrogen costed at £3·75 per 100 units and the wheat grain valued at £30 per ton, then the figures given in Table 4.2 result.

From Table 4.2 it can be seen quite clearly that at the lower levels of nitrogen application the extra (marginal) revenue (column (*d*)) from the wheat considerably exceeds the extra (marginal) cost (column (*e*)) of the increment of nitrogen fertiliser applied, e.g. by increasing the level of nitrogen per acre from 30 to 40 units the extra wheat produced was worth £1·5, while the cost of the 10 units of nitrogen applied to produce this increase in yield was only £0·375. Towards the other end of the scale, when the nitrogen fertiliser application is increased from 90 to 100 units nitrogen per acre, the marginal revenue was only £0·15, while the marginal cost was £0·375 – obviously not a profitable proposition.

In any production process, if profit margins are to be maximised, then the optimum point to which inputs should be employed is where marginal revenue equals marginal cost. In this particular example (see Table 4·2) the amount of nitrogen fertiliser that should have been applied was

Table 4.2   Response by winter wheat to different levels of nitrogen applied in
the spring

Rate of nitrogen applied (units) (a)	Yield of grain (cwt/acre) (b)	Marginal increase in yield (cwt/acre) (c)	Marginal value* of increases in yield of grain (d)	Marginal cost of nitrogen (£†/acre) (e)
0	21·2	—	—	—
10	22·2	1·0	1·50	0·375
20	23·8	1·6	2·40	0·375
30	25·1	1·3	1·95	0·375
40	26·1	1·0	1·50	0·375
50	26·9	0·8	1·20	0·375
60	27·5	0·6	0·90	0·375
70	28·0	0·5	0·75	0·375
80	28·3	0·3	0·45	0·375
90	28·5	0·2	0·30	0·375
100	28·6	0·1	0·15	0·375
120	28·5	−0·1	−0·15	0·375

* Wheat at £30 per ton   † Nitrogen at £3·75 per 100 units

somewhere between 80 and 90 units per acre. At 80 units of nitrogen per acre marginal revenue (£0·45) was greater than marginal cost (£0·375), and at 90 units of nitrogen per acre marginal cost (£0·375) exceeded marginal revenue (£0·30).

Marginal analysis permits the location of the point in a production process where marginal revenue equals marginal cost. When this position has been located, then the question raised earlier as to how much of an input should be employed in a production process can be answered – assuming that capital is available and profit margins are to be maximised.

Some would try to argue that this marginal concept is too theoretical and would therefore dismiss it as being irrelevant to farming. This is dangerous: obviously the principle applies in farming as in any other business – too high levels of input can be employed. It follows, therefore, that the doctrine of maximising output (i.e. produce up to the level of the technical limit) does not make economic sense and will consequently affect profit margins.

The effect on final profit margins of increasing inputs beyond the point where marginal revenue equals marginal cost can be shown by calculating a margin of 'wheat sales minus nitrogen cost' (this is similar to the efficiency measure calculated in Chapter 1 – Worksheet 7, Table 1.14, 'margin of milk sales minus concentrates fed to cows'). Taking the figures given in Table 4.2, margins of wheat sales minus nitrogen cost have been calculated and are presented in Table 4.3.

Table 4.3   *Responses by winter wheat to different levels of nitrogen fertiliser applied in the spring – margin of wheat sales minus nitrogen cost at different levels of nitrogen application*

Units of nitrogen (a)	Yield in cwt/acre (b)	Value of grain at £30/ton (c)	Cost of nitrogen at £3·75/100 units (d)	Margin of wheat sales minus nitrogen cost (e)
		£	£	£
20	23·8	35·70	0·75	34·95
60	27·5	41·25	2·25	39·00
70	28·0	42·00	2·63	39·37
80	28·3	42·45	3·00	39·45
90	28·5	42·75	3·38	39·37
120	28·5	42·75	4·50	38·25

Note: The optimum level of nitrogen inputs is between 80 and 90 units of nitrogen where the margin of wheat sales minus nitrogen cost is greatest. After this point the margin decreases

The optimum level of nitrogen input so as to maximise margin of wheat sales minus nitrogen cost is the same point as was located in Table 4.2, i.e. between 80 and 90 units per acre of nitrogen fertiliser. Where higher levels of nitrogen fertiliser are used, although the total yield may increase, the margin decreases.

Average returns

Farmers are usually very much concerned with averages – average levels of outputs, average levels of costs, and so on. Now that the concept of marginal analysis has been explained and it has become evident that to maximise profit margins the optimum level of input to aim at in any production process is that point where marginal revenue equals marginal cost, it is important to examine the concept of average levels of results.

If the data used earlier (Tables 4.1 and 4.2) are re-examined, average levels of responses can be calculated for the various levels of nitrogen fertiliser inputs – these are given in Table 4.4. In column (c) it will be seen that the best average level of response made by the winter wheat to the nitrogen fertiliser applied in the spring was obtained at the lower level of nitrogen application. As larger amounts of nitrogen were applied the average level of response fell – because of the effect of the law of diminishing returns.

It follows, therefore, that where maximum profit margins are being sought, the optimum level of input can only be determined by reference to marginal analysis, and averages, by themselves, can be misleading.

Table 4.4   *Average response by winter wheat to different levels of nitrogen fertiliser applied in the spring*

Rate of nitrogen fertiliser applied (units/acre) (a)	Yield of grain (cwt/acre) (b)	Average grain yield per 10 units of nitrogen (cwt/acre) (c)
0	21·2	—
10	22·2	2·22
20	23·8	1·19
30	25·1	0·84
40	26·1	0·65
50	26·9	0·54
60	27·5	0·46
70	28·0	0·40
80	28·3	0·35
90	28·5	0·22
100	28·6	0·29
120	28·5	0·24

Conclusions on marginal and average analysis

1. As levels of an input are increased in a production process, a certain level of yield is attained after which any further increases in input result in diminishing increases in output.

2. If profit margins are to be maximised, the optimum level of input to employ in a production process is where marginal revenue equals marginal cost and not where the highest average level of response is achieved. This optimum level of input will obviously be affected by changes in price of input and value of output.

3. Since the greatest response per unit of input is obtained in the early stages of the production process, then where capital is limited, it will be better to apply small amounts of an input over the whole enterprise rather than the optimum amount to only part of the enterprise (i.e. it is better to apply 30 units per acre of nitrogen fertiliser on all acres of winter wheat rather than an optimum amount of, say, 85 units per acre of nitrogen fertiliser on some acres of winter wheat and none on the remaining acres!).

4. Maximum profit margins will not be realised by maximising output, i.e. by producing the greatest possible output. Maximum profit margins will always be short of the 'maximum output' or 'technical limit' of a production process – unless, of course, the input being employed costs nothing.

Average and marginal returns on capital

Farmers and managers should clearly distinguish in their minds between average and marginal returns on capital. Average returns relate to the return on all the capital invested in an enterprise while marginal returns relate to the return on an extra (added or marginal) sum of capital. The figures in Table 4.5 may help to illustrate this difference.

Table 4.5   Average and marginal returns on capital in different enterprises

	Pigs	Poultry	Cows
Capital invested	£5000	£5000	£5000
Return on £5000	500	250	1000
∴ Average return =	10%	5%	20%
Increase capital invested by	£1000	£1000	£1000
Return on extra £1000	300	100	50
∴ Marginal return on extra £1000 invested =	30%	10%	5%
Total return on £6000	800	350	1050
∴ Average return on £6000	13·3%	5·8%	17·5%

In Table 4.5 results are given for three farm enterprises on the same farm. The average capital invested in each enterprise (in buildings, stock, equipment, etc.) is £5000. The present returns are such that the average percentage return on the £5000 average capital invested in each enterprise is 10 per cent from pigs, 5 per cent from poultry and 20 per cent from cows. Each enterprise can be extended and a sum of £1000 is being considered for investment in one of the enterprises. The expected results are budgeted and the anticipated return (marginal return) on this £1000 is £300 (30 per cent) from pigs, £100 (10 per cent) from poultry and £50 (5 per cent) from cows. (This may be due to the fact that most of the £1000 if invested in the cow enterprise would need to go into buildings and equipment while most of the £1000 if invested in the pigs' enterprise could go into stock – the present buildings being suitable and containing spare pig space.) The total return (average return) on the total £6000 would be 13·3 per cent from pigs, 5·8 per cent from poultry and 17·5 per cent from cows.

If the average return on capital was considered without reference to the marginal return figures, then the indication would be to invest the extra £1000 in the cow enterprise, since at both the £5000 and £6000 levels of investment the cows yield the greatest average percentage return on capital. This is, of course, misleading since the greatest marginal return on capital comes from the pigs' enterprise at 30 per cent, and so the £1000 should be invested in the pigs' enterprise. Average figures, taken in isolation, can obviously be misleading.

Equimarginal returns and opportunity cost

From the earlier consideration of maximising profit margins it was assumed that farmers had adequate capital to employ inputs up to the level where marginal revenue equals marginal cost. If, however, capital is limited then the concept of equi-marginal returns is a relevant principle.

In essence, the principle of equi-marginal returns means that the last £1 spent on an enterprise or factor of production will yield a marginal return exactly equal to the last £1 earned from all other enterprises or factors of production. This is common sense: if £1 spent buying feed will return more than £1 spent buying fertiliser, then the additional feed should be purchased up to that point where the last £1 spent on feed will return exactly the same as the last £1 spent on fertiliser.

Underlying the principle of equi-marginal returns is the concept of opportunity cost. Opportunity cost evaluates the product that was not produced because resources were used for some other purpose. Suppose, for example, that a farmer can grow wheat or barley on a field on his farm. Budgeted outputs and costs for these two crops are as follows:

Table 4.6   Budgeted costs and outputs of wheat or barley on a given field

	Wheat	Barley
	£	£
Output	100	90
Cost	80	60
Margin	20	30

The comparative margin in favour of barley is £10, this being the difference in their budgeted margins. If wheat is grown in place of barley, the opportunity cost of making this choice is £30, this being the margin forgone from the barley crop. Conversely, if barley is grown in preference to wheat, the opportunity cost of so doing is £20, i.e. the margin forgone from the wheat crop.

Comparative advantage or comparative costs

This economic principle explains the reason why any economic unit, whether a farm, county or regions, concentrates on the production of those items for which its relative advantage is the greatest (or its relative disadvantage is least). It is the basic reason why arable cropping predominates in the East of England and grass production is common in the West. The principle can be simply explained by reference to two farms both in the same area each growing 200 acres of cereals in their cropping programme, but because of different soil types the following average levels of cereal yields are obtained:

	Farm A per acre	Farm B per acre
Oats	2·0 tons	1·25 tons
Barley	1·75 tons	1·5 tons

From these average yield figures it can be seen that Farm A has a comparative advantage in favour of oats (the land will yield more oats per acre than barley). Farm B has a comparative advantage in favour of barley (the land will yield more barley per acre than oats). The tendency therefore will be for Farmer A to specialise in oat growing and for Farmer B to grow barley. The fact that Farmer A has an absolute advantage over Farmer B in growing both oats and barley (i.e. the yields are higher than on Farm B) does not affect the principle of comparative advantage.

In deciding whether or not to specialise, both farmers would reason along the following lines – Farmer A must sacrifice $\left(\dfrac{2.0}{1\cdot75} = 1.14\right)$ tons of oats if he wants one ton of barley (because the oats on his farm yield 2·0 tons per acre, but the barley only yields 1·75 tons per acre). Farmer B, on the other hand, must sacrifice $\left(\dfrac{1\cdot5}{1.25} = 1\cdot2\right)$ tons of barley, if he wants one ton of oats. It follows, therefore, that it will be to each farmer's advantage to specialise, especially if Farmer A can acquire a ton of barley for less than 1·14 ton of oats, and if Farmer B can acquire a ton of oats for less than 1·2 ton of barley.

In addition to the advantages to each of the farmers that result from specialisation, the total output that results from specialisation is greater (? an advantage to the national economy). The figures given in Table 4.7 (Case (ii)) show this, where Farmer A grows only oats and Farmer B grows only barley. The result of this specialisation is a total output of 700 tons of grain from the two farms compared with only 650 tons when each grew 100 acres of each crop.

Clearly, then, the resulting total output is greater, and this is explained by the principle of comparative advantage where each farm specialises in growing that crop which yields best under its own particular conditions.

Specialisation

Consideration of the principle of comparative advantage has led on to the question of specialisation on farms. This involves the concentration and

Table 4.7   The principle of comparative advantage – the case for specialisation

Case (i): Farmers A and B growing 100 acres each of barley and oats

Acreage	Farm A		Farm B		Total
	tons/acre	tons	tons/acre	tons	tons
Oats: 100	at 2·0 =	200	at 1·25 =	125	325
Barley: 100	at 1·75 =	175	at 1·5 =	150	325
					650

Case (ii): Farmers A and B specialising

Acreage	Farm A		Farm B		Total
	tons/acre	tons	tons/acre	tons	tons
Oats: 200	at 2·0 =	400			400
Barley: 200			at 1·5 =	300	300
					700

efforts of a farm into one or two specific enterprises on the farm. There are a number of advantages in specialising.

Labour utilisation may well be better on farms which specialise; skilled labour can often be employed for specific jobs. Similarly, specialisation may lead to better machinery use. Managerial efforts can be concentrated into one or two particular enterprises more easily than over a whole range of different ones and so make better use of specialist machinery. Economically, specialisation also offers the advantage of reducing overheads; fixed costs per acre tend to be lower on larger farms – being one of the advantages of scale.

While specialisation leads to certain definite advantages there are also a number of risks that may be incurred. Risks such as market fluctuations for the limited number of products being produced, unfavourable weather conditions, and pest and disease attack. Some of these risks can be insured against, but obviously the consequences of some of them could be financially crippling to a farm business which has a high degree of specialisation.

Diversification (non-specialisation)

This is the opposite of specialisation and is often called mixed farming. Despite the adage 'mixed farming and muddled thinking' there are a number of positive advantages in running a number of enterprises in a farm business. Risks are spread by diversification – not all the eggs are in the same basket. Although setbacks may occur, the impact is not so great as where there is a high degree of specialisation.

Another advantage of diversification is the utilisation of by-products from other enterprises, e.g. beef animals utilising pea-haulm silage, pigs eating chat potatoes. Furthermore, many farms have a range of buildings, and if the farm carries a number of enterprises this may mean better use is made of these buildings.

In summary, the arguments for and against specialisation or diversification essentially revolve around the nature of the farmer himself and his ability to control the enterprises on his farm so as to produce a high enough level of gross margin to cover his fixed costs and to leave a reasonable profit margin at the end.

Type of enterprise

Any consideration of the economic principles relating to farming would not be complete without reference to the interrelationships of enterprises within a farm business. Basically, farm enterprises can be classified as follows:

1. *Complementary enterprises*

These are enterprises which aid or contribute towards the success of each other, e.g. leys and cereal production, cheese-making and whey fed to pigs, pigs being fed chat potatoes.

2. *Supplementary enterprises*

These are enterprises which do not compete with other enterprises but may use up superfluous resources available on the farm, e.g. pigs and poultry enterprises using spare labour and buildings.

3. *Competitive enterprises*

These are extremely well known, especially on grass farms, since these enterprises compete with each other, e.g. sheep and dairy cows competing for grass, dairy cows and dairy followers competing for grass on the same farm.

Any business management appraisal must consider a farm business as a whole and the interrelationships between enterprises in that business must not be ignored, neither should individual enterprises be examined in isolation. When the farm business is regarded as a whole, then the basic principles of economics outlined in this chapter can be applied and their likely effects anticipated since basic principles of economics will influence every farm business.

5 | Capital in agriculture

Capital is said to be the key to progress at all times. It is the basic resource and the life-blood of all industry, without which no form of business or development can ever materialise.

Land, labour and capital are the three basic resources or factors of production and the successful organisation of a farm business involves the best possible use being made of these resources under any set of circumstances, which means that at all times they should be employed in the correct proportions according to the basic economic principles discussed in the previous chapter.

This chapter considers the problems of financing a farm business and of planning capital investment to ensure an optimum or at least an adequate return.

The general inflationary trends which beset our economy during the 1960s have led to a very considerable increase in the value of agricultural land and buildings and also to a significant increase in the cost of borrowing money. At the same time the modernisation, development and mechanisation of the industry has led to an increasing demand for further capital investments.

These factors have all contributed towards making capital a scarcer and more valuable resource, therefore necessitating an adequate return from its employment.

The farmer must consequently learn to employ capital, and if necessary credit, to their fullest possible extent. He must regard capital in much the same way as he would land and labour, namely as a resource carrying a hire charge which must always be kept usefully and gainfully employed and never left idle if it can be made to yield a return.

While becoming increasingly expensive and difficult to obtain, capital has the advantage of being a 'fluid' resource in that it has a wide range of possible uses and can be used to substitute for labour (by replacing labour with machinery), and also to obtain land. Nevertheless, capital in any set of circumstances will always have its own limits or boundaries which will in turn impose restrictions on the size and form of business which can be conducted.

Measuring capital in the farm business

Capital invested in the farm business can be considered in two basic categories:

1. Landlord's capital;
2. Tenant's capital.

Landlord's capital comprises investment in the land itself, in roads, buildings and improvements.

Tenant's capital is that which is invested by the tenant in a farm and comprises all those items necessary for running the farm business which are not provided by the landlord, i.e. machinery, tenant's fixtures (buildings and fixed equipment provided by the tenant with the agreement of the landlord), livestock, stores, tenant right and cash float (if any).

Owner occupier's capital embraces both landlord's capital and tenant's capital under the one heading.

The farm trading account (Chapter 1, Table 1.4) showed the margin obtained from a year's trading, and also showed the tenant's opening and closing valuations. In order to assess the capital position of the farmer at the end of the trading year, further information is required, i.e.:

(*a*) how much he owes (sundry creditors);
(*b*) how much is owing to the farm (sundry debtors);
(*c*) the amount of cash at the bank and in hand;
(*d*) any outstanding long-term loans;
(*e*) any other assets or liabilities.

This information is not shown in the trading account, but will appear in the balance sheet. A balance sheet can be drawn up at any time and its basic layout is as follows:

LIABILITIES		ASSETS	
Sundry creditors	⎫ Liquid	Cash in hand	⎫
Bank overdraft	⎭ liabilities	Cash at bank	⎪
		Sundry debtors	⎪
		Valuation of crops and saleable stores	⎬ Liquid assets
		Livestock for sale	⎪
		Shares and other realisable investments	⎭
Loans, mortgages, etc.	⎫ Fixed	Valuation of farm buildings	⎫
	⎭ liabilities	Fixed equipment	⎪ Fixed
		Machinery and livestock not for sale	⎬ assets
		Land and houses	⎭
Balance being	Net capital		
	Total assets		Total assets

The balance sheet can be drawn up either to show the net capital of the farm business or to show the net capital of the proprietor. Shares and investments outside the farm business will only appear on the balance sheet in the latter instance.

Functions of the balance sheet

1. To indicate the net capital or net worth of the business or individual on a given date.
2. To show the distribution of net capital between partners in a business.
3. To indicate the liquidity of the business at a given date.

Before the balance sheet can be discussed further, some terms must be clearly defined:

Net capital or Net worth = Total assets – Total liabilities.

Solvency = The state of financial affairs which exists when net capital is shown on the balance sheet, i.e. when total assets exceed total liabilities.

Insolvency = When total liabilities exceed total assets (i.e. bankrupt).

Liquidity = Liquid assets – liquid liabilities. This is a measure of the amount of 'ready cash' that can be raised from the business at a given time. It is the difference between realisable assets and immediate commitments, but is by no means synonymous with 'solvency', since it is possible to be solvent yet unable to raise ready cash.

Equity = The capital owned by an individual expressed as a percentage of the total assets of the business. It is a measure of the farmers' personal investment or 'stake' in the farm business.

N.B. It is important to distinguish between 'profitability' and 'solvency'. Although a business may show profits which are acceptable by comparative standards, it will only remain solvent if it can retain a portion of its profit to maintain or increase net capital. (To maintain net capital or net worth in real terms an increase of at least 3 per cent per annum will be required in order to keep pace with the effect of inflation.)

Where 'drawings' exceed 'profits' then the level of net capital will diminish and if this continues the business will eventually become insolvent.

The income generated by capital invested in a farm business must therefore provide for the following:

1. living expenses of the farmer and his family;
2. taxation;
3. interest on capital outstanding;
4. private drawings;
5. repayment of loan capital.

Living expenses, taxation, interest and private drawings will all diminish the net capital position.

Repayment of loan capital will leave the net capital position unaltered, since this results in a corresponding reduction in the loan liability on the balance sheet, but the necessary liquidity must be available to allow such repayments to be made on schedule.

In order to show the distribution of capital between partners in a business a capital account is drawn up. This also serves to prove the account by reconciling opening and closing net capital with the trading account profit and drawings.

Table 5.1 Littledown Farm: Balance sheet and capital account at end of Year 2

LIABILITIES	£	£	£	ASSETS	£	£	£
Capital account				Livestock			10 621
Partner (A) (farmer)				Crops & cultivations			6 931
Balance at beginning				Stores			324
Year 2	9 333			*Machinery account*			
Plus half share profit	735			O.V.		5 500	
		10 068		+purchased tractor		1 000	
Less	£					6 500	
Private draw-				*Less*			
ings	762			Sale tractor		450	
Tax	170			Depreciation		790	
Rental value of						1 240	
farmhouse	38						5 260
Own consump-				*Car account*			
tion & private				O.V.		400	
use car & elec.	55			Less depreciation		50	
		1 025					350
Balance at end of Year 2		9 043		*Tenant's fixtures account*			
Partner (B) (wife)				O.V.		1 000	
Balance at beginning				+purchases		150	
Year 2	9 333					1 150	
Plus half share profit	735			*Less*			
		10 068		Sales		60	
Less	£			Depreciation		150	
Private draw-						210	
ings	363						940
Rental value of				*Sundry debtors*			
farmhouse	37			December milk			700
Own consump-				Cash in hand			30
tion & private							
use car & elec.	55						
		455					
Balance at end of Year 2		9 613					
Total net capital		18 656					
Private loan		4 000					
Bank overdraft		2 000					
Sundry creditors (feedingstuffs)		500					
		25 156					25 156

Summary of balance sheet

	£
Total assets	25156
Total liabilities	6500
Net capital	18656

∴The business is solvent.

Joint equity of farmer and his wife in business:

$$= \frac{\text{Net capital}}{\text{Total assets}} \times 100 = \frac{18656}{25156} \times 100 = 74 \cdot 2 \text{ per cent}$$

Their individual equities are as follows:

$$\text{Partner A } \frac{9043}{25156} \times 100 = 35 \cdot 9 \text{ per cent}$$

$$\text{Partner B } \frac{9613}{25156} \times 100 = 38 \cdot 3 \text{ per cent}$$

N.B. Net capital of the two partners falls by £10 during the year since total drawings are £1480 and total profit £1470.

Although the two partners start the year with equal shares of the net capital, the net worth of Partner A (the farmer) diminishes while that of Partner B (his wife) improves. This is because, although their shares of profit are equal, Partner A's drawings exceed his share of profit, while Partner's B drawings are less than her share of profit.

In this example it should be noted that although the total profit for the year was £1470, which is fairly satisfactory by comparative standards, the net capital decreased over the year because total drawings exceeded this sum.

Liquidity

The liquidity of the business can be assessed as follows:

Liquid assets	£	£
Pigs for sale	135	
Crops for sale – Wheat	945	
Barley	1440	
Potatoes	2250	
Sundry debtors	700	
Cash in hand	30	
		5500
less Liquid liabilities		
Bank overdraft	2000	
Sundry creditors	500	
		2500
Net liquidity		3000

This means that the farmer could if he wished raise £3000 without having to sell any of his permanent assets.

Capital gearing

Where a business is run both on owner's or proprietor's capital together with loan capital, this is a means of expressing the proprietor's equity as a ratio.

Table 5.2   Example of capital gearing ratios

	No gearing	Low gearing	High gearing
Loan capital (A)	—	2 000	6 000
Proprietor's capital (B)	10 000	8 000	4 000
Total assets	10 000	10 000	10 000
Level of equity	100%	80%	40%
Capital gearing B : A	—	4 : 1	1 : 1·5

The gearing ratio is easily determined from the balance sheet and can be of value in making a quick appraisal of the proprietor's likely position under different rates of return on the total capital invested in the business.

When the return on total capital in the business is greater than the interest charged on borrowed capital, then the proprietor's net worth will increase if all profits are re-invested, and the margin after paying interest charges will be high when expressed as a percentage of the proprietor's capital. Under these circumstances the higher the gearing the more profitable the business will be to its proprietor.

But if the overall return on capital is lower than the rate of interest charged on loan capital, then the proprietor's net worth will quickly be eroded when the gearing is high, but may be maintained at a low level of gearing as the extension of Table 5.2 illustrates – see table 5.3.

High gearing may well be justified if the asset is expected to generate a high return, e.g. a machine for contracting. Where the asset can only be expected to generate a moderate or low return, e.g. buying land, then a policy of high capital gearing could well be financial suicide.

Measuring return on capital in the farm business

Figures of percentage return on capital are frequently quoted, but unless a clear definition is made as to (a) the form of return, and (b) the type of capital invested, then such measures can only be extremely misleading.

In order to appraise investment of capital accurately it is necessary to make valid comparisons between the returns made on capital by different enterprises or alternative investments. It is therefore absolutely essential, as with all efficiency factors, to compare like with like.

In expressing return on capital, the following margins could be used:

1. Net margin or management and investment income.
2. Gross margin.

Table 5.3 The cases for high and low capital gearing

	No gearing	*Low gearing*	*High gearing*
Gearing ratio:	—	4 : 1	1 : 1·5
Total assets:	10 000	10 000	10 000
Situation 1			
Assuming 15% return on total capital invested			
Profit before deducting interest	1 500	1 500	1 500
Less interest on loan capital at 10%	—	200	600
Profit after deducting interest	1 500	1 300	900
Profit expressed as % of proprietor's capital	15%	16·25%	22·5%
New level of equity if all profit re-invested	100%	82·3%	44·9%
Situation 2			
Assuming 3% return on total capital invested			
Profit before deducting interest	300	300	300
Less interest on loan capital at 10%	—	200	600
Profit after deducting interest	300	100	−300
Profit expressed as % of proprietor's capital	3%	1·25%	—
New level of equity if all profit re-invested	100%	80·9%	38·1%

3. Budgeted margin or 'marginal return' on a section of the business as the result of a budgeted plan or change of policy.
4. Net cash flow.

At the same time the capital employed could be expressed as follows:

1. tenant's capital;
2. landlord's capital;
3. owner occupier's capital;
4. initial capital – the capital required to start a business or to initiate a change of policy;
5. average capital – half initial capital in machinery, buildings and depreciating assets + value of livestock and share of working capital (*see* pigs enterprise);
6. fixed capital – that which is tied up in land, buildings, fixed equipment and breeding livestock, and not easily realisable;
7. working capital – the capital required to finance the production cycle, e.g. to provide seed, fertilisers, feedingstuffs, fattening stock and to cover labour and fixed costs. The absolute amount depends on the length of the production cycle;

8. marginal capital – the extra capital required to initiate or change a policy.

By using the formula

$$\% \text{ return on capital} = \frac{\text{margin} \times 100}{\text{capital employed}}$$

it is now possible to calculate 32 possible ways of expressing return on capital – all of them different and none of them of any value unless used in the right context and compared with figures calculated on the same basis. The need for care in interpreting such measures will now be obvious.

The rates of return most frequently used and generally accepted are:

(a) *Return on initial capital* $= \dfrac{\text{Management and investment income} \times 100}{\text{Initial capital}}$

This is used in appraising the return on a long-term investment and is of particular value where the asset itself does not depreciate.

(b) *Return on average capital* $= \dfrac{\text{Management and investment income} \times 100}{\text{Average capital}}$

This is the most appropriate measure when assessing the return on a depreciating asset, e.g. a machine, the margin being expressed as a percentage of half the initial capital when the asset is completely written off.

This will of course always give a higher per cent return than the rate of return on initial capital.

(c)   *Marginal return on marginal capital* $= \dfrac{\text{Budgeted margin} \times 100}{\text{Marginal capital}}$

This may in some cases be the same as $\dfrac{\text{Gross margin} \times 100}{\text{Marginal capital}}$

The use of marginal return on capital was explained more fully in Chapter 4.

Discounted cash flow calculations

A viable investment in the farm business must during its life repay its initial capital and also generate a yield equivalent to or better than that which could be obtained by investing elsewhere at compound interest.

Since capital always has a value or opportunity cost, it must be regarded as a constantly growing or moving commodity. Discounted cash flow techniques are therefore used to appraise the return on an investment over a period of time and are based upon compound interest.

They have the further advantage of being able to make an accurate assessment of return obtained on capital when the income or net cash flows fluctuate throughout the life of the investment.

The principle of 'discounting' or conversely of 'compounding' can be explained as follows:

If £1 is invested for five years at 10 per cent compound interest, it will at the end of that period be worth £1·611. The growth of £1 over five years at 10 per cent compound interest can be shown as follows:

The value of £1·0 at the end of 1 year is £1·1 $\quad= £1·100$
The value of £1·0 at the end of 2 years is $(£1·1)^2 = £1·210$
The value of £1·0 at the end of 3 years is $(£1·1)^3 = £1·331$
The value of £1·0 at the end of 4 years is $(£1·1)^4 = £1·464$
The value of £1·0 at the end of 5 years is $(£1·1)^5 = £1·611$

One could therefore say that the present value of £1·611 receivable in five years' time at 10 per cent compound interest is £1·00, or that £1·611 discounted for five years at 10 per cent will be worth £1·00.

The present value of £1 receivable at a future date is clearly less than £1 and can be calculated as follows:

Present values of £1 discounted at 10 per cent are:

in one year $\quad \dfrac{£1}{1.100} = £0·9091$ (multiplying factor)

in two years $\quad \dfrac{£1}{1·210} = £0·8264$ (multiplying factor)

in three years $\dfrac{£1}{1·331} = £0·7513$ (multiplying factor)

in four years $\dfrac{£1}{1·464} = £0·6831$ (multiplying factor)

in five years $\quad \dfrac{£1}{1·611} = £0·6207$ (multiplying factor)

The present value of £1 received in five years at 10 per cent is £0·6207. This means that £0·6207 if invested now at 10 per cent compound interest will be worth £1·00 in five years' time.

Since these calculations are cumbersome, tables are published in Appendix B from which it is possible to obtain these appropriate discount factors and reciprocals.

If a forward budget indicates the likely net cash flows from a given investment, then two measures may be used in appraising the profitability of the investment using discounted cash flow techniques.

The two methods are:

(a) the present net worth of the investment;
(b) the discounted yield of the investment.

The present net worth is the capital gain or growth that can be obtained from an investment after discounting the net cash flows at a predetermined rate of compound interest and deducting the initial capital. If an investment shows a positive net worth it is, therefore, deemed to be viable or worth while.

The discounted yield is the rate of compound interest that will equate the present value of the net cash flows of a project over a given period back to the value of the initial investment. It is, in other words, the equivalent rate of compound interest earned by the investment during its life.

Two thousand pounds invested in a pigs' enterprise produces the following results over a ten-year period:

Table 5.4 Budgeted financial results of a pigs' enterprise

Year	1	2	3	4	5	6	7	8	9	10
	£	£	£	£	£	£	£	£	£	£
Sales	1000	1100	1000	1050	1200	1200	1200	1250	1200	1300
Expenses	700	700	650	700	700	750	800	800	900	800
Net cash flow	300	400	350	350	500	450	400	450	300	500
− Depreciation	200	200	200	200	200	200	200	200	200	200
Net margin	100	200	150	150	300	250	200	250	100	300

These figures can be summarised as follows:

	£
Initial capital invested	2000
Average capital invested	1000
Average annual net cash flow	400
Average annual net margin	200

$$\text{Rate of return on initial capital} = \frac{\text{Average net margin} \times 100}{\text{Initial capital}}$$

$$= \frac{200 \times 100}{2000} = 10\%$$

$$\text{Rate of return on average capital} = \frac{\text{Average net margin} \times 100}{\text{Average capital}}$$

$$= \frac{200 \times 100}{1000} = 20\%$$

The present net worth of the project is found by calculating the present value of the forecast incomes after discounting them at a given rate. The rate of compound interest or discount factor chosen is usually the opportunity cost of the capital and for the sake of illustration this is taken to be 10 per cent.

A discounted cash flow for the project can be calculated as follows:

Table 5.5   Discounted cash flow for budgeted pigs' enterprise

Year	Forecast income before depreciation or net cash flow	Discount factor at 10% (See Appendix B.1)	Present value of forecast income or N.C.F.
	£	£	£
1	300	0·909	272·70
2	400	0·826	330·40
3	350	0·751	262·85
4	350	0·683	239·05
5	500	0·621	310·50
6	450	0·564	253·80
7	400	0·513	205·20
8	450	0·467	210·15
9	300	0·424	127·20
10	500	0·386	193·00
Total	4000	—	2404·85

	£
Present value of Net cash flow	2404·85
Less initial capital	2000·00
Present net worth of investment	404·85

Since this is positive, the investment is worth while and clearly produces a return which at compound interest is greater than 10 per cent. However, in order to compare and appraise the viability of alternative investments, a figure of percentage return on capital is more valuable than an absolute figure such as the present net worth, and for this purpose the discounted yield is used.

The discounted yield is the rate of compound interest that will discount the net cash flows to the value of the investment over a period of years.

If the net cash flows are constant or fluctuate around a mean, this involves a simple calculation to find the appropriate discount factor:

$$\text{Discount factor} = \frac{\text{Initial capital}}{\text{Annual net cash flow}}$$

$$= \frac{2000}{400} = 5·00$$

By referring to the table for calculating the present value of a future annuity (see Appendix B.2) this factor is found to correspond to a return of just over 15 per cent, i.e. almost exactly half-way between the return on initial capital and the return on average capital.

When the cash flows are not constant but fluctuate from year to year, then a discount factor based on the average net cash flow is unreliable and the full discounted cash flow calculation must be made. Finding the actual discounted yield is in practice largely a matter of trial and error. However, since it is known that the discounted yield is greater than the rate of return on initial capital and less than the rate of return on average capital, the actual discount rate can be obtained by interpolation.

This can be calculated as follows for the pigs enterprise:

Table 5.6   Calculation of discounted yield for budgeted pigs enterprise

Year	Net cash flow	Discount factor at 10%	Present value	Discount factor at 20%	Present value
	£	£	£	£	£
1	300	0·909	272·70	0·833	249·90
2	400	0·826	330·40	0·694	277·60
3	350	0·751	262·85	0·579	202·65
4	350	0·683	239·05	0·482	168·70
5	500	0·621	310·50	0·402	201·00
6	450	0·564	253·80	0·335	150·75
7	400	0·513	205·20	0·279	111·60
8	450	0·467	210·15	0·233	104·85
9	300	0·424	127·20	0·194	58·20
10	500	0·386	193·00	0·162	81·00
			2404·85		1606·25

Interpolation

		£
	Present value at 10%	2404·85
less	Present value at 20%	1606·25
		798·60

	Present value at 10%	2404·85
less	Capital	2000·00
		404·85

$$\frac{404·85}{798·60} \times 10 = 5·07$$

Discounted yield $= 10\% + 5·07\% = 15·07\%$

Where the net cash flows are fairly constant or fluctuate around a predictable mean then the discounted yield is approximately half-way between the rate of return on initial capital (R.R.I.C.) and the rate of return on average capital (R.R.A.C.).

E

The discounted yield is less than $\dfrac{\text{R.R.I.C.} + \text{R.R.A.C.}}{2}$ – the longer the life of the investment, the higher the R.R.I.C. and the more the cash flow is weighted towards the latter years of the investment. When the opposite conditions prevail, then

$$\text{Discounted yield is greater than } \dfrac{\text{R.R.I.C.} + \text{R.R.A.C.}}{2}$$

Discounted cash flow is a sophisticated technique which has long been used in appraising investment in industry and is a fundamental process in making actuarial calculations. As the cost of capital continues to rise and need also increases to substitute capital for other resources, e.g. labour, then these techniques are likely to assume greater importance in relation to the farm business.

Sources of agricultural capital

The main sources of capital in the agricultural industry can be summarised as follows:

Accumulated profits from within the industry itself

This is indeed the major source of farming capital but it is not always in a liquid or readily realisable form since it is mainly in the form of appreciated land and capital values. The farmer's net worth and likewise his credit worthiness is improved as his land and fixed assets appreciate, but he has no ready cash unless he sells his land or uses it to secure a loan.

Public investment

Unlike other forms of business, very little public shareholders' capital has entered the industry. Only about 4 per cent of the holdings in the United Kingdom are in the hands of limited companies. Farm businesses tend to occur in small units, mostly centred around the family farm.

Government grants

These are many and varied, and since they are subject to frequent revision the National Agricultural Advisory Service should always be consulted as to the availability of Government aid for any proposed project. Eleven schemes for providing capital grants to agriculture have now been unified under the Farm Capital Grant Scheme, which provides grants for capital improvement rising to as much as 70 per cent for drainage on hill land.

Credit

There is an increasing demand for credit facilities for the farming industry, which becomes more pressing with the increasing need to modernise and re-structure farms.

At the same time, the farmers themselves hold about 90 per cent of the equity of the industry and while the banks claim that they now have over £500 million on loan to agriculture, the farmers themselves lend up to three-quarters of this amount back to the banks in the form of their current credit balances.

A change seems to have occurred in recent years in the average farmer's attitude or philosophy towards borrowing money. At one time there was a strong body of opinion amongst farmers which regarded borrowing almost as a cardinal sin, and to admit to having a bank overdraft was almost a public admission of disgrace. These attitudes were probably conceived in the terrible depression years in the late 1920s and 1930s when farming bankruptcies were all too frequent and farm businesses survived mainly as a result of utmost frugality and tenacity of purpose.

Today attitudes are changing. Other industries need to borrow capital in order to finance their development and to progress, and so also must agriculture. An overdraft is no longer something only to be admitted in deep confidential undertones, but more an expression of the risk that the bank manager is prepared to take on an individual.

Because of the awe and distrust with which any form of borrowing has long been regarded by certain sectors of the community, an unnecessary aura of mystery has grown up around the whole subject. In fact there are no gimmicks about finance. £1 borrowed is £1 which must eventually be repaid with interest. Any additional return after this is profit for the borrower.

There are, however, certain fundamental principles in relation to borrowing which must be clearly understood. These can be summarised:

Rules of Borrowing

1. The loan must show a profit – do not borrow for the purpose of providing amenities.
2. Be sure that interest and capital can be repaid out of income while maintaining liquidity.
3. Plan and budget conservatively and accurately when negotiating a loan.
4. Consider all possible alternative sources of credit.
5. Never borrow to bolster a dying or failing enterprise.
6. Aim to repay the loan during the life of the asset for which it is borrowed, e.g. if borrowing to buy a tractor make sure that the money is repaid before the tractor needs replacing.
7. Borrow from the smallest number of sources.
8. Agree on sound arrangements for repaying the loan. If possible, make special arrangements for repayment privileges to enable the loan to be paid off in a shorter time than that originally planned, should the borrower be in a position to do so. Also make provision for reduced repayments under extenuating circumstances. Arrange if possible an automatic system of repayment such as by banker's order.

9. Make all arrangements the subject of a written agreement.

A prospective lender will want to know the following about a prospective borrower:

(a) Who is he, what is his background and past business record?
Personal reputation is of paramount importance in agriculture where businesses are mostly small and based on the family unit. While this may put newcomers at a disadvantage, it is in the main a fair question. Small struggling dairy farmers of fifty seldom become dynamic entrepreneurs at fifty-five.

(b) How much does he want?

(c) What is the loan for?
Is the loan required for something that will depreciate and soon become worth nothing, e.g. a machine, or is it for land or stock which will appreciate in value?

(d) Can he meet the interest payments and repay the principal in a reasonable amount of time, while at the same time maintaining his liquidity?

(e) What security can he offer against the loan?
This involves proof of the borrower's net worth, of his equity within his present business interests and of any other creditors having prior claim on his assets.

The borrower's equity is in this connection just as important as his absolute net worth, as the example in Table 5.7 illustrates:

Table 5.7   The equity and net worth of two prospective borrowers

	Initial situation		Situation after a 10% setback of assets	
	A	B	A	B•
	£	£	£	£
Assets	110 000	15 000	99 000	13 500
Liabilities	100 000	5 000	100 000	5 000
Net capital	10 000	10 000	−1 000	8 500
Equity	9·09%	66·67%	nil	62·97%

In this case two prospective borrowers A and B each have the same net worth, but A has only a small stake in his business so that when a 10 per cent setback occurs to the value of both their assets, A is left insolvent, whereas B's equity is only marginally reduced.

As a prospective borrower, then, A is by far a greater risk than B, although his business is much larger and superficially more impressive.

A prospective borrower who has insufficient security of his own may find a guarantor to secure the loan on his behalf. The guarantor undertakes to carry the risk of the loan and to repay the capital, should the borrower find himself unable to do so.

A prospective lender will also be well advised to study the balance sheet of his prospective borrower and also to study in detail with him a capital budget of his proposed policy (*see* Chapter 2).

Credit facilities

Credit available for agriculture can be considered in three categories:

Long-term credit (over 10 years)

Mainly for the purchase of land and buildings and to carry on long-term improvements.

Medium-term credit (1–10 years)

For the purchase of plant, machinery, tenant's fixtures, breeding stock and short-term improvements.

Short-term or temporary credit

To maintain liquidity through a normal year's trading operations, e.g. to bridge the gap between sowing the crop and selling the harvest, buying store stock and selling them fat and to provide something to live off in the meantime and pay the tax man.

A farmer may well need to use all three of these forms of credit in his business at the same time.

The available facilities are now considered in their respective categories:

Long-term credit

Agricultural Mortgage Corporation
Lands Improvement Company
Private mortgages
Insurance companies
Banks

Agricultural Mortgage Corporation

The A.M.C. is Government backed and will give a mortgage for ten to sixty years on the freehold of up to two-thirds of their valuation of a property (land and buildings).

Interest is payable throughout the life of the loan at the ruling rate at the time of its acceptance by the A.M.C. Repayment is made in the form of a combined half-yearly payment covering both interest charges and capital repayment. This is so arranged that at the outset the payment is mainly interest on outstanding capital (allowable as a deductable expense for the purpose of assessing income tax commitments) and in the latter years the half-yearly payment is mainly in the form of capital repayment (not deductable for tax purposes).

Table 5.8   Breakdown of half-yearly payments on £1000 loan from A.M.C. at 9·75 per cent over three different loan periods

Year	Length of loan								
	20 years			25 years			30 years		
	Total	Interest	Capital	Total	Interest	Capital	Total	Interest	Capital
	£	£	£	£	£	£	£	£	£
1	57·291	48·341	8·950	53·733	48·516	5·216	51·733	48·612	3·120
5	57·291	42·887	14·404	53·733	45·341	8·391	51·733	46·712	5·020
10	57·291	34·104	23·187	53·733	40·225	13·508	51·733	43·650	8·083
15	57·291	19·966	37·325	53·733	31·987	21·745	51·733	38·725	13·008
20	57·291	2·670	54·620	53·733	18·729	35·004	51·733	30·795	20·937
25	—	—	—	53·733	2·525	51·208	51·733	18·033	33·700
30	—	—	—	—	—	—	51·733	2·420	49·312

If the borrower wishes to foreclose a loan before it has run to full term, he may do so upon payment of a redemption fee to compensate for the loss of interest incurred by the Corporation.

Loans are normally required to run to their full term. The final amounts repaid per £1000 borrowed initially at a rate of interest of 9·75 per cent are shown in Table 5.9.

Table 5.9   The cost of borrowing £1000 through the A.M.C.

Term in years	Half-yearly instalments per £1000 principal	Equivalent gross payment per annum %	Total amount repaid per £1000 principal
	£	£	£
40	49·862	9·983	3989
30	51·733	10·350	3104
20	57·291	11·462	2291·6
10	79·400	15·883	1588

Thus although the gross payment per annum is smaller on the long-term loan, the total repayment is very considerably more.

In the event of a borrower being unable to raise the first third of the capital required to purchase the land, the A.M.C. are now prepared to accept as collateral an endowment policy on the life of the borrower.

2. *The Lands Improvement Company*

This company was set up under the Improvement of Land Acts of 1861 and 1899. Loans are granted for periods up to 40 years at a predetermined rate of interest. This is not a mortgage as the deeds are retained by the landowner.

The security of the loan lies in the increased rent charge placed by the Minister of Agriculture on the land improved. The improvements carried out must be authorised and inspected by one of the Ministry's Land Commissioners.

The number of new loans granted each year under these arrangements is now very small.

3. *Life insurance companies*

Some companies will provide a mortgage for up to 60 per cent of their valuation of the property. These companies normally insist on the borrower covering his loan with an endowment policy. This tends to be an expensive form of borrowing but does ensure that, in the event of the borrower's death, his dependants will be protected.

4. *Private mortgages*

Next to the main clearing banks, private loans are the principal source of agricultural credit. Since farming is essentially a family concern and in many cases businesses are passed on from father to son, many new entrants to the industry are financed by their relatives or through executors or trustees of benefactors.

For example, a farmer with a family of three may die leaving his estate to be divided equally amongst his children. One of these may wish to continue to run the business and so he arranges a mortgage by which he pays out the other two over a given period during which he pays them interest on their share of the capital in the business.

5. *Clearing banks*

Although in the past the banks have been able to assist with long-term farm financing, their activities in this field of credit are now strictly limited and at present they are reluctant to negotiate credit for loans of more than ten years.

6. Other Sources

There will always be someone willing to supply credit at a price. Whether or not the price is economic is another matter.

The Industrial and Commercial Finance Corporation do undertake agricultural loans provided that they are for £5000 or more. These account for less than 1 per cent of total lending to agriculture.

Medium-term credit

Banks
Hire purchase companies
Syndicates and co-operatives
'Lease-back' arrangements

1. Clearing banks

Bank credit is by far the most convenient form of borrowing and, since interest payments are calculated on a day-to-day diminishing balance, it is also one of the cheapest. The normal rate of interest is 1 per cent above the current bank rate and is deductable for tax purposes.

Since negotiation of a bank loan is usually a personal matter between a farmer and his local bank manager, a great deal of importance is attached to the borrower's reputation and integrity. It is therefore extremely important that such agreements – often only verbal – should be honoured and overdrafts paid back on time and not allowed to drag on and on. The manager's permission and approval should always be sought if it is intended to overdraw on a bank account, however short the period, and however great the security.

2. Hire purchase companies

This is almost invariably an expensive form of borrowing for two reasons. Interest rates are usually higher than those charged by banks, and interest is calculated for the period of the loan upon the basis of the principal and not the diminishing balance.

An example is given in Table 5.10, where £1000 is repaid in equal instalments over three years. In case A (as with a bank) the interest is payable on the diminishing balance. In case B (as with a hire purchase company) the interest is calculated for the whole period on the basis of the principal.

Table 5.10   Borrowing from a bank compared with a hire purchase loan

	Sum borrowed	Length of loan	Rate of interest	Interest paid
Case A	£1 000	3 years	8%	£120
Case B	£1 000	3 years	8%	£240

Note: The advertised rate of interest is the same in both cases

This form of credit is not popular in agriculture, but some may justifiably be driven to it in order to maintain their liquidity during a programme of expansion when their assets are in an unrealisable form, or if it is used for purchasing assets with very high earning power, e.g. machinery used for contracting.

3. *Syndicates and co-operatives*

Government backed loans and also direct grants for approved projects are available through the Central Council for Agricultural and Horticultural Co-operation.

4. *Lease-back arrangements*

This form of investment arises when a farmer wishing to raise capital, sells the freehold of his farm to an investor and then leases it back on a full repairing lease at a rent equivalent to 4–5 per cent of the sale price. The price paid for the land is seldom its full market value since vacant possession is not given.

This provides a sum for expansion or re-investment for the farmer and gives the investor a secure investment with a guaranteed income, while at the same time affording him the opportunity of considerable capital appreciation. He will also gain tax relief on capital expenditure on capital improvements and modernisation, 45 per cent of the agricultural value of the land will be free of estate duty and his income will be treated as earned (i.e. eligible for two-ninths earned income relief for taxation purposes).

Short-term credit

Banks
Merchants
Co-operatives
Creditors

1. *Banks*

The main clearing banks are still the principal source of short-term credit since this is both a convenient and cheap form of borrowing and can usually be well secured.

Since the main short-term requirement will be to meet commitments during seasonal shortages of working capital, it is essential that the farmer and his bank manager should clearly understand the form of seasonal fluctuation to be expected. This is most easily illustrated by a simple cash flow diagram or capital profile as explained in Chapter 2.

2. *Merchant's credit*

This is mainly accounted for by a surcharge on the sale price or by loss of discount on a delayed payment. The interest charged here can be as high as 20 per cent. While this is obviously excessive it is the merchant's way of ensuring that his bills are paid on time. Cheaper credit can usually be negotiated between a farmer and his merchant, provided that a properly organised plan of buying and selling can be arranged in advance and that any such agreements made are strictly honoured by both parties.

3. *Co-operatives and marketing organisations*

Few co-operatives have the facilities for offering credit to farmers. Some co-operative marketing organisations (e.g. British Wool Marketing Board) do, however, allow forward payments to be made on produce which has yet to be sold and which is being held in store on the farmer's behalf.

F.M.C. will provide credit for buying stock which they will then undertake to market.

4. *Sundry creditors*

Anyone supplying goods or services without receiving immediate payment is supplying credit. Farmers seem to be notoriously bad at settling accounts unless they carry a surcharge or discount rebate. Agricultural contractors in particular appear to suffer from this form of calculated oversight.

Planning capital investment in the farm business

One advantage of capital as a resource is its fluidity and adaptability for different purposes. Capital invested in the farm business suffers from two general restrictions: (i) the slow rate of turnover of most farm enterprises, and (ii) the high proportion of fixed costs.

Both these factors limit the possible return on capital. Slow rates of turnover require high margins from each production cycle if the overall rate of return is to be adequate and high fixed costs will impose restrictions on the business, usually committing it to a narrow range of alternative enterprises.

In planning investment a fundamental aim must always be to keep capital as fluid and as mobile as possible, by keeping the largest possible proportion in productive or working capital which will be capable of earning a return and remain realisable. At the same time the proportion of capital invested in buildings and fixed equipment should be minimised since it is committed for long periods and cannot show a direct return.

When investing capital in the farm three considerations must be made:

1. What will the capital cost?
2. What must the capital earn if solvency and liquidity are to be maintained?

3. What is the opportunity cost of the capital? i.e. how much could it earn if invested elsewhere at a similar level of risk?

The cost of borrowing capital has already been discussed.

The margin from a farm business or from an investment must be sufficient to cover the following commitments if the business is to remain solvent:

(*a*) living expenses;
(*b*) repayment of borrowed capital;
(*c*) interest on capital;
(*d*) taxation.

(The net cash flow of the business must also be sufficient to cover provision for depreciation in addition to these commitments.)

It follows therefore that there is a minimum finance charge or earning rate which must be achieved by capital invested in the farm business if that business is to remain solvent. The actual finance charge will vary according to individual circumstances.

Example

A young farmer with a wife and two small children inherits a smallholding and wishes to borrow sufficient money to set up a pig unit. He needs £10000 for buildings and equipment to set up a unit which will use his labour fully.

In the initial years of the loan this investment must provide the following:

	£	
(*a*) Living expenses at £15 per week	750	£1750 taxable
(*b*) Repayment of loan over 10 years	1000	
(*c*) Interest on £10000 at 8 per cent	800	
(*d*) Income tax on £1750.		

less allowances

	£	
(*i*) depreciation	1000	
(*ii*) personal	465	
(*iii*) two children	230	
(*iv*) earned income relief $\frac{2}{9}$ of £750	166	
Total allowances	1861	
Taxable income	nil	
Tax		nil
Total commitments		£2550

The loan must generate a net cash flow of £2550 if the business is to remain solvent. In terms of immediate commitments this represents a finance charge of 25·5 per cent on the initial capital.

Suppose that a much larger loan were contemplated, e.g. to build and stock a large intensive poultry unit requiring say £100000. The return now necessary is as follows:

		£	
(*a*)	Living expenses	750 ⎫	£10750
(*b*)	Repayment of capital over 10 years	10000 ⎭	taxable
(*c*)	Interest on capital at 8 per cent	8000	
(*d*)	Taxation: Income tax on £10750		

less allowances

	£	
(*i*) depreciation	10000	
(*ii*) personal	465	
(*iii*) two children	230	
(*iv*) earned income relief $\frac{2}{9}$ of £750	166	
Total allowances	10861	
Taxable income		nil
Tax		nil
Total commitments		£18750

In this case a net cash flow of £18750 is required if the farmer is to remain solvent, and this represents a finance charge of only 18·75 per cent of the initial capital, since in this case living expenses assume a much smaller proportion of the total commitments.

Repayment of borrowed capital is regarded as profit and is liable to be taxed. On the other hand, depreciation of the asset will be set against this in calculating taxable income.

If an asset is depreciated over ten years and the initial capital is repaid over the same period, then at the end of ten years the loan will all have been paid back and the asset will be worth nothing. The farmer's capital position is thus the same as it was before embarking on the loan. But if the asset depreciates at a slower rate than the capital is repaid, then the difference will represent an increase in net worth and be taxable.

Conversely, if the asset depreciates at a more rapid rate than the loan is repaid, the borrower will enjoy considerable tax relief in the early years of the investment but would be taxed more heavily in the later years of the loan since the rate of loan repayment would be constant but the amount of depreciation would be progressively less. The net result in terms of tax paid over the whole period would be the same in either case provided that the rate of tax remained constant throughout the life of the loan.

The most important point emerging from these two examples is the need for liquidity in order to be able to repay the loan and to pay living expenses, interest and commitments.

The loan of £10000 must generate a net cash flow which can pay out £2550 a year in the early years of the loan. Similarly the loan of £100000 must produce a net cash flow of at least £18750.

Suppose now that a loan of £10000 is negotiated but this time for land and breeding stock which will not depreciate in value. In order to maintain liquidity the yield of this investment must be much larger since all repayments of capital will be regarded as income and taxed accordingly.

In order to maintain his liquidity this loan must cover the following:

			£	
(a)	Living expenses at £15 per week		750	£1750
(b)	Repayment of loan over 10 years		1000	taxable
(c)	Interest at 8 per cent		800	

		£	
(d)	Taxation on	1750	

Less allowances

	£		
(i) depreciation	nil		
(ii) personal	465		
(iii) two children	230		
(iv) earned income relief			
$\frac{2}{9}$ of £1750	388		
Total allowances		1083	
Taxable income		667	
Tax at £0·4125 in £1 on £667			275
Total commitments			2825

A finance charge of £2825 a year is now required if the farmer is to maintain his liquidity, but his net worth or credit worthiness will increase during this period by £1000 a year (i.e. the amount of capital repaid).

These examples quoted are an extremely rough and ready attempt at illustrating the concept of 'finance charge' on invested capital. To be strictly correct these examples should be subjected to discounted cash flow in order to find the appropriate average financial charge for the whole of the loan period. These examples only apply to the first years of the loans in question – but then the first years are always the most difficult.

It has also been assumed for purposes of illustration that the loans in question must provide for all the farmer's living expenses and commitments. In most cases the loan will be of a marginal nature and only be required to pay back its own capital and interest plus the extra income tax on the marginal income resulting from its employment.

The need for liquidity is illustrated more clearly by this next example.

A tenant farmer on 200 acres is making a steady annual profit of £10 per acre and is paying £5 per acre rent. He has the opportunity of buying the farm for £200 per acre. He already owns all his tenant's capital and has sufficient working capital in hand to meet his working capital requirements. He has also saved £20000, i.e. half of the purchase price and more than sufficient security for a mortgage through A.M.C.

He thus needs to borrow £20000 from A.M.C. to be repaid over 20 years at 9·75 per cent equivalent to a gross rate of £11·46 per cent (*see* Table 5.9). His annual profit is now £10 per acre+£5 per acre (rent saved) = £3000 per year. But this will have to meet the following finance charge:

		£
(*a*) Living expenses	say	750
(*b*) Taxation on £3000 per year less allowances	say	750
(*c*) Annual repayment to A.M.C. on £20000 at £11·46 per cent		2292
Total annual commitment		3792

At £15 profit per acre this cannot be done for even though the farmer's net worth or credit worthiness continues to increase at £1000 per year (the equivalent annual capital repayment), he simply has not sufficient ready cash to meet these commitments and to keep his business running. He may therefore be forced to borrow elsewhere to meet these immediate requirements.

How large a loan could he then carry? He has the following amount per year available for loan repayment and interest:

		£
Profit		3000
less living expenses	say 750	
Income tax	say 750	
		1500
		1500

At a gross rate of £11·46 per cent for a 20-year loan, £1500 per annum will service a loan of $£\dfrac{1500}{11\cdot46} \times 100 = $ *approx. £13000.*

The maximum loan that he can afford to service from his present profit of £3000 is therefore £13000. So unless he has £27000 towards the cost of the farm, he cannot afford to buy the farm and to run it at its present level of profitability.

It is important to distinguish clearly, in planning capital investment, between borrowing for a depreciating asset such as a machine and borrowing for an asset such as land which will retain or increase its capital value.

The essential differences are summarised below:

	Depreciating assets, e.g. machinery	*Non-depreciating assets, e.g. land*
Net worth	Remains unaltered as result of loan, provided that loan is repaid during the life of the asset, since annual depreciation = annual repayments	Will increase by an amount equivalent to the annual repayment of capital
Taxation	On income generated by loan less depreciation, personal and earned income allowances	On income generated by loan but no depreciation allowance is given so rate of taxation is correspondingly higher
Finance charge	Must cover: (a) Living expenses, (b) Loan repayment, (c) Interest on capital, (d) Taxation	Must cover the same items but will be greater due to the higher level of income tax payable
Capital appreciation	None	In land, this should keep pace with inflation and is currently in the order of 3% per annum
Capital gains Tax	Not liable	Liable

Opportunity cost of capital

When tying up capital in a farm business it is advisable to consider the opportunity cost, i.e. the income that the capital might generate if invested elsewhere. Income from investments outside one's own business would be regarded as 'unearned' and would be taxable at the full rate. Alternative investments outside agriculture will vary in their return according to:

(a) the risk involved, i.e. the security of the capital;
(b) the length of the loan;
(c) the amount of expected growth of the investment.

Examples of such investments

1. *Building Societies* – completely secure; no growth of capital; 4·5–5 per cent after tax deducted by building society; tax is not reclaimable.
2. *Corporation and council loans* – secure; up to 9·5 per cent interest (gross); tax deducted at source but is reclaimable; no growth of capital.
3. *First mortgage debenture stocks* – secure; up to 9·5 per cent depending on length of loan; no growth of capital.
4. *Unsecured notes* – a higher rate of interest than 1st mortgage debenture stocks but less security; no growth.
5. *shares* – less secure; chance of growth; interest or dividend usually proportional to risk; transferable; preference shares the safest.

6. *Unit trusts* – a form of share, but with a wide spread of investment in large number of different businesses; growth reflecting general trend of share market and property values; interest only moderate and fully taxable.

To invest money as securely as in the farm business one could expect a return of 10 per cent before tax. On this basis then money invested in farming must show a return of at least 10 per cent or it will pay to invest elsewhere if one's objective is purely financial.

Agriculture as an investment

The figures given in Table 5.11 illustrate the current earning power of capital invested in Agriculture.

Table 5.11   Return on capital for farms in S.E. England

	Investment per acre	Average return on capital	Premium return on capital
	£	%	%
Tenant's capital	50–55	12	20
Landlord's capital	250–300	approx 1·5*	1·5*
Owner occupier's capital	300–355	3	4·5

* Excluding capital gains and amenity values

(*Source:* Nix, J. *Farm Management Pocketbook*, 3rd Edition 1969 – Wye College, Department of Economics)

While average and premium returns on tenant's capital compare well with the opportunity cost of capital invested, it is clear that the return on capital invested in land and buildings is in general very poor indeed.

A landlord or owner occupier can obviously not afford to borrow capital at 9–10 per cent in order to achieve a return of 1·5–4·5 per cent. Similarly if the rent charged on farm land were appropriate to the interest charged at say 10 per cent on £250–300 per acre this would be an excessively heavy charge for the tenant to pay at £25–30 per acre.

There must clearly be other financial reasons for investing in agricultural land. Land is firstly a very secure investment and since approximately 100 acres a day are removed for non-agricultural purposes it is rapidly becoming scarce.

Investment in land provides a hedge or buffer against the effects of inflation, since land prices tend to follow the general trend of rising prices and thus money invested in land retains its real value or purchasing power. There is also the possibility of very significant capital gain if the land can be sold for non-agricultural development.

Government grants are available for capital improvements and in addition there are very considerable tax benefits to be obtained in that

(*a*) all income is considered as earned and therefore subject to two-ninths earned income allowance;

(*b*) agricultural land is eligible for 45 per cent estate duty rebate;

(*c*) the net cost of improvements is added to the initial value for the purpose of computing Capital Gains Tax.

During the 1960s agricultural land increased in value very considerably, and the value of land with vacant possession increased approximately two and a half times between 1959 and 1969, whereas the *Financial Times* Industrial Ordinary Share Index increased by only 54 per cent over the same time.

The same rate of appreciation of land values cannot be expected to continue, but this does explain why landlords can accept a rental value for their land which is far below the appropriate interest charge on the value of their capital invested.

6 | Livestock enterprise studies

The dairy enterprise

Milk and dairy products constitute the major output of British agriculture, the gross value of these products amounting in 1969 to 22·4 per cent of total agricultural sales in Great Britain (£447 million out of £1 988·5 million).

The dairy industry is currently undergoing great changes both in its structure and in its methods of production.

If one follows the more spectacular developments in the field of milk production one might easily be tempted to imagine that the more traditional methods of cow keeping are rapidly being discarded for mammoth units or 'cotels', as they have popularly been called, containing very large herds of a hundred or more cows. However, if one examines the statistics which are published each quarter by the Ministry of Agriculture or from time to time by the Milk Marketing Board, this is seen to be far from the truth.

Numbers of dairy cows have been increasing slowly but steadily over the last few years, but at the same time numbers of herds have dwindled, with the result that the average dairy herd is becoming larger. In spite of the occasional and much publicised 'cotel' the average size of herd in the U.K. is still only 30 cows. A wide variation exists between regions from an average of 12 cows per herd in Northern Ireland to an average of 50 cows per herd in Scotland. England and Wales average 33 cows per herd, the region having the bigger herds being the South-East with an average of 38 cows per herd.

The recent trend of rising dairy cow numbers is the cause of great concern amongst dairy farmers, for it is felt that an increase in milk production is inevitable, and then a fall in the pool price paid to the producer is bound to follow.

Although herd numbers have decreased, milk production has compared well with other farm enterprises in recent years. Figures for South-East England published recently by Wye College[1] indicate that, apart from intensive pigs and poultry production and horticulture where capital requirements are extremely high, dairying gives the best net farm income per acre and also the best return on tenant's capital for the smaller farms.

[1] *Farm Business Statistics for S.E. England*, 1969 – Wye College (Department of Economics)

Initial capital requirements for dairy farming are high, but milk production has the important advantage of being less dependent upon seasonal working capital than arable, stock rearing or fattening enterprises, due to the regular nature of its sales in the form of the monthly milk cheque.

When judged on the basis of gross margins produced per forage acre, dairying would seem to be one of the most efficient ways of converting grass and forage crops into cash. Standard gross margins (Nix, J. op. cit.) illustrates this point.

	Gross margin £/forage acre		
	Low	*Average*	*High*
Dairying: Friesians	40	52	64
Channel Island	35	49	62
Other breeds	34	44	54
Fat lamb production	14	19	29
Rearing dairy replacements	15	18	22
Beef: Single suckling	19	23	28
Multiple suckling	23	28	32
Fattening store cattle	15	18	24
18 month beef	27	—	32

Great care is necessary in interpreting measures of profitability for the dairy herd. The gross margin comparisons quoted above must be used with great reservation since they only refer to one aspect of the enterprise and comparative gross margins are not necessarily an indication that the final profitability of the enterprise will be in the same proportions, since levels of fixed costs and capital investment will not be the same in all cases.

Basic cost structure of milk production

A wide range of factors are involved in determining the ultimate profitability of milk production and consequently much confused thinking persists as to the relative importance of each.

The significance of any one factor will vary from farm to farm and each case must be judged upon its own merits and special circumstances.

The most useful measure of profitability within an enterprise is the return on tenant's capital, since this single factor involves and is influenced by just about every other possible factor of production.

However, profitability is more frequently expressed for comparative purposes as gross or net margin per cow or gross or net margin per acre.

Interpretation of profitability expressed in this way will depend largely upon the farm in question.

As already stated, a high overall return on capital is the aim. In order to achieve this, it will be necessary to obtain the maximum possible margin within the limits that are imposed. Thus if physical factors, e.g. buildings, labour, etc., limit the number of cows to be kept, then it is necessary to achieve a high margin per cow in order to achieve a good return on capital for the enterprise.

However, if land is the only factor imposing a limit on the enterprise, then it may be possible to achieve the same or even better return on capital from a lower margin per cow, but with a lot more cows on the same acreage, provided that the stocking rate is increased sufficiently to result in an increased margin per acre.

Final profitability or 'net margin' will be the difference between

(*a*) gross margin,
(*b*) fixed costs,
whether expressed per cow or per acre.

The factors affecting these two important aspects of profitability are therefore considered systematically according to the following diagram of cost structure (see Figure 6.*a*).

Factors affecting gross margin

1. *Gross output per cow*

```
                              ┌ (i)  Yield
               ┌ Quantity sold ┤
               │              └ (ii) Calving index
 (a) Milk sales┤
               │              ┌ Quality
               └ Price obtained┤
                              └ Seasonality
```

The value of milk sold per cow per year is the result of a number of factors, which are now considered in turn.

Quantity of milk sold

Quantity of milk sold per cow per year is a function of (*i*) yield per cow per lactation and (*ii*) calving index.

(*i*) *Yield per cow per lactation.* Yield per cow per lactation has increased steadily in recent years as Table 6.1 indicates.

Lactation yield is subject to the influence of many factors. The most important of these are health, management, level of feeding and environment, the technical implications of which would require many volumes to cover adequately, and cannot be discussed here. Breed of cows has an important influence upon yield as the following summary, Table 6.2, from the National Milk Records for 1969 indicates:

Figure 6.a. Factors affecting the profitability of milk production

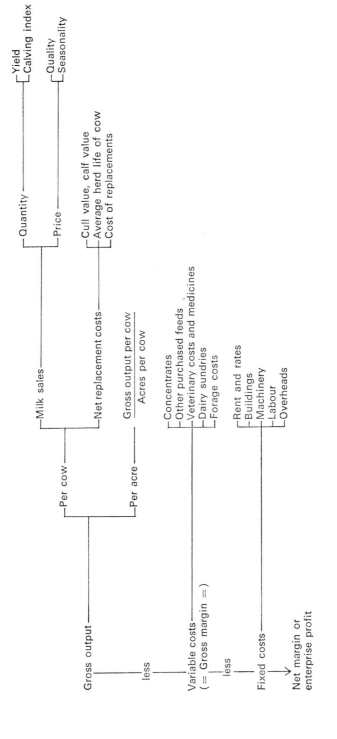

Table 6.1   U.K. average annual milk yield per cow for all breeds
(Recorded and non-recorded)

	Gallons
1961–62	774
1962–63	779
1963–64	765
1964–65	775
1965–66	795
1966–67	790
1967–68	810
1968–69	815

(*Source;* U.K. Dairy Facts and Figures, 1969)

Table 6.2   Influence of breed of cow on milk yield

Breed	Lactation yield gallons	Annual yield gallons	% National herd
Friesian	998	982	65·8
Ayrshire	905	862	11·1
Guernsey	763	732	5·9
Jersey	725	691	6·3
Shorthorn	868	832	2·5
Red Poll	793	767	0·5
Others	—	—	7·9
			100·0

Equally important is the strain within the breed and the level of genetic improvement within the herd.

National Milk Records also indicate that certain areas of the British Isles have a higher average lactation yield per cow, the West and West Midlands generally showing a better yield per cow per annum than the South-East and extreme West. This is a function of climate and managerial skill, as well as breed and system.

Seasonality of calving will considerably affect yield, the optimum time of calving for maximum lactation yield being September to October for heifers and November to December for cows.

(*ii*) *Calving index.* Calving index is the interval in days between calvings. Ideally this should be 365, i.e. one lactation per cow per year, and is made up as follows:

Cow calves
                    4 days – interval between calving and commencement
                                    of milk recording
                    305 days – recorded lactation
                    56 days – dry period
Cow calves
              $\overline{365 \text{ days}}$

However, the ideal calving index of 365 days is seldom achieved in practice and the average calving index is about 395 days.

This means that the recorded 305-day lactation yield is not the same as the milk sold per cow per year, i.e. since the milk sales are spread over 395 days instead of 365 days the milk sold per cow per year will be:

$$\text{Lactation yield} \times \frac{365}{395}.$$

Table 6.3 shows the effect of calving index upon actual milk output per cow per year:

Table 6.3   Influence of calving index upon milk output

	Output/cow/year		
	Calving index		
Lactation output	*365*	*380*	*400*
	£	£	£
700 gallons at £0·15	105	101	96
800 gallons at £0·15	120	115	109
900 gallons at £0·15	135	130	123
1 000 gallons at £0·15	150	144	137
1 100 gallons at £0·15	165	158	150
1 200 gallons at £0·15	180	173	164

In this way the effective output of a 1 100 galloner is reduced to that of a 1 000 galloner if the calving index slips from 365 to 400, see figures underlined in Table 6.3.

An approximate relationship exists between the calving index, the percentage dry cows in a herd, the average lactation length and the average number of days in a year when a cow is dry. These can be expressed by the formulae:

I. Percentage dry cows in herd $= \dfrac{\text{days dry in cycle} \times 100}{\text{calving index}}$

e.g. at the ideal calving index of 365

Percentage dry cows in herd $= \dfrac{56}{365} \times 100 = \text{approx. } 16$

II. Lactation length $=$ calving index $-$ days dry

III. Lactation output $=$ output per cow per year $\times \dfrac{\text{calving index}}{365}$

Thus if sufficient basic information is available for a dairy herd, it is possible to calculate a number of factors relating to breeding efficiency and frequency. This can be an extremely useful exercise in pinpointing management weaknesses within a dairy enterprise. For example, if recorded lactation output is greater than output per cow per year, then the calving index must be greater than 365.

If percentage dry cows is high, i.e. more than 16, then this will be due to either: (*i*) poor calving index; (*ii*) short lactations.

In this way a process of elimination will reveal the basic weaknesses, the technical or managerial causes of which will then need investigation and rectifying.

Price per gallon

Price received per gallon depends upon three main factors:

(*a*) *Quality* of milk produced;
(*b*) *Seasonality* of production;
(*c*) *Bonuses* for which the producer is eligible.

(*a*) *Quality* affects price per gallon and can be considered under two headings: (*i*) compositional quality; (*ii*) hygienic quality.

(*i*) *Compositional quality.* All milk sold to the Milk Marketing Board is paid for on a set scale according to its analysis for total solids. The scale set out in Table 6.4 pays the basic monthly price for milk containing 12·0–12·1 per cent total solids. Above this level price per gallon increases on a sliding scale; below this level the price is reduced.

Milk produced by Jersey, Guernsey or South Devon cows may be eligible for a special Channel Island Premium. This is not set at a standard rate for the whole country, but has to be negotiated between the producer and the dairy he supplies, and will depend upon the demand for this type of milk in a given area. A rough indication of the level of premiums paid above basic price is as follows:

	New pence
October to January	+5·83
February	+5·42
March	+3·75
April	+2·08
May	+1·67
June	+1·67
July	+2·50
August	+3·96
September	+4·17

Table 6.4   Compositional quality scheme

Payment class code	Annual average total solids content %	Addition to or deduction from basic price (new pence per gallon)
29	14·50 and over	3·125
28	14·40 and less than 14·50	3·000
27	14·30 and less than 14·40	2·875
26	14·20 and less than 14·30	2·750
25	14·10 and less than 14·20	2·625
24	14·00 and less than 14·10	2·500
23	13·90 and less than 14·00	2·375
22	13·80 and less than 13·90	2·250
21	13·70 and less than 13·80	2·125
20	13·60 and less than 13·70	2·000
19	13·50 and less than 13·60	1·875
18	13·40 and less than 13·50	1·750
17	13·30 and less than 13·40	1·625
16	13·20 and less than 13·30	1·500
15	13·10 and less than 13·20	1·375
14	13·00 and less than 13·10	1·250
13	12·90 and less than 13·00	1·125
12	12·80 and less than 12·90	1·000
11	12·70 and less than 12·80	0·875
10	12·60 and less than 12·70	0·750
9	12·50 and less than 12·60	0·625
8	12·40 and less than 12·50	0·500
7	12·30 and less than 12·40	0·375
6	12·20 and less than 12·30	0·250
5	12·10 and less than 12·20	0·125
4	12·00 and less than 12·10	Basic price
3	11·90 and less than 12·00	− 0·333
2	11·80 and less than 11·90	− 0·667
1	Less than 11·80	− 1·000

The scheme is based on the annual average composition of the milk of each dairy farmer over the preceding 12 months with a reclassification every 6 months

Prices received for milk produced in the months March–September will depend upon the level of milk production during the peak months October to January.

(*ii*) *Hygienic quality.* A scheme is operated to ensure that the hygienic quality of milk reaches very high standards. The scheme is based on the results of regular testing at the dairy. Deductions are made as follows for milk failing the hygienic quality test:

1st month containing a failure – no deduction
2nd month containing a failure – − 0·417 new pence per gallon
3rd month containing a failure – − 0·833 new pence per gallon
4th and subsequent months
    containing a failure   – − 1·250 new pence per gallon
Unmarketable milk is rejected.

(b) Seasonality of production

Milk prices paid to the producer vary from month to month as a direct result of supply and demand. Production of milk is at its highest level in April, May and June, and prices are consequently at their lowest. During the months October to January milk production is low and prices are at their highest. Consequently the higher the proportion of winter milk produced on a farm the higher the average price received per gallon throughout the whole year.

Table 6.5 illustrates the way in which the proportion of winter milk (October–March) can affect the average price per gallon and value of milk sales per cow per year.

Table 6.5   Effects of seasonality of milk production on price per gallon

Percentage winter milk		Av. price per gallon (new pence)	Difference from average £/cow		
			Low	Average	High
56	Mainly winter	15·70	+2·2	+2·5	+2·9
48	Average seasonality	15·41	—	—	—
42	Mainly summer	15·25	−1·2	−1·5	−1·7
45	Summer specialist	14·95	−3·4	−4·0	−4·6

(*Source: Farm Management Pocketbook*, 3rd Edition, John Nix, 1969. Wye College, Department of Economics)

It is frequently claimed that summer milk production should be more profitable than winter milk production, since costs of producing milk off grass in the summer are very much lower than those of producing winter milk. A survey of the relative economics of summer and winter milk production carried out by the low cost production service of the Milk Marketing Board (ref. L.C.P. Report, M.M.B. 1967) showed this is not the case when assessed on a gross margin basis. There are, however, circumstances where specialised summer milk production could be more profitable than all the year round or winter milk production. Since it is impossible to generalise this can only be assessed by careful budgeting for the specific conditions existing on the individual farm.

(c) Bonuses

Bulk tank bonus. In order to encourage farmers to co-operate in bulk handling of milk, a bonus which varies from 0·208 to 0·833 new pence per gallon according to quantity and frequency of collection is paid for three years following the installation of a bulk tank.

Brucellosis incentive scheme. This scheme, announced in the 1970 Annual Price Review, proposes to pay a premium on all milk from accredited *Brucella*-free herds.

Net herd replacement cost

This is sometimes considered as an item of variable cost, but should strictly be deducted from sales at this stage in calculating the gross output per cow.

The net herd replacement cost is the difference between the cost of replacement animals brought into the herd and any livestock sales in the form of calves and culls from the dairy herd. This will depend on four main factors:

1. Rate of replacement.
2. Value of livestock sales from the herd.
3. Cost of replacement animals.
4. Difference in opening and closing valuations for the herd.

Since this is a large subject and involves a further enterprise, i.e. heifer rearing, the factors affecting herd replacement costs are dealt with more fully in the section on Dairy Young Stock Enterprise (p. 154).

Enterprise gross output per forage acre

This measure is simply a function of gross output per cow and stocking density. Gross output per acre will increase as stocking density increases since it is not affected by extra feeds costs which usually accompany a heavier stocking density.

Enterprise net output per forage acre

This is a far more valuable measure upon which to compare output per acre, since it relates to the margin achieved per acre after deducting the cost of purchased and home-grown feeds from the gross output. It is easy enough to increase gross output per acre, simply by buying in large quantities of feeds and thereby increasing stocking density. Any ultimate profit will come from the net output, i.e. the difference between gross output and feeding-stuffs cost.

Variable costs

1. Concentrates

Concentrates, whether purchased or home grown, are usually the principal item of variable cost incurred in milk production, and represent one section of expenditure over which the farmer has some degree of immediate control. Because of this a great deal of confused thinking exists over the economics of concentrate feeding.

A great deal of publicity has been given to the need for increased milk production from cheap bulk feeds and because of the national need for a reduction in imports the use of concentrate feeds has been officially discouraged. A doctrine has subsequently evolved which condemns the excessive or unnecessary use of bought concentrated feeds. Unfortunately, like all doctrines, this has become seriously misunderstood to such an extent that to many the use of concentrates has become an anathema and their universal condemnation almost a religion.

The milk producer has to try to see through the propaganda which is issued from both sides by those with vested interests – the ardent grassland enthusiasts on the one side and the feedingstuffs manufacturers on the other and to adopt the concentrate feeding policy most likely to maximise the margin from his herd. He knows that excessive feeding of expensive concentrates is likely to be wasteful, but he also knows that a severe reduction in concentrate feeding is likely to result in a correspondingly greater fall in milk production and a drop in the net output of his herd.

He must therefore try to pursue a middle course in order to obtain the best possible margin of milk sales over concentrates.

Before considering the use and interpretation of feed economy figures, it is first necessary to clarify the purpose of concentrate feeding.

Concentrates, as their name implies, supply nutrients in a concentrated form. At high levels of daily yield it is necessary, particularly during winter, to supply much of the animal's daily requirement of nutrients in this form, otherwise the cow's appetite is satisfied long before her nutrient requirements have been fulfilled and production will consequently fall. The recent recommendations published by the Agricultural Research Council[1] emphasise the need for a more highly concentrated diet at high levels of yield.

The feeding of concentrates is, therefore, practised in order to sustain or increase the level of yield. The most economic level of concentrate feeding will depend upon the response of the herd to concentrates, which in turn will depend upon the quality of their bulk diet, upon their genetic potential and upon the level of yield already being obtained.

Provided that a given value of concentrates when fed produces milk of a greater value, then the overall margin of milk sales over concentrates will be increased. In short, concentrate feeding is economic if it produces an improvement in net output. In theory the feeding of concentrates is economic up to the point when the cost of extra concentrates fed is equal to the value of extra milk produced. Until this point on the diminishing returns curve is reached, then the margin of milk sales over concentrates will be increased.

This all sounds fine in theory, but how does one assess the correct level at which to feed in practice? Once again there is no universal answer. The

[1] The Nutrient Requirements of Farm Livestock, No. 2 Ruminants, Agricultural Research Council, London 1965

optimum level of feeding will not be the same for any two herds and will depend entirely upon the level of response obtained for any given level of bulk feeding. This can only be assessed individually and the overall economy of concentrate feeding will in the final analysis depend upon the cowman's knowledge of his individual animals, upon knowing each cow's individual response and then feeding to it.

Feed economy measures. Much of the confusion over concentrate feeding arises from the way in which feed economy measures for the herd have been calculated and interpreted.

Probably the easiest measure to calculate for a herd is:

Pounds concentrates fed per gallon of milk produced

This can be calculated for any period of time simply by dividing the number of gallons of milk produced into the number of pounds of concentrates fed during the same period. The simplicity of its calculation has led to the widespread use of this measure and to its frequent misinterpretation, since it is often used as a means of comparing feed efficiency between herds and between production achieved in different years for the same herd.

This can be dangerous and misleading, for if one examines the situation objectively it is clear that the one really important factor influencing profit at any level of yield is the difference between the value of milk produced and the cost of concentrates fed. If adequate records are available this can be calculated for any period of time and is expressed as *margin of milk sales over concentrates*. This is an absolute figure and can be compared quite fairly with results obtained by other herds and by the same herd in previous years. A number of factors are embodied in this measure and consequently it is closely related to the gross margin for the herd and to herd profit. Margin of milk sales over concentrates should, therefore, be used whenever possible if a reliable measure of feed economy is required.

Other measures of calculating, expressing and comparing feed economy are based upon the ratio of concentrates fed to milk produced and not on the difference between their values. They can be summarised as follows:

(*a*) Pounds concentrates fed per gallon;
(*b*) Cost of concentrates fed per gallon;
(*c*) Index of concentrate feeding.

This last measure is based upon the assumption that 28 cwt of concentrates are required per 1 000 gallons of milk produced.

$$\text{Index of concentrate use} = \frac{\text{Concs. required at 28 cwt per 1 000 gallons} \times 100}{\text{Concs. actually used}}$$

The higher the index the higher the assumed efficiency of concentrate use, but once again this is merely a way of expressing a ratio – just a little more complicated.

The ratio of milk produced to concentrates fed can only be a valid measure of comparing the efficiency of food use between herds when their levels of yield are the same. Since this is seldom likely to be the case, a more absolute and direct measure is required.

The graph (Figure 6.*b*) illustrates this point more clearly. Margins over concentrates are plotted at different levels of yield per cow per year and for

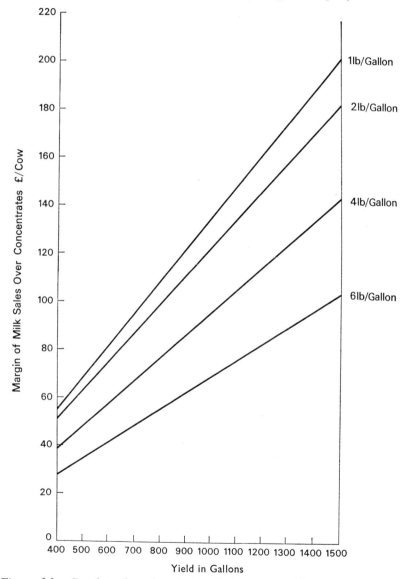

Figure 6.b   *Graph to show the relationship between yield, concentrates fed per gallon of milk produced and margin of milk sales over concentrates (Milk price £0·15/gallon, concentrates – £30/ton).*

different ratios of pound concentrates fed per gallon. As the yield of milk rises so also does the margin of milk sales over concentrates. This will be the case as long as the value of concentrates fed per gallon is less than the value of the gallon of milk produced.

The margin rises most sharply with increasing yield at the lower levels of concentrate feeding, and more slowly as the rate of concentrate feeding rises.

Margin of milk sales over concentrates is clearly a function of yield per cow and level of concentrate feeding. Equal margins can be achieved at different levels of yield and concentrate feeding. For example a margin of £100 milk sales over concentrates can be obtained from a yield of –

732 gallons per cow per year at 1 lb concentrates per gallon
812 gallons per cow per year at 2 lb concentrates per gallon
1037 gallons per cow per year at 4 lb concentrates per gallon
1436 gallons per cow per year at 6 lb concentrates per gallon

A superficial examination of feed economy figures might lead one to believe a herd using 6 lb of concentrates per gallon to be far less efficient than one using only 1 lb of concentrates per gallon, yet 6 lb concentrates per gallon at a yield of 1436 gallons is just as efficient in real terms as 1 lb concentrates per gallon at 732 gallons, 2 lb per gallon at 812 gallons, or 4 lb per gallon at 1037 gallons. The difference between costs and output is the main factor affecting profit in any enterprise so beware of slick and superficial comparisons based solely on ratios.

2. *Other purchased feeds*

Concentrates account for only part of the total feedingstuffs' costs. Bulk foods may also be purchased and under some circumstances can if used wisely be a means of improving the profitability of a dairy enterprise.

It has already been shown that net output per acre must be high in order to produce a satisfactory gross margin and subsequently an acceptable profit per acre.

Any increase in the cost of purchased feedingstuffs per cow will, at a given yield, result in a reduction in the net output per cow and consequently in a reduction in the gross margin per cow.

If net output per cow falls and stocking densities remain the same, then the net output per acre will fall and income will be reduced, but if the stocking density can be improved as a result of buying in more feed, then it may be possible to increase net output per acre and eventually to improve the farm income.

A yardstick to be applied to the practice of purchasing bulk foods is simply this, 'Will it or will it not increase net output per acre?'

Net output per acre will be increased in the following circumstances:

(*a*) when net output per cow is increased and stocking density remains the same;
(*b*) when net output per cow remains the same and stocking density is improved;
(*c*) when both net output per cow and stocking density are improved;
(*d*) when net output per cow is reduced but stocking density increases to compensate.

Consideration of this fourth case is important when deciding upon the most economic level of purchased feedingstuffs for a given farm. A reduction in net output per cow can be justified if it is compensated by an improvement in stocking density which results in increased net output per acre.

Example

Original situation

Stocking density	2 acres per cow
Net output per cow	£100
Net output per acre	£50

An extra £45 is spent per cow on purchased feedingstuffs, but as a result of this stocking density is doubled.

New situation

Stocking density	1 acre per cow
Net output per cow	£55
Net output per acre	£55

A very large reduction in net output per cow is thus justified by an improved net output per acre.

This is the basic theory behind the successful feeding of purchased bulk feeds, e.g. stockfeed potatoes, wet brewers' grains, sugar-beet pulp, straw and balancer or even hay. Many farmers have found that this pays well in practice and that by purchasing their winter feed they can use a limited grassland acreage for grazing only, thereby keeping up to three cows per acre and maximising their farm income.

However, if purchased feeds are used to supplement an inefficient conservation programme and do not result in an improved stocking rate, then costs will increase for no increase in output and profitability will be bound to suffer.

3. *Miscellaneous variable costs*

It is always difficult to pinpoint any single factor in this group of costs and to isolate it for specific criticism. These costs are not very controllable and are usually fairly constant at around £7 per cow per year. Average figures per cow are approximately:

	£
Veterinary and medicines	1·5
Service and recording fees	1·5
Dairy stores, etc.	4·0
	7·0

If these items when grouped are greatly in excess of £7 per cow, then further investigation may be of value. High veterinary charges may indicate some basic fault in stockmanship, herd management or policy.

Service and recording charges will vary slightly according to proportion of A.I. and nominated A.I. services, system of recording and size of herd.

Dairy stores are very difficult to pinpoint accurately and a very efficient system of accounting and stocktaking is required if the trading account figure for these commodities is to be really reliable. Economies may be effected in this direction, particularly in the field of cleaning material and detergents, but their effect on the final gross margin will be small.

4. *Forage costs*

Only the annual variable costs of grassland and forage crops are included here and comprise:

(*a*) Seeds;
(*b*) Fertilisers;
(*c*) Sprays;
(*d*) Consumable materials used in fodder conservation and utilisation;
(*e*) Casual labour and contract (e.g. silage and haymaking).

Forage costs are difficult to standardise and vary enormously according to situation, soil, climate, etc., but as stocking rate increases, forage costs are bound to rise not only per acre but also per cow. The following figures provide a guide to average lowland conditions:

Table 6.6 Forage costs at various stocking rates

	Seeds and fertiliser costs	
Forage acres/cow	(1) £/acre	(2) £/cow
1·0	19·0	19·0
1·2	14·0	17·0
1·4	10·0	14·0
1·6	7·5	12·0
1·8	5·5	10·0
2·0	4·0	8·0
2·2	3·0	6·5

(*Source:* Nix, J. *op. cit.*)

F

As stocking density increases, the main cost to rise will be that of fertilisers, particularly of nitrogenous fertilisers.

Forage costs per cow increase with increased stocking density. Consequently gross margin per cow will decrease with increased stocking density, but gross margin per acre will rise.

Since forage costs can amount to £20 per cow or even more they account for a large proportion of the variable costs incurred by the dairy enterprise. However, in gross margin analysis, forage variable costs are usually calculated from the difference between total seeds, fertilisers, sprays and other crop costs, and those allocated directly to cash crops. They are thus subject to accumulative error and must be interpreted with reservation.

Because of the difficulty of obtaining sufficient information upon which to calculate forage costs, many costings' agencies base their results on 'standard costs' of forage production. Such results can seldom be accurate, are extremely dangerous and should never be treated seriously.

Having discussed the factors affecting gross margin per cow and per acre, it is necessary now to construct some standard figures which can be used as a yardstick against which to compare the results obtained on individual farms. The following table illustrates the levels of gross margin to be expected per cow (before deducting forage costs) for different breeds and at different levels of performance.

Fixed costs

The basic principles affecting fixed costs have already been discussed in Chapter 3.

Final profit for any business or enterprise will depend upon the difference between the gross margin obtained and the fixed costs incurred. The dangers and pitfalls of careless gross margin planning have already been discussed in Chapter 2. However, it is again emphasised that while it is convenient for some purposes to regard fixed costs as a separate unit they are by no means constant and will almost certainly change with changes in stocking density and changing proportions of farm enterprises.

The graph (Figure 6.*c*) shows the results of costings carried out by L.C.P.[1] for the years 1964–68. During these years a considerable improvement occurred in the average level of stocking density achieved on the costed farms, accompanied by a very significant increase in the gross margin obtained per forage acre.

It would be most unwise, however, to assume that the final level of profitability would have risen in the same proportions as the gross margin. This would only be true were the fixed costs to remain constant.

[1] Report of the Breeding and Production Organisation of the M.M.B., 1967–1968

Table 6.7   Standard gross margins for milk production

Breed:	Friesians			Channel Island			Other breeds		
Performance level:	*Low*	*Av.*	*High*	*Low*	*Av.*	*High*	*Low*	*Av.*	*High*
Yield* (Galls/cow/yr)	700	900	1 100	500	700	900	700	800	900
Milk sales† (£/cow/year)	105	135	165	96	134	162	105	120	135
Net herd replacement cost‡	5	5	5	12	12	12	7	7	7
Gross output/cow	100	130	160	84	122	150	98	113	128
Concentrate costs	34	34	34	34	34	34	34	34	34
Margin over Concentrate costs	66	96	126	50	88	116	64	79	94
Misc. variable costs	7	7	7	7	7	7	7	7	7
Gross margin/cow (before deducting forage costs)	59	89	119	43	81	109	57	72	87

* Computed from National Milk Records for 1967–68
† Friesian and other breeds at £0·15 per gallon, Channel Island at £0·191 per gallon
‡ See Dairy Young Stock Enterprise (p. 156)

Surveys of farm costings show that the level of fixed costs is steadily rising for all types of farm, the average levels of fixed costs per acre for dairy farms in the South-East varying from £25 per acre to £37 per acre in 1969, depending upon the size of the holding.

One of the main drawbacks of the dairy enterprise is the high capital cost involved in stock, buildings and equipment. The annual charge for servicing this capital is excluded for comparative purposes when calculating management and investment income, but it is nevertheless a very real charge, and one which is bound to rise if the dairy enterprise increases.

Labour costs per cow are difficult to determine, particularly on mixed farms, but the following figures from a survey published by L.C.P.[1] in 1967 show that their allocated labour costs per cow were very similar over a wide range of herd sizes, savings in man-hours per cow on the larger herds being offset by a higher labour cost per man-hour commensurate with the higher level of skill and responsibility required.

More cows per acre will usually result in higher fixed costs per acre, even though some items, e.g. rent, rates, overheads, etc., remain constant. The

[1] Low Cost Production Report, M.M.B., 1967, p. 42, Table 17

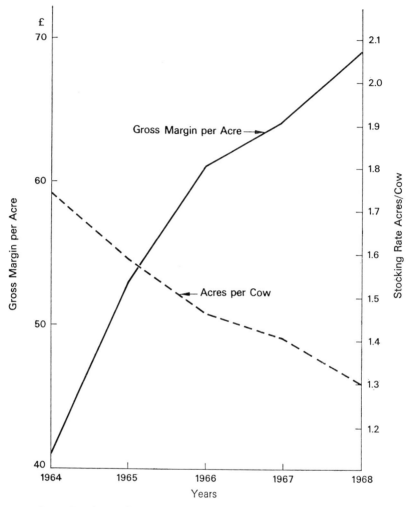

Figure 6.c   *Graph to show effect of improvement in stocking rate on gross margin per acre in 200 low cost production costed herds selected at random*

	Size of herd		
	30 cows	*50 cows*	*Over 100 cows*
Labour hours per cow per year	85	66	61
Labour cost per cow per year	£22·0	£18·3	£18·3
Average cost per labour hour	£0·258	£0·275	£0·30

full extent to which fixed costs will be affected by changes in stocking density will depend on changes in the actual size of the herd. If, for example, improved stocking rate enables the dairy herd to be concentrated on to a smaller acreage without altering its size, then total fixed costs will not change. If, on the other hand, an increase in stocking density is achieved by increasing the size of the herd, then extra capital buildings charges will be incurred and fixed costs will rise. The general trend towards an increase in the size of dairy herd indicates that this is more likely to be the case.

The fixed cost items which will be most affected by changes in the dairy enterprise are:

1. Labour.
2. Buildings costs.
3. Capital charges.

Table 6.8 shows how fixed costs could be affected by changes in stocking density. It is assumed that accommodation is required for all cows and that rent, overheads and machinery charges remain constant at £14 per acre (the average level for dairy farms in South-East England).

Table 6.8   Effect of buildings and equipment costs and stocking density upon fixed costs per acre

Buildings and equipment cost/cow	£ 25	£ 50	£ 100	£ 150	£ 200
Depreciation on buildings at 10%	2·5	5·0	10·0	15·0	20·0
Interest on capital in buildings $\dfrac{Capital}{2} \times 8\%$	1·0	2·0	4·0	6·0	8·0
Interest on capital in cow, £100 at 8%	8·0	8·0	8·0	8·0	8·0
Labour cost/cow	20·0	20·0	20·0	20·0	20·0
Annual cost/cow	31·5	35·0	42·0	49·0	56·0

Stocking rate (acres/cow)	*Cost/acre including £14/acre rent, overheads and machinery*				
	£	£	£	£	£
2·0	30	31·5	35	38·5	42·0
1·5	35	37·5	42	46·5	51·5
1·0	45·5	49	56	63	70
0·5	77	84	98	112	126

These are not the levels of fixed costs to be expected when increasing the level of stocking density on an existing unit but would be a fair guide as to the level of fixed costs incurred in setting up a new unit. At high levels of stocking density fixed costs per acre of £60 and above are to be expected and correspondingly higher gross margins are necessary in order to achieve a satisfactory final profit.

In planning changes in farm policy involving the dairy enterprise it is necessary to consider very carefully any changes that are likely to occur to the fixed costs, since these will represent a large proportion of the total cost changes and will have an important bearing upon the ultimate level of profit.

Do not under any circumstances plan changes involving the dairy enterprise solely upon the basis of changes in gross margins.

The dairy young stock enterprise

Statistics for the National Dairy Herd suggest that the average productive life of a dairy cow is only four years. Replacement heifers must therefore be available if the total number of dairy cows is to be maintained or increased and on the basis of present numbers 600000–700000 heifers are required annually.

As this number of animals represents no small proportion of our total grazing livestock, it is necessary to look critically at replacement rearing as an enterprise.

The numbers of replacements required for a herd each year will depend on (*a*) the size of the herd, (*b*) whether the herd is constant or increasing in size, (*c*) the rate of replacement.

The rate of replacement is closely linked with culling policy and will depend upon a wide range of factors.

The basic purpose of culling is to remove animals which are uneconomic in order to maintain or increase the productivity of the herd.

Principles of culling

Certain basic principles must be borne in mind when culling stock:

1. A rigorous system of culling will increase the depreciation rate of the herd and must be justified by increased productivity.
2. Removal of animals by culling will not result in a reduction of fixed costs. If culling leaves a smaller number of animals, then each must carry a larger share of fixed costs.

   Total herd output must therefore be maintained if the level of productivity is to be maintained or improved. This usually means that total numbers must be kept up.

   There is always a danger that while output per animal may be increased by culling, output for the herd or flock may be reduced.
3. When replacing an animal always replace with something better.

   Replacing an old cow with a heifer will result in an increase in costs, so unless the heifer's first lactation is better than the potential next lactation of the cow she replaces, then the old cow should be kept.

   For example, an old cow giving 700 gallons per year is a better financial proposition than a heifer giving the same yield providing that she remains healthy and that concentrate and veterinary bills are the same in each case.

Bearing these principles in mind, it is now necessary to consider the factors which affect the rate of replacement in practice.

These can be broadly subdivided as Husbandry factors and Economic factors.

Husbandry factors affecting rate of replacement

The main causes for replacement of stock in practice will come under this heading. There is usually less difficulty in deciding whether or not to keep an animal where such factors are involved since the answer is normally clear cut.

Husbandry factors can be grouped as follows:

1. Disease, e.g. mastitis, brucellosis.
2. Infertility – cows persistently returning to service, not worth keeping.
3. Incapacity, e.g. legs and feet.
4. Injury, e.g. cut teats etc.
5. Temperament, e.g. slow milkers, kickers, fence-busters (these usually get culled on some other pretext but the basic cause is the same).
6. Genetic quality, e.g. an animal of exceptional breeding may be kept in spite of other failings in order to produce further stock.

Economic factors affecting rate of replacement

In any herd there will be a level of production below which it is not worth keeping an animal. It is necessary therefore to set a minimum tolerance level for both quality and yield below which an animal must be replaced.

The acceptable level of milk quality will depend on the type of herd. If compositional quality is a problem, then any individual animals which are particularly poor in this respect may have to go.

Yield is the main factor to consider since this has the greatest single effect upon output.

The problem now is to determine where to draw the line. What is an economic yield and what is not? Once again there is no universal answer to this question. The economic level can only be assessed in the light of the particular circumstances of the individual farm and will depend upon the following factors:

1. *The level of fixed and overhead costs incurred by the farm*

Where the fixed cost background is high then high yields are essential if a margin is to be obtained. If fixed costs are low then a lower level of yield can be tolerated as it will still leave a margin.

2. *The amount of capital available*

Replacement stock will require working capital. If this is very limited, then it may be necessary to cull more lightly and to accept a lower level of yield.

3. *The cost of making a replacement*

Table 6.9 *Net herd replacement costs*

	Costs £/cow/year		
	Friesians	*Channel Island*	*Others*
Cost of replacements ¼ herd/year	at 120 30	at 85 21·5	at 90 22·5
Less value of cull cows ¼ herd/year (allowing for deaths)	at 56 14	at 25 6·5	at 40 10·0
Herd depreciation	16	15·0	12·5
Less value of calves (allowing for deaths)	11	3·0	5·5
Net replacement cost	5	12·0	7·0

Net herd replacement costs are summarised in Table 6.9 and depend on three main factors:

(*a*) *Cull value of the animal replaced.* This depends on:

(*i*) *Age and condition of animal*

(*ii*) *Breed of animal*

Heavier fleshier animals, e.g. Friesians and Shorthorns command a much better cull price than the lighter and more angular Ayrshire or Channel Island breeds.

(*iii*) *Method of sale*

This must be budgeted according to local preference, time of year and feed available. Possible to sell bare as a chopper or freshly calved with or without calf or it may even pay to feed the cow up and sell her fat.

(*iv*) *Time of year*

Fat and cull cow prices vary with season but usually follow the general trend of the clean beef market, i.e. maximum price March to April, minimum price September to October. Exports of fat cows to the Continent can have a very significant effect on this general pattern.

(*b*) *Sale value of calves* This depends on:
   (*i*) *Age and condition when sold*
   (*ii*) *Breed*
      Beef cross calves and those suitable for intensive rearing, e.g. Friesian, South Devon, command the best prices. Channel Island calves are worth very little.
   (*iii*) *Sex*
      Bull calves preferred to heifers for fattening.
   (*iv*) *Time of year*
      Calf prices are usually at their best in the spring.

(*c*) *The cost of replacement heifer.* If the replacement heifer is reared on the farm, then the costs of providing a down calver can be subdivided as under fixed costs and variable costs.

Table 6.10   Standard feed costs for calf rearing

	£	£
0–6 weeks		
56 lb Milk substitute at £6·5/cwt	3·25	
30 lb Weaning pellets at £2·1/cwt	0·55	
28 lb Hay at £12/ton	0·15	
		3·95
6–12 weeks		
Concentrates		
42 days × 4 lb at £42/ton		
168 lb = 1·5 cwt	3·15	
Hay		
42 days × 2 lb = 84 lb at £12/ton	0·45	
		3·60
Cost to 12 weeks		7·55
3–6 months		
Concentrates		
90 days × 4 lb = 360 lb		
= 3·25 cwt approx. at £32/ton	5·20	
Hay		
90 days × 3 lb = 2·5 cwt at £12/ton	1·50	
		6·70
Cost to 6 months		14·25
6–12 months or any winter		
Concentrates		
180 days × 2 lb = 3·25 cwt at £32/ton	5·20	
Hay		
180 days × 7 lb = 1260 lb		
= 11 cwt at £12/ton	6·05	
		11·25
Cost to 12 months		25·50

The principles affecting fixed costs and forage costs have already been discussed in the dairy enterprise study. Of the remaining variable costs, by far the most important is that of foodstuffs. Rearing methods vary and it is impossible to discuss the technical aspects of rearing in the chapter, but a rough guide to the feedingstuffs costs incurred in rearing a heifer on a conventional six-week weaning system using milk substitute is given in Table 6.10.

Miscellaneous variable costs include veterinary and medicine costs and usually amount to approximately £5 per heifer reared.

If costs of hay and conserved grass are included as forage costs from six months onwards, then the variable costs (excluding forage) of rearing a heifer are approximately as follows:

	£	£
Foodstuffs		
All foods to 6 months	14	
Concentrates 6–12 months	5	
Concentrates in second winter	5	
Total foodstuffs	—	24
Miscellaneous		
Vet. and Miscellaneous		5
Total costs		29

The heifer will also require the use of land during this period and will incur forage costs.

By using grazing livestock units it is possible to assess the land required for rearing a heifer.

Grazing livestock units for young stock are as follows:

0–6 months   0·1 grazing livestock units
6–12 months   0·2 grazing livestock units
12–24 months   0·6 grazing livestock units
2 years and over   0·8 grazing livestock units.

For every heifer required to join the dairy herd each year it will be necessary to have on the farm at any one time a succession of 'followers' consisting of:

1 heifer-in-calf backed up by younger animals coming forward to calve in subsequent years,

i.e.   1 heifer   1 year to 2 years old
       1 heifer   under 1 year old.

The necessary young stock to provide one down-calving heifer each year is known as one replacement unit and contains the following number of grazing livestock units:

g.l.u's

$$1 \text{ Replacement unit} = \begin{cases} 1 \text{ heifer 2 years and over} \times 0{\cdot}8 \times \tfrac{1}{2} = 0{\cdot}4 \\ 1 \text{ heifer 1–2 years} \times 0{\cdot}6 \qquad\quad = 0{\cdot}6 \\ 1 \text{ heifer 6–12 months} \times 0{\cdot}2 \quad\;\; = 0{\cdot}2 \\ \qquad\qquad\qquad\qquad \text{Total} \;\; = \overline{1{\cdot}2} \end{cases}$$

So for each heifer that calves down, it is necessary to carry 1·2 grazing livestock units of young stock. At a stocking rate of 2·0 forage acres per livestock unit this would represent a requirement of 2·4 acres to rear each heifer. The forage cost incurred on this acreage must therefore be added to the variable costs of producing a replacement heifer.

Gross margins from rearing dairy followers

Once the variable costs of heifer rearing have been calculated, it should be possible to credit this group of livestock with a gross margin, provided that a satisfactory figure can be assessed for their gross output.

Since no actual sale takes place when a heifer is brought into the herd, the gross output per heifer reared has to be based on an estimate of the market value of the down-calving heifer, less the value of the calf and an allowance for mortality and losses incurred during the rearing period.

An approximate gross margin account for rearing a heifer is as follows:

	£
Market value of down calver	100
less value of calf + losses	15
Gross output/down-calving heifer	85
less food and miscellaneous costs	29
Gross margin/heifer reared (excluding forage costs)	56

From this figure it is possible to calculate the final gross margin and the gross margin per forage acre from dairy replacements.

For example: if the stocking rate is 2 acres per livestock unit then

$$1 \text{ replacement unit requires } 1\cdot2 \times 2 = 2\cdot4 \text{ forage acres}$$

$$\therefore \quad \text{Gross margin per forage acre} \quad = \frac{£56}{2\cdot4} \text{ less forage costs per acre.}$$

Assuming forage costs of £4 per acre at this level of stocking density,

$$\text{Gross margin per forage acre} = \frac{£56}{2\cdot4} - 4$$

$$\therefore \quad \text{Gross margin per forage acre} = £19\cdot3$$

Similarly for a range of stocking densities at the levels of forage costs used in the dairy enterprise study, gross margins per forage acre from dairy replacements are as shown in Table 6.11.

These gross margins per forage acre are obviously much lower than those obtained from dairy cows at the same stocking densities and at an average level of output.

Assuming that the rate of replacement is 25 per cent, i.e. the national average, then for every four cows in the herd one replacement unit must be carried.

Table 6.11   Gross margins from rearing dairy young stock

Acres/livestock unit	1·0	1·4	1·6	2·0
	£	£	£	£
Gross margin/replacement unit	56	56	56	56
Gross margin/acre = $\dfrac{56}{1\cdot2\times\text{acres/livestock unit}}$	46·6	33·3	29·1	23·3
less Forage costs/acre	19·0	10·0	7·5	4·0
Gross margin/forage acre	27·6	23·3	21·6	19·3

Therefore for every four livestock units as cows, 1·2 livestock units are required as followers.

That is: for every 10 livestock units (cows)
3 livestock units (followers) are required.

Therefore at the same overall level of stocking density, for every ten acres devoted to dairy cows, three acres will be required for heifer rearing.

Therefore 10 cows with their followers will require as much land as 13 cows with replacements bought in.

When replacement stock and dairy cows are competing for the same land, the advisability of rearing replacements compared with buying in replacements needs to be critically examined.

The following partial budget is based on the assumption that 50 cows and their followers will require the same amount of land as 65 cows with replacements bought in. It is also assumed that (*i*) existing labour can handle either 50 cows plus followers or 65 cows; (*ii*) extra buildings must be erected for the 15 extra cows; (*iii*) straw costs will be the same for the extra 15 cows as for the replacements.

Under these conditions the farmer would be £378 a year better off if he were to give up rearing replacements and buy in all his down-calving heifers at £90 a head.

By working out the break-even point on this budget it is apparent that buying in replacements would be more profitable than home rearing provided that they could be acquired at less than $\left(£90+\dfrac{378}{16}\right) = £113\cdot6$.

Under intensive conditions of dairy management and with expensive land and high levels of fixed costs it may be considered uneconomic to rear replacements on the farm, using conventional rearing methods.

If this is so then the following three alternatives are worth considering:

1. Buy in all replacements.
2. Reduce the cost of rearing replacements.
3. Have replacements reared away from the farm on a contract basis.

Budget: 65 cows with replacements bought in v. 50 cows with replacements reared on the farm.

EXTRA COSTS	£	COSTS SAVED	£
Replacement heifers		*Variable costs* on 12·5 replace-	
16 per year at £90	1440	ment units at £29	363
Concentrates			
15 extra cows at 1 ton at £32	480		
Vet., medicines and sundries			
15 extra cows at £7	105		
Buildings' costs			
15 cows at £100/head			
Depreciation £1500 at 10%	150		
Interest $\dfrac{£1500}{2} \times 8\%$	60		
REVENUE FOREGONE		EXTRA REVENUE	
37·5 calves at £10	375	*Milk sales*	
12·5 culls at £50	625	15 extra cows at 800 galls at	
		£0·15	1800
		Calves	
		65 at £10	650
		Culls	
		16 at £50	800
EXTRA INCOME	378		
	3613		3613

1. Buying in replacements

Although this appears the more profitable alternative in the budget, it would only be so if (*a*) level of yield were maintained, (*b*) replacement rate were to remain at 25 per cent. In practice this may not be achieved as stock, whether bought in as down-calving heifers or at a later stage, tend to be of unknown quality and can never be expected to yield above breed average. It is impossible in this way to carry on any programme of genetic improvement.

There is also always a danger of introducing disease when buying in stock, and a change to a policy of buying in all replacements is frequently accompanied by an increase in the herd replacement rate.

Prices of down-calving heifers vary enormously, it is impossible to rely upon stock being available when required and travelling round to markets and sales in the hope of finding suitable stock at a reasonable price can be costly, frustrating and a time-consuming occupation.

2. Reducing the cost of rearing replacements

This can be attempted in four ways:

(*a*) Reducing foods costs;
(*b*) Reducing land requirements;
(*c*) Reducing rearing time by early calving;
(*d*) Reducing fixed costs.

(*a*) *Reducing foods costs.* (*i*) Early weaning techniques reduce the cost of milk substitute but usually require a higher quality concentrate to be fed. These may save work but effect little saving in total feeds costs to 12 weeks which remain at £7 to £8 on all systems.

(*ii*) Use of more grass. Experiments carried out by Great House E.H.F.[1] showed significant savings in foods costs from early weaning on to grass. The Grassland Research Institute at Hurley[2] have also been successful with weaning calves straight onto grass.

(*b*) *Reducing land requirements.* The use of straw feeding with barley and a balancer is claimed to be satisfactory for rearing calves right up to calving time.

Calves can be intensively stocked on a paddock grazing system and their normal land requirements for grazing and conservation can be successfully reduced. Far more trials are needed on the intensive stocking of calves under farm conditions before this can be recommended for general practice.

(*c*) *Reducing time to calving.* Clearly by calving earlier the rearing period is shortened and the cost of rearing should be reduced. Where a calving policy is established requiring the majority of calvings at a given time of year, a heifer will have to calve down at a time very close to her own birthday i.e. at either two years old or at three years old (since calving interval is likely to slip and the cow calve a little later each year as she gets older, then her first calf needs to be born a little before she reaches two years old or three years old). With all-the-year-round calving this is unimportant and it is possible to calve heifers at their most suitable age. While a great deal of lip-service is paid to the theory of early calving, very few farmers seem to achieve this ideal in practice. An experiment on early calving carried out at the Great House E.H.F.[3] with Ayrshires showed that by attempting to calve too early (20 months) the growth and production of heifers was permanently impaired. Early calving requires the highest possible standards of husbandry in calf rearing and subsequent management and should only be attempted where heifers are really well grown for their age and breed.

(*d*) *Reducing fixed costs. Labour* required for calf rearing can be reduced in several ways.

Once-a-day feeding using either whole milk or milk substitute is now an accepted and perfectly satisfactory technique.

Automatic feeders are being improved and perfected by several firms and have been shown to be most successful in practice.

---

1 Great House Review, 1963
2 J. C. Tayler, Technical Report No. 3, Grassland Research Institute, Hurley, Berkshire. March 1966
3 Great House Review, 1967, 1966, 1965, 1964

The Grassland Research Institute at Hurley[1] has shown that calves can be satisfactorily reared on *ad libitum* feeding of cold milk.

It should be noted that while these developments remove a lot of the drudgery of calf rearing, feeds costs are not reduced and are, in fact, usually a little higher than when two supervised feeds of warm milk are given per day.

Buildings costs for calf rearing have been ingeniously and successfully reduced by making 'disposable' calf houses of straw bales, thus also avoiding diseases being carried by the building from year to year.

3. *Contract rearing*

There are many benefits to be obtained from getting someone else to rear dairy replacements on a contract basis.

This enables the breeder to follow a planned breeding programme of livestock improvement since his own calves will eventually return to the herd. With a well-organised contract scheme it is possible to plan the availability of replacement heifers at a reasonable cost, to avoid buying in diseases and to make the best possible use of all suitable land by stocking it with dairy cows and maximising its output.

The system should also be of mutual benefit to both the breeder and the rearer. A farmer with limited capital may well find contract rearing of heifers to be a profitable way of using land and making a living without heavy investment in stock.

Many different contract rearing systems are at present operating satisfactorily, and can be considered broadly in two categories: (*i*) where the breeder retains ownership of the heifer and pays the rearer to keep the animal until it is ready to return home; (*ii*) where the rearer buys the heifer from the breeder but the breeder has the first option of buying her back.

An actual working example of each of these two systems is summarised below.

Example I

Breeder retains ownership of calf.

Calf is in the charge of the rearer from 10 days to at least 15 months.

Calves taken by rearer in autumn and returned to breeder in the spring, 15 to 18 months later.

Breeder pays rearer on following scale:

£1 per head per week for first 12 weeks
£0·8 per head per week for next 15 months

$$£$$

i.e. 12 weeks at £1   = 12
   60 weeks at £0·8 = 48

Cost to 15 months   60

£0·75 per week for every week kept after 18 months.

[1] Tayler, J. C., Technical Report No. 3, Grassland Research Institute, Hurley, Berkshire. March 1966

Calves reared on milk substitute and weaned at 5 weeks. Fed on high plane for bulling at 15 months. Four pounds cake per day plus Rumevite with grazing.

Breeder and rearer share losses.

Rearer pays £1 towards vaccination against husk.

Example II

Breeder sells calves to rearer off colostrum.

Rearer brings up calves on multiple suckling system.

Calves ear marked by breeder for later recognition.

Price of calves fixed by agreement for 12 months ahead.

Rearer provides a beef bull and undertakes to get heifers in-calf.

Heifers calve at 2·5–2·75 years old.

Breeder has first option to buy heifers back one month before calving.

Breeder buys heifers back at ruling market prices, usually about £80 per head.

Rearer has the heifer's first calf by the beef bull.

Rearer, as owner, stands all losses.

Rearer dehorns calves and is responsible for them receiving vaccination against brucellosis.

Breeder pays carriage on calves to rearer.

Rearer pays carriage on heifers to breeder.

It is essential on the outset of such an undertaking to draw up a comprehensive contract agreement to be signed by both parties, i.e. the breeder and the rearer. Numbers of points need to be covered by this agreement and an example of a typical contract is reproduced below:

Suggested contract for heifer rearing

1. The breeder will retain ownership of the heifer.
2. An instalment system of payment will be undertaken, e.g. 3 months, 6 months or even 1 month.
3. The owner to have right of access to inspect the heifers at any time and the right to withdraw the animals if in his opinion the husbandry is not satisfactory. Any argument to be referred to an independent arbitrator, e.g. cattle valuer or auctioneer.
4. Any outstanding payments to be made before an animal is removed.
5.* Reciprocal visits of veterinary surgeons to be made to establish suitability of rearing farm and risk of introduction of disease from the owner's farm.
6. The rearer will be responsible for having all calves vaccinated with S.19 under the free scheme of the Ministry of Agriculture. Other precautions, e.g. against husk, warble fly, etc., could also be undertaken and presumably paid for by the owner.

7. The rearer will be responsible in the case of sickness, for calling the vet and also notifying the owner. It should be decided who will pay the veterinary fees: normally it would be the rearer. Any outbreaks of disease should be reported promptly.

8.* The rearer will be responsible for getting the heifer in calf, but the owner will decide when the heifer will be served and with which bull.

9. The owner may remove the heifer, when springing to calve, in order to acclimatise to the dairy herd environment and allow steaming up.

10. Should the heifer, at any age, prove to be unfit to rear further, it may be removed by the owner on payment of any outstanding charge.

11. If for any reason the heifer dies on the rearer's farm, the rearer loses all his payment for that particular instalment period. A veterinary certificate could be obtained. If negligence is established, the rearer should reimburse the owner for all payments to date *and* the value of the calf when taken. If the heifer is injured or killed outside the rearer's farm (e.g. the New Forest), the full loss to the owner will be met by the rearer. (The rearer would normally insure against this risk.)

12. Feeding will be left to the discretion of the rearer; but the system of feeding will, presumably, have been agreed by the owner before the calf is placed on the rearer's farm.

13.* Every effort will be made to get the heifer in calf. If necessary the fertility of the bull should be checked before use. Pregnancy diagnosis could be made by the owner. The rearer will contact the owner as soon as possible if he has any reason to suspect infertility and/or abortion.

14. Transport to and from the rearing farm will be met by the owner.

15. The calf from the calved heifer will be the property of the owner of the heifer.

16. The identification of the heifer will be made before placing on the rearing farm, e.g. by ear tags, cold branding or by the usual breed identification sketch prepared by the owner, signed by the rearer, and retained by the owner.

17. The rearer has the right to refuse taking a particular animal for rearing.

18. The contract to run in the first instance for a minimum of two years thereafter renewable annually.

Signed .... (Owner)

.... (Rearer)

**Note.* It is strongly recommended that the veterinary surgeons for each party should in fact meet each other. It is impossible to eliminate all risks of venereal disease, but providing one accepts that they are not going to be transmitted deliberately the matter should be covered in 5, 8, and 13, i.e. the owner deciding which bull is used (if A.I. is used the risk is negligible) together with the veterinary surgeons meeting to discuss the risk of the introduction of disease.

The beef production enterprise

A world shortage of beef is developing so beef is one agricultural product for which the future currently appears bright. Home consumption of beef is slowly increasing and, in order to improve upon our balance of payments position, it is imperative that as much of this as possible should be produced at home.

The programme of 'Selective Expansion' for agriculture which was founded in the National Plan of 1965, laid great emphasis upon the future importance of beef production and in fact pledged the Government to maintaining beef prices over a period of three years. During this time and since, beef has been particularly favoured at annual price reviews. Between the years 1967 and 1970 the guaranteed price of beef rose by over 20 per cent – more than any other agricultural commodity experienced over the same period.

Numbers of beef cattle have also been on the increase. It must be remembered, however, that only about one-third of the cattle slaughtered in the United Kingdom are bred out of specialist beef breeding herds. The remaining two-thirds are by-products of the national dairy herd together with imported stores from southern Ireland.

As there are nearly three dairy cows for every beef cow in the United Kingdom and as a large proportion of male calves from dairy herds are still slaughtered as bobby calves, any immediate increase in beef production in the United Kingdom must arise from better use being made of calves from the dairy herd, rather than from an increase in the number of beef-breeding cows. At the same time, however, beef-breeding herds are being encouraged, particularly by the Hill Cow Subsidy and Winter Keep Allowance and by the more recently introduced Beef Cow Subsidy. In addition to this, the Calf Subsidy is payable on all calves of eight months and over, which are suitable for beef production. (Heifers of Friesian, Ayrshire and Channel Island breeds are excluded from subsidy on the hoof, but if subsequently certified, calf subsidy can be claimed on the carcase.)

The hill areas benefit considerably from these subsidies which are both a social as well as an economic necessity if many of the less accessible and poorer areas of the U.K. are to be kept in agricultural production.

Much publicity has been given to recent developments in beef production, particularly to intensive methods of producing immature beef, and there is evidence to show that an increasing proportion of cattle slaughtered in the U.K. are immature beasts, slaughtered at less than 2 years of age. This general trend towards finishing cattle at an earlier age is due to four main reasons:

1. Cereals have become cheaper since the 1950s and intensive fattening systems based on cereal feeding, e.g. barley beef, are now an established commercial practice.

2. Dairy-cross calves which of necessity are being more widely used for beef production are better suited to systems using a high-energy diet and early slaughter than to more traditional methods involving a store period. This type of beast needs to be kept on a high plane of nutrition at a rapid rate of liveweight gain in order to produce a satisfactory carcase.

3. Traditional systems of fattening where cattle are slaughtered at 2–3 years of age show an extremely slow turnover of capital. Increasing interest charges have favoured intensive systems which have a quicker turnover and provide more opportunity for improving return on capital.

4. The Government has endeavoured to stabilise marketing of fat cattle throughout the year by adjusting the weekly standard price (and consequently the fatstock guarantee payment) to favour the period when slaughterings of cattle are normally at their lowest, in late winter and early spring. This has meant that most intensive systems have been geared towards spring sales when prices are at their highest and fewer animals now experience a winter store period.

The pattern of slaughterings has tended to become more even in the last two years and as a result the differential between market prices of Spring and Autumn sold cattle has become less marked. The final price inclusive of subsidy, however, still strongly favours the spring-killed beast.

Production economics

The economics of beef production are considered in two broad sections –

(*a*) Beef breeding herds;
(*b*) Beef fattening systems.

Beef breeding herds

Numbers of cows kept primarily for the production of beef calves have increased in recent years in response to the general encouragement which this section of the industry has received. There has also been a need in many arable areas to introduce a grazing enterprise which will effectively use rotational grass and produce satisfactorily gross margins without involving heavy fixed capital expenditure.

Single suckling herds

The majority of beef breeding herds fall into this category and follow a traditional system of spring calving to produce a weaned calf for sale as a store animal by the following autumn. This has been the practice with most Hill and Moorland breeding herds for generations and the store calves produced are usually taken onto arable units for fattening.

Table 6.12   Gross margin standards for single suckling herds

	Upland	Lowland		
		Spring calving	Autumn calving	Intensive
Sale of calf (or transfer value)	45	50	50	55
Calf subsidy	—	—	10	10
Maximum calf output	45	50	60	65
Calving percentage	90	95	95	95
Effective calf output/cow	40·50	47·50	57·00	61·75
Hill cow subsidy	18·50	—	—	—
Winter keep allowance	5·00	—	—	—
Beef cow subsidy	—	11·00	11·00	7·00
Sale of cull cows	¼ at £40	⅕ at £60		
	10·0	12·0	12·0	12·0
Total livestock sales	74·0	70·5	80·0	80·75
Replacement calves		1·0	1·0	1·0
Bull depreciation or hire*	1·0	1·0	1·0	1·0
Replacement heifers	20·0	16·0	16·0	16·0
Total livestock purchased	21·0	18·0	18·0	18·0
Gross output/cow/year	53·0	52·5	62·0	62·75
Variable costs				
1. Concentrates	4·0	4·0	6·0	10·0
2. Purchased bulk feeds	4·0	—	—	2·0
3. Misc. variable costs	2·0	2·0	2·0	2·0
Total var. costs (excluding forage)	10·0	6·0	8·0	14·0
Gross margin (excluding forage)	43·0	46·5	54·0	48·75
Forage costs/cow	?	8·0	8·0	17·0
Gross margin/cow	<43·0	38·5	46·0	31·75
Gross margin/acre	?	19·25	23·0	26·5
Forage acres/cow	?	2·0	2·0	1·2

* Bull depreciation is calculated as follows:

    1 bull to 30 cows over 5 years

		£
Purchase price	=	£200
less Cull value	=	50
∴ Depreciation	=	150
Annual depreciation	=	30
Deprec./cow/year	=	1

In recent years there has been a tendency to adopt, wherever possible, an autumn calving policy for single suckling herds.

The advantages of such a policy are:

1. A bigger and better calf is produced for the calf sales in the following autumn.
2. The calf being older, is better able to utilise spring and early summer grazing.
3. Calves are usually stronger at birth due to a higher plane of nutrition in late pregnancy on summer and autumn pasture.
4. More milk is produced by the dam, the spring grass gives a boost to the dam's milk production which can be fully utilised by the calf.
5. There is generally a lower mortality rate for both calves and cows, provided that shelter and supplementary feeding are available in mid-winter. Calving in the autumn does not coincide with the period of maximum risk for hypomagnesaemia.

The disadvantages of autumn calving are:

1. It is necessary to provide more shelter and more supplementary feed to calves and cows during winter. This involves additional expense and may well eliminate the possibility of autumn calving on many true hill farms.
2. Cows must conceive at the most difficult time of the year, i.e. January to February for September to October calvings. Spring calving is more natural and allows bulling at a time when fertility is naturally at its highest.

Factors affecting the profitability of the breeding herd

The beef-breeding enterprise is now heavily supported by subsidy. In specified areas, the Hill Cow Subsidy of £18·5 a head plus £5 Winter Keep Allowance can be claimed and in areas not qualifying for Hill Cow Subsidy, a special Beef Cow Subsidy of £11 a head is payable provided that the cows are not stocked more densely than 2 acres per cow. These rates were set at the Annual Price Review in 1970. (At higher densities the subsidy is proportionately reduced.)

A systematic breakdown of the cost structure of single suckling is shown in Figure 6.*d.*

These principles are best illustrated by reference to typical gross margin accounts and standards for single suckler enterprises. Three separate situations are taken as examples.

(*a*) A hill farming system, qualifying for full rate of subsidy. This herd would normally follow a spring calving policy and produce a weaned calf for sale the following autumn. Calf subsidy will not normally be claimed by the breeder but since the calves are 'clean-eared' they will command a proportionately higher market price. Figures are not expressed on an acreage

Figure 6.d. Factors affecting the profitability of the beef breeding herd

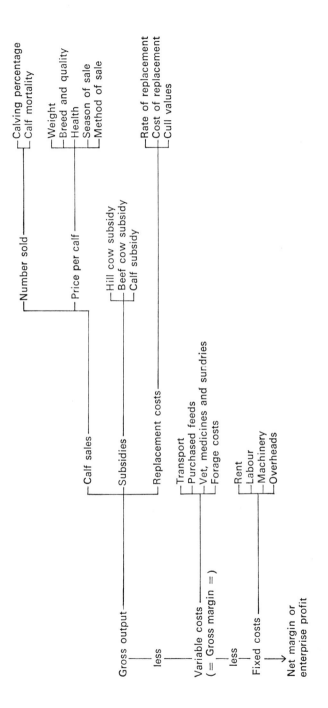

basis since this will depend on the proportion of true hill and 'in-bye' land which vary enormously.

(*b*) A lowland single suckler enterprise. No hill cow subsidy is payable but the beef cow subsidy partly compensates for this. This type of enterprise is examined in two forms: (*i*) autumn calving; (*ii*) spring calving.

(*c*) An intensive lowland single suckling herd. In this case cows are stocked at high density similar to that of a dairy enterprise on good quality land and beef cows subsidy is proportionately reduced.

Recent trials (I.C.I. Henley Manor)[1] have shown that if really well managed, an intensive lowland single suckling enterprise can be competitive with any other grazing livestock enterprise (except perhaps dairying).

In the examples which follow (Figures 6.*e* and 6.*f*) an attempt is made to plot the seasonal capital profiles or cash flow diagram for each enterprise. Output and expenditure tend to follow a seasonal pattern requiring wide variations in working capital at different times of the year. To avoid confusion the capital profiles have been restricted to requirements for marginal working capital only and fixed costs, e.g. labour, buildings, interest, etc., have been omitted.

Multiple suckling

This is essentially a system for the better land and the milkier strain or breed of cow. Many variations of this technique have been practised, the basic idea being to make full use of the cow's milking abilities by allowing her to suckle more than one calf at a time.

While appearing on paper to be an admirable system, it is in practice fraught with difficulties. Firstly, there is the problem of obtaining the right type of calves at the right time to foster on to the cow; then there is the job of persuading the cow to take to the extra calves, and furthermore, there is always the danger of producing two or more light calves at the end of the season which will not be forward enough to fatten at the end of their first winter.

Properly done, this can be worth another £10 gross margin per acre, but the system is demanding upon labour and the extra gross margin may not justify the extra time, trouble and risk involved.

Capital profiles

Single suckling enterprises are considered here and it is assumed that all calves are sold off in the autumn.

With a spring-calving herd, it is assumed that replacement heifers are bought in early summer in time for bulling, and with the autumn-calving

---

[1] *Modern Beef Production* (Autumn 1969) (I.C.I. Agricultural Division). Henley Manor Farm – I.C.I. Farming Service

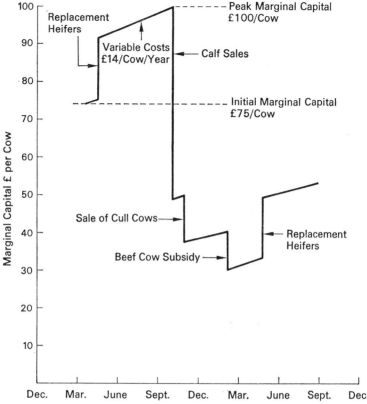

Figure 6.e   Marginal capital profile for single-suckling herd (spring calving)

herd that replacement heifers are bought in late autumn for bulling at around Christmas.

Cull cow sales are divided between two times of the year:

(a) empty cows are sold after pregnancy testing (November for spring calves and June for autumn calves);

(b) old cows not bulled are sold off after weaning their calves.

A high proportion of the marginal working capital for this enterprise is tied up in the breeding stock themselves. The profiles indicate that an average capital requirement of approximately £85 to £90 per cow is required with a peak requirement of approximately £100 per cow occurring September to October in the case of the spring-calving herd and in the late winter in the case of the autumn-calving herd.

Beef fattening systems

The economics of beef fattening are considered as follows:

A. Immature cattle;

B. Mature cattle.

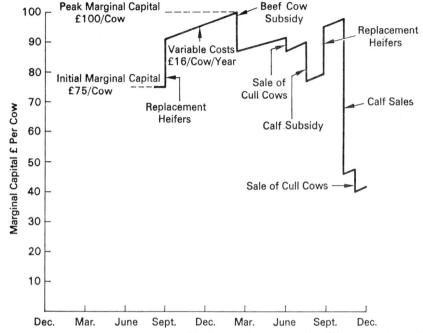

Figure 6.*f   Marginal capital profile for single-suckling herd* (*autumn calving*)

Immature cattle

This broad term is intended to include cattle which are sold fat before they have cut their permanent incisor teeth, i.e. before 20 months of age. This form of fattening has become more popular for reasons already discussed and is most commonly employed in the following circumstances:

1. Fattening single suckled beef calves in their first winter.
2. Finishing by-product calves from the dairy herd either on: (*a*) full intensive system, e.g. barley beef; or (*b*) a semi-intensive system, e.g. grass and cereal beef (18-month beef).
3. Veal production.

Fattening single suckled calves in their first winter

The aim is to finish a single suckled calf in late winter or early spring when fat cattle prices are usually at their highest. This means that an autumn-born calf will finish at 14–18 months and a spring-born calf at 12–15 months. The most important single factor affecting the success of this venture is the suitability of the store calf at the beginning of the fattening period. It is essential that the calf should be strong and in good health and that it should already have reached at least 500 lb liveweight without losing its calf flesh. This type of animal can be kept going on a moderate level of concentrate feeding supplementing good quality silage and can be expected to finish at 800–900 lb liveweight by the spring. Smaller calves which so often result from calving too late or from poor suckler management, multiple suckling, or the use of unsuitable breeds cannot be expected to finish in time using this system and must be regarded as non-starters which are best wintered as stores.

If a fattening period of 180 days (mid-October to mid-April) is assumed, then the Table 6.13 indicates the necessary combinations of starting weights and liveweight gain required to produce a certifiable beast (minimum liveweight being 672 lb for special lightweight heifers and 784 lb for special lightweight steers).

Table 6.13   Starting weights and liveweight gain to produce a certifiable beast

| | Weight at mid-April (lb) | | | |
| | Rate of liveweight gain | | | |
Weight at mid-October (lb)	*0·5 lb/day*	*1 lb/day*	*1·5 lb/day*	*2 lb/day*
300	390	480	570	660
350	440	530	620	710
400	490	580	670	760
450	540	630	720	810
500	590	680	770	860
550	640	730	820	910
600	690	780	870	960
650	740	830	920	1010

There is a wealth of evidence both from trials and commercial enterprises to show that with good management, liveweight gains of 1·5 lb to 2 lb per day can be achieved on this system from silage and barley without exceeding 8 lb per day of cereals.

A higher rate of gain requires a more concentrated diet and has three major disadvantages:

(a) High cost.
(b) Digestive disorders are more likely and consequently there is a higher level of risk.
(c) With early maturing breeds and particularly with heifers, there is a danger of animals becoming 'overripe', i.e. too fat too soon, necessitating their sale at too light a weight and thereby reducing output.

Accounting problems arise when silage is fed since there are many possible ways of allocating suitable forage costs to the gross margin account. This can be overcome either by assuming a value for the silage (e.g. £3 per ton) or more correctly by debiting the cattle with the variable costs incurred in producing the silage and at the same time allocating a proportion of the farm forage acreage to the enterprise. In the examples in Table 6.14 the latter alternative has been adopted.

Table 6.14   Feeders' margins and gross margins for single suckled beef calves, fattened in their first winter

	7 cwt heifer	8 cwt steer
	£	£
Sale price at £11·25/cwt liveweight	78·75	90·00
Calf subsidy	9·00	11·25
Total receipts	87·75	101·25
Less value of suckled calf	50·00	55·00
Gross output or 'feeders' margin'	37·75	46·25
Variable costs		
Concentrates 8 lb × 180 days = 13 cwt rolled barley and minerals at £23/ton	15·00	15·00
Silage 40 lb × 180 days = 3 tons = ⅓ acre at £15 v. costs/acre	5·00	5·00
Vet., medicines, sundries, drenches, warble dressing, etc.	1·50	1·50
Total variable costs	21·50	21·50
Gross margin/beast	16·25	24·75
Weight of store calf	500 lb	550 lb
Rate of liveweight gain	1·6 lb/day	1·9 lb/day

This is a short-term fattening enterprise and, for the purpose of calculating a cash flow, can be considered in the same way as a pig-fattening enterprise, provided that concentrates are bought in as required. If home-grown cereals are used, then the working capital requirements will be slightly less, but spread over a longer period.

N.B. 'Feeders' margin' is the livestock output obtained by whoever fattens or finishes the stock. It is calculated simply as gross sales less cost of store stock or replacements and is exactly the same as gross output.

2.(a) Intensive fattening on a 'barley-beef' diet

This technique now has an established place in beef production, and can be used for calves born at any time of the year. The system has the advantage of being completely independent of forage acreage and as such is comparable in many respects with 'Concrete' enterprises such as pigs and poultry.

Calves are reared on an early weaning system and are kept on a high level of concentrate feeding throughout their lives. Rolled barley and a small quantity of protein supplement is available *ad libitum* from about 4 months of age. Rapid rates of gain are experienced and the calves usually reach slaughter weights at 11 to 14 months.

Factors affecting profitability

These are illustrated diagrammatically (*see* Figure 6.*g*).

Gross output or 'Feeders' margin' is the difference between livestock receipts including subsidies, and calf purchases.

Sale price is a function of weight and price per pound, and since food conversion efficiency drops rapidly after the animal reaches about 6·5–7 cwt, barley beef animals are usually marketed as soon as they reach certification weights. Provided that animals maintain the necessary rate of liveweight gain to finish at 12–14 months, then quality of carcase is fairly uniform. The main danger of the system is over-finishing, which often results from using early maturing breeds, especially heifers.

Price per pound is usually at its highest in the spring and consequently most barley beef systems are geared to a spring sales programme using spring-born calves. If an all-the-year-round price can be negotiated on a contract basis, then the system may well be integrated with a dairy herd producing calves throughout the year. A fairly standard product is produced which is consequently well suited to contract marketing with all its adherent benefits.

Calf subsidy provides an interim source of income in the production cycle and significantly increases output while at the same time providing an injection of ready cash at a critical stage in the programme.

Barley beef is essentially a high-risk business and a mortality rate of about 7 per cent should be allowed when budgeting.

Cost of suitable calves for barley beef fattening is variable. Steer calves of large fast-growing breeds, e.g. Friesian and South Devon are preferred and the best prices are usually paid in the spring.

Feedingstuffs are by far the greatest single item of expenditure. The cost of early weaning feeds is predictable at about £8 per head, but after this food costs are influenced by a number of factors. Total requirement depends on conversion rate which for the fattening period should average 5·0–5·5 lb of concentrate per pound of liveweight gain. The heavier the animal at slaughter, then the poorer the overall conversion rate, since efficiency of food use falls steadily after 6·5–7 cwt due to an increase in intake coupled with a decrease in liveweight gain. Overall growth rate also seems to be better during the summer months than that of winter-fed cattle at similar weights and stage of growth. However, this is partly offset by an increase in the cost of barley due to storage, and so final feed costs of autumn- and spring-sold cattle are very similar.

Figure 6.g.   Factors affecting the profitability of barley beef

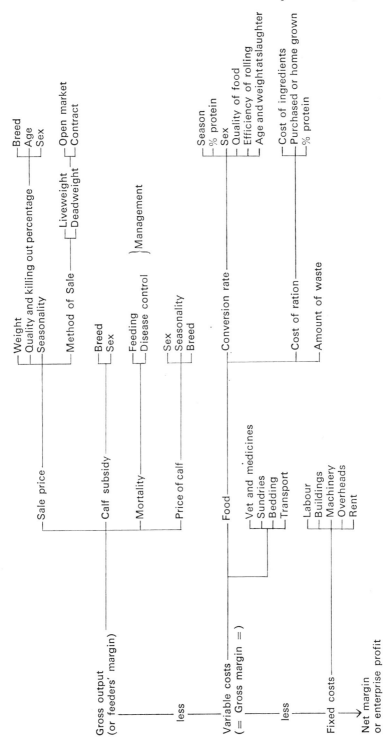

Deaths can occur at any stage in the production of barley beef and because of this some share of production cost must be allowed against the 7 per cent budgeted mortality.

This has been assumed in Table 6.15 as one-half of the variable costs of production, incurred by the animals which are lost and no allowance has been made for their carcase value.

Table 6.15   Gross margins for Friesian steer calves fattened on a barley beef system

	Sold in spring	*Sold in autumn*
	8 cwt at £11	8 cwt at £10
Sale of fat beast	88·0	80·0
Calf subsidy	11·25	11·25
Total possible sales	99·25	91·25
Less 7% mortality	6·95	6·37
Actual sales	92·30	84·88
Less cost of calf	15·00	12·00
Gross output	77·30	72·88
Variable costs		
1. Concentrates and milk:		
(a) Early weaning	8·0	8·0
(b) Barley 28 cwt at £23/ton	32·0	32·0
(c) Beef concentrate 4 cwt at £45/ton	9·0	9·0
(d) Hay 2 cwt at £10/ton	1·0	1·0
2. Miscellaneous	4·0	4·0
Total variable costs	54·0	54·0
Less $\frac{1}{2} \times 7\%$ mortality	1·9	1·9
Effective variable costs	50·1	50·1
Gross margin	27·2	22·8

Capital profile (*see* Figure 6.*h*). Provided that calf subsidy can be claimed on all cattle then a peak marginal capital requirement of £58·0 per head is required, with an average of $\dfrac{£58+15}{2}$ = £36·5. If one month's merchant's credit could be arranged, then the peak marginal capital requirement (excluding labour and fixed costs) would fall to £50–55 per head.

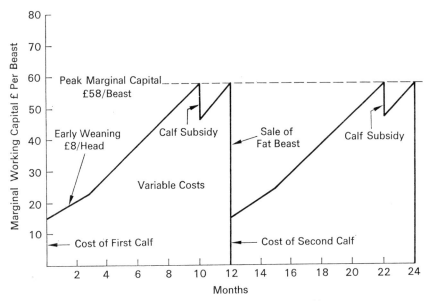

Figure 6.h   Barley beef – marginal working capital profile

2.(b) Semi-intensive or 'Grass and Cereal' beef

This system, which is also known as '18 month beef', has increased in popularity for the following reasons:

(a) Satisfactory gross margins are obtainable from grazing livestock without heavy capital investment.
(b) Autumn-born calves, which are usually in good supply, can be finished in the spring when prices are at their highest.
(c) The system is sufficiently intensive to finish by-product calves from the dairy herd.

Autumn-born calves are early weaned and kept growing at about 1·5 lb per day until turnout the following spring, when they will weigh about 400 lb. Intensive summer grazing for the next six months results in yearlings being re-housed in the following autumn at about 700–750 lb liveweight. If a steady rate of liveweight gain of 1·5–1·8 lb per day can be maintained, the beasts will finish by the following spring weighing 850–1 100 lb.

The factors affecting profitability are in essence the same as those for barley beef, but since forage acres are involved, efficiency of forage utilisation in the form of stocking density, liveweight gain from grazing and conserved forage and costs of forage production must also be considered.

Difficulties arise in apportioning a suitable forage acreage to such an enterprise, particularly where grazing and conservation acreage is shared with other grazing livestock. Trials have shown that with intensive grassland management it is possible to provide summer grazing and sufficient silage to finish one beast from 0·8 acre.

Grazing requirements increase as the summer progresses and as the cattle grow, but this allows for a large proportion of spring and early summer grass to be conserved for fattening in the following winter. If summer grazing requirements are considered exclusively, these will amount to an average requirement of 0·3–0·5 acre per beast for the whole summer.

Table 6.16   *Gross margin for Friesian steer calves bought in autumn and sold in spring at 18 months*

		£
Sale of fat beast	8·5 cwt at £11·0	93·50
Calf subsidy		11·25
Total possible sales		104·75
Less 4% mortality		4·19
Effective output		100·56
Less value of calf		12·00
Gross output		88·56

Variable costs		
1. Concentrates:	£	
(*a*) Early weaning	8·0	
(*b*) Weaning to 6 months	5·0	
(*c*) Cereals at grass	5·0	
(*d*) Finishing ration 8 lb barley × 180 days = 13 cwt at £23/ton	15·0	
		33·0
2. Bought hay		1·0
3. Vet. and medicines		3·0
4. Bedding and sundries		4·0
Total variable costs		41·0
Less share mortality $\frac{1}{2} \times 4\%$		0·82
Effective variable costs		40·18
Gross margin (excluding forage costs)		48·38

Effect of stocking density on gross margin/forage acre

Acres/beast	0·80	1·00	1·20
Gross margin/acre excluding forage G.M./beast × beasts/acre)	60·0	48·0	40·0
Less forage costs/acre	18·0	15·0	12·0
Gross margin/acre	42·0	33·0	28·0
Final gross margin/beast (G.M./acre after forage × acres/beast)	33·6	33·0	33·6

Capital profile. When calf subsidy is paid at 8–12 months, the peak marginal capital on this enterprise (*see* Figure 6.*i*) amounts to approximately £78 per head including forage and conservation costs.

The average working capital for the 18-month cycle is thus:

$$\frac{£78+12}{2} = £45$$

At the end of the cycle the marginal capital will be completely repaid by the sale of the first batch of cattle, leaving a margin to cover fixed costs and profit.

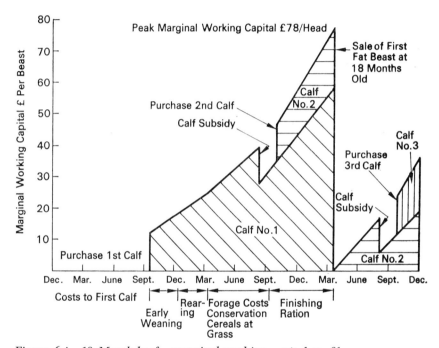

Figure 6.i   18-Month beef – marginal working capital profile

3. Veal production

The practice of forcing calves on an all-milk diet, for slaughter at about 3 months of age, has long been popular in Continental countries and has recently gained popularity in the U.K.

A limited number of calves are slaughtered annually for veal. The market is small as yet but is capable of expansion, particularly through increased sales to the Continent.

Calves are usually kept under conditions of controlled environment and are fed on milk or reconstituted milk with no dry feed. Rapid growth is possible and the conversion rates achieved are comparable with those obtained by fattening poultry, i.e. 1·4–1·5 lb dry matter per pound of liveweight gain.

G

Veal production is essentially a high-risk business because of the decimating effect of infectious disease, e.g. bacterial scour, under conditions of controlled environment and a successful unit demands an extremely high level of stockmanship.

The example given in Table 6.17 relates to a heavyweight carcase of 300 lb liveweight killing out at 60 per cent, suitable for the restaurant or 'weiner schnitzel' trade and is based on an assumed 4 per cent mortality.

Table 6.17   Gross margin for veal production

Sales	£
180 lb carcase at £0·25/lb	45·0
Less 4% mortality	1·8
Effective sales	43·2
Less cost of calf	12·0
Gross output	31·2
Variable costs	
2·7 cwt high fat milk substitute at £142/ton	19·2
Vet. medicines and sundries	0·5
Total variable costs	19·7
Less ½ × 4% mortality	0·4
Effective variable costs	19·3
Gross margin	11·9

This type of calf would be slaughtered at 12–14 weeks of age. Capital costs for controlled environment buildings are approximately £15 per calf housed, with a throughput of four batches of calves per house per year.

B. *Mature cattle*

This loose definition is intended to cover all cattle of 18 months and over, which are fattened by less intensive methods than those so far mentioned.

Two broad systems can be considered:

(*a*) Summer fattening off grass.
(*b*) Winter fattening.

(*a*) *Summer fattening off grass.* Grass fattening accounts for the majority of cattle sold at this stage, and in examining the profitability of this enterprise a large number of factors need to be considered as Figure 6.*j* will illustrate.

Variable costs are minimised, being only transport, a small veterinary and medicines charge and the forage costs incurred in providing grazing.

Figure 6.j. Factors affecting the profitability of grass fed beef

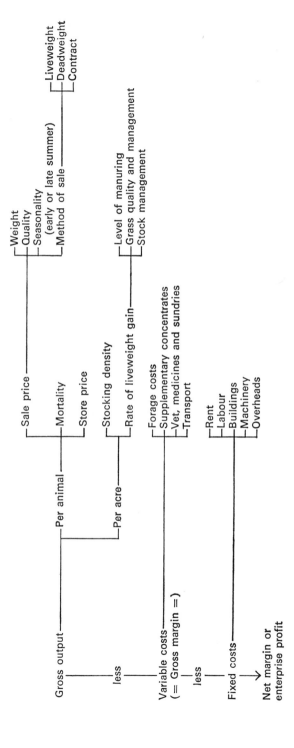

Output is the difference in value of the store animal at the beginning of the fattening period and that of the fat beast and is usually expressed by the term 'Feeder's margin'.

Three main factors affect this:

(*i*) Mortality;
(*ii*) Increase in weight, i.e. speed of growth with time;
(*iii*) Difference in price per pound of the store animal and the finished beast.

Price differences are extremely important. Standard prices for fat cattle are so regulated that the producer's final price tends to fall steadily throughout the summer grazing period and a beast can only maintain or increase its value by a compensatory weight increase, since the producer's price usually falls by about £1 per live hundredweight during this period.

An 8-cwt store in good forward condition would therefore lose £8 in value without any liveweight increase. At 1 lb l.w.g. per day over a grazing period of five and a half months, he will gain approximately 1·5 cwt and increase his final value by about £5. At 2 lb l.w.g. per day the same beast would increase in value by about £18. This then is the feeder's margin and the final level of profit will depend upon stocking rate and levels of costs incurred.

No satisfactory standards can be calculated for this type of enterprise since so much of the success of this type of business depends upon marketing skill – mainly in buying suitable store cattle at the right price.

Indeed, it would be fair to concede that the real art of fattening mature cattle lies in the sale ring rather than in the feed lot.

The final feeder's margin must be sufficient to cover the following:

(*a*) Forage and agistment costs;
(*b*) Transport;
(*c*) Any supplementary feeds costs;
(*d*) Veterinary, medicines and sundries;
(*e*) Fixed costs, e.g. rent if appropriate;
(*f*) Interest on capital tied up in the cattle;
(*g*) Profit margin.

Unless one possesses the necessary skill at buying store cattle it is easy to tie up capital in stock without showing any return at all. It is therefore necessary to assess very carefully the maximum price that can be paid for store cattle, above which it will pay to invest the money elsewhere – see Table 6.18 where only if suitable cattle can be obtained at £85 a head or less, will there be any point in going ahead with such a venture.

(*b*) *Winter fattening.* The basic principles listed above will also apply to winter fattening.

Table 6.18   Calculation of maximum store price payable when fattening mature cattle

		£	£
Expected sale price	10 cwt at £10·0/cwt		100
Less Transport		1·5	
Vet. and medicines		1·0	
Hay at turnout		0·5	
Forage and agistment		7·0	
Interest on capital, say £90 at 10% for 6 months		4·5	
			14·5
Maximum store price at NO profit			85·5

Price per hundredweight will tend to increase during the fattening period (whereas in summer it does the reverse) but fattening variable costs will be higher since concentrates will be required to finish this type of beast.

Once again standards are of little value, since buying skill is the major factor determining final feeder's margin and profit.

Conclusions on beef production

In an increasingly affluent society the demand for meat, particularly beef, is likely to increase. Beef producers are thus assured of a long-term market. The U.K. producer is faced with competition from the vast temperate and semi-tropical grasslands of the world where an extensive system of beef production allows a cheaper carcase to be produced. Even under continued Government support at home, a very strict cost control is essential if margins from beef production are to be attractive to the small producer.

A growing supermarket trade is now showing preference for a much larger carcase with a high lean content, since this is better suited to providing a large number of small joints (all made with the knife) than the small blocky animal of the fatstock shows.

If the producer is given sufficient incentive to produce this larger carcase, then a return to a higher age of slaughter is likely together with use of imported breeds with higher growth potential and greater emphasis upon the use of grass and forage crops in fattening, particularly if entry into the E.E.C. renders cereal feeding uneconomic.

The sheep enterprise

Sheep are to be found in every county of the British Isles, yet they only produce about 5 per cent of our national agricultural output. Mutton and lamb sales constitute the greater part of this, wool sales amounting to only one-sixth of the total sheep output.

Since 1966, sheep numbers in the U.K. have been falling steadily. The Ministry of Agriculture claim that the decline has occurred mainly in the lowland areas and on the better quality grass, and that in the hills and on the poorer quality land and marginal grazing areas, sheep numbers are being maintained.

Further statistics show that three-quarters of the flocks kept in this country are of less than three hundred ewes, and that distribution of the national flock is approximately one-third of the total sheep in flocks of less than 300, one-third in flocks of 300–700 and one-third in flocks of 700 ewes or more. One can gather from this that on most farms sheep are a subsidiary enterprise and only in a small number of cases are the sheep the principal source of income.

Government policy, since the announcement of the National Plan in 1965, has been to encourage sheep production, particularly in the hill areas, where maintenance of flocks is a social rather than an economic necessity.

Falling sheep numbers, coupled with a fairly constant home demand for mutton and lamb, have resulted in increased imports of sheep meat mainly in the form of frozen lamb from New Zealand. The Government wishes to keep these imports to a minimum and has increased the guaranteed price of mutton and lamb at each price review since 1966. The Hill Sheep Subsidy and Winter Keep Allowance have also been increased and now stand at £1·05 and £0·175 per ewe respectively. (The full rate of subsidy is restricted to pure breeding flocks of certain breeds in specified areas, but since the 1967 Review, a much larger number of sheep kept on marginal upland areas have become eligible for the subsidy at half-rate, i.e. £0·525 per ewe.) The Hill Sheep Subsidy makes a very significant contribution to farm income in these areas.

A superficial examination of gross margin figures obtained from sheep enterprises on lowland areas is likely to give the impression that sheep are something of a 'Cinderella' enterprise and have very little part to play in the economy of farms on better quality land. At traditional stocking densities of 2·5–3 ewes per acre the gross margin from sheep is extremely disappointing at £12 to £16 per acre and compares very unfavourably with the average level of gross margins obtainable from other grazing enterprises or from cereals.

Great care is required, however, in interpreting such information for the sheep enterprise, whose influence is reflected in the outputs of other enterprises on the same farm. On a mixed farm, for example, the sheep themselves may not show a very brilliant gross margin per acre, but their presence on the farm may well be reflected in increased crop yields resulting from better soil fertility and disease control when a grass break is introduced into the rotation.

Sheep on a general farm may also contribute indirectly to the economy of the farm by helping to establish leys and utilise by-products and by the technical advantages accruing from mixed grazing.

Apart from making the farm economy more diversified and thereby spreading risk, the sheep enterprise has the added advantage of requiring very little fixed capital investment, and unless winter housing is contemplated, almost all the capital tied up in the sheep enterprise is that invested in the sheep themselves, i.e. working capital in every sense of the word and fully realisable.

Being lightfooted, sheep can often fit in well on a mixed farm, because of their ability to graze late into the winter without causing excessive poaching. They are frequently able to utilise outlying and inaccessible fields and those with an inadequate water supply for cattle.

It is often claimed that a small flock can be handled between the main jobs on a mixed farm and will contribute to the economy without requiring additional labour. On the other hand, fencing must be of a higher standard than that usually required for cattle, and some of the routine work involved in flock management does require certain very specialised skills.

Although specialised shepherding services will now carry out this work on a contract basis, good sheep-men are still scarce in the U.K., and as stocking densities become heavier, risks become greater and managerial skill more critical – hence the old adage 'the only trouble with sheep is men'.

Systems of sheep farming

Before the economics of the sheep enterprise can be discussed further, it is necessary to appreciate that sheep enterprises on farms in the U.K. exist in a wide variety of possible forms.

With a wide range of topographical and climatic conditions prevailing, with over 30 recognised breeds and with several possible products from the flock, sheep farming systems are extremely diverse and cannot be easily classified.

One can generalise broadly, in order to avoid considering an unnecessary number of combinations and permutations and divide sheep farming systems into three main groups:

1. *Hill flocks*

Full-rate subsidy flocks, breeding pure under true hill and moorland conditions and supplying their own replacements in a normal year.

2. *Marginal and cross-breeding flocks*

These are mainly 'flying flocks' relying upon bought-in cast-for-age ewes from the hill areas as replacements. They are still on marginal and upland grazing but do not qualify for subsidy at full rate. Long-wool rams are used to produce hybrid females for sale to better quality land and store wethers for fattening.

3. *Lowland flocks*

Producing mutton, fat lamb or store sheep from good quality grassland or in conjunction with an arable rotation. These may breed their own female replacements or they may rely on purchased replacement stock.

Factors affecting the profitability of the sheep enterprise

The basic principles of costing the sheep enterprise remain the same, however diversified the individual systems may be.

Factors affecting the ultimate profit are numerous and are expressed diagrammatically in Figure 6.*k*. (The diagram relates to a breeding flock but can be suitably modified to deal with enterprises which rely on purchasing and re-selling sheep.)

Individual factors affecting profitability can now be discussed systematically.

Factors affecting gross margin

GROSS OUTPUT PER EWE

A. *Lamb sales*

1. *Numbers sold per ewe.* This combines two factors: (*i*) lambing percentage; (*ii*) post-weaning lamb mortality.

Lambing percentage can be expressed in several ways and a very fair method of making this calculation is as follows:

$$\text{Lambing percentage} = \frac{\text{Number of lambs in flock at weaning} + \text{lambs sold before weaning} \times 100}{\text{Number of ewes tupped}}$$

This allows for ewe mortality and pre-weaning lamb losses. Lambing percentage is itself affected by a wide range of factors, e.g. fertility of ewes and rams; level of environment (feeding, protection, attention at lambing); breeding (fertility is partly a genetic factor); management before tupping (flushing, etc.); ewe mortality; pre-weaning lamb mortality.

Under exposed hill conditions a lambing percentage of 80–100 is usually considered good, whereas in the lowland, with a higher level of nutrition, better protection against the elements and closer shepherding, the same breeds have been shown capable of up to 200 per cent.

2. *Price obtained per lamb*

(*a*) *Weight of lamb sold.* For the greater part of the year, lambs produced at home are in competition with imported New Zealand lamb which is a fairly standard product at 30–40 lb dead carcase weight. Our main market tends to be geared to this weight range and butchers usually show preference

Figure 6.k.   Factors affecting the profitability of the sheep enterprise

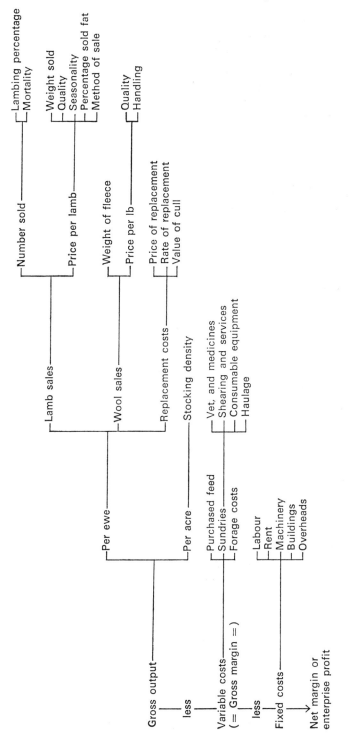

for this type of carcase. Under some conditions carcases outside this weight range may be preferred. In early spring there is usually a high demand for 'Easter Lamb' and high prices per pound will often be paid for carcases of less than 32 lb dead carcase weight. Conversely, markets in the industrial areas of the Midlands and North and the now growing export trade provide a good outlet for heavier carcases. At constant quality the price per pound tends to be inversely proportional to the weight. It is, therefore, important to choose a breed or cross which will produce the type of carcase best suited to the available market.

(*b*) *Quality.* The most important consideration here is that the carcase should be well enough finished to qualify for fatstock guarantee payment by being certified as suitable by an inspector of the Ministry of Agriculture.

Both the liveweight and the deadweight market will also pay a premium for the 'Q' or top-quality carcase. When marketing on a liveweight basis, evenness of quality throughout a group of lambs will increase the demand from the butcher, and careful penning and sorting is often well justified.

(*c*) *Seasonality of production.* Lamb production in the U.K. tends to be seasonal in nature and with a relatively constant demand only partly satisfied by imports, lamb prices tend to follow a predictable seasonal pattern.

The bulk of the home produce crop is marketed in the late summer and early autumn and consequently prices are at their lowest at this time of the year. As production falls off in the autumn, a steady rise in price is usually experienced until a maximum is reached at around Easter, after which a steady decline is once again apparent.

The producer has therefore to assess the market to which his system of production is best suited. He must decide whether it is more profitable to go for the high-priced product by lambing out of season and by the costly hand feeding to produce a fat lamb for the Easter trade, or whether to lamb later and aim to produce a more cheaply fed lamb to be marketed at a lower price. Such a decision can only be made by careful budgeting in the light of all the circumstances affecting the individual farm business.

The best prices on a conventional grassland system of fat lamb production are obtained when a high proportion of lambs are finished and marketed before the end of June. This form of marketing is particularly well suited to intensive grassland management, since the first lamb sales coincide with the peak of grassland production and thus enables numbers of grazing stock to be better equated with falling grassland production as the season progresses.

(*d*) *Percentage of lambs sold fat.* On many farms, lambs which are not finished by the autumn are sold as stores to be fattened elsewhere. The price of a finished animal, certified and with subsidy, will almost certainly be higher than that of a store animal sold at the same time of the year. The higher the proportion of animals sold fat, therefore, the higher the overall price per lamb sold.

As stocking densities become heavier, it becomes increasingly difficult to maintain a satisfactory proportion of lambs sold fat. All too frequently the result of increasing the number of ewes kept per acre is a higher proportion of store lambs and no real increase in net output. At the same time it must be remembered that some situations, for example in the hills and marginal grazing areas, are better suited to store production, and production is aimed primarily at the store market. This inevitably means a lower return per animal, but could still leave a satisfactory margin provided that costs were kept at a sufficiently low level.

(e) *Method of sale.* Lamb is a seasonal product and consequently organisation of orderly marketing is more difficult than with all-the-year round products such as pigmeat or poultry.

A properly organised contract system which allows suitable bonuses for quality will generally realise a better price than short-term haphazard selling on the open market. Long-term contracts are as yet only offered to the larger producer and a great need exists for co-operative marketing organisations which allow the smaller producer to gain more benefit from planned and orderly marketing of his lambs.

B. *Wool sales*

Wool is essentially a by-product of the British sheep industry, whereas in some countries, e.g. Australia and South Africa, wool is the most important output of the flock.

British wools do not generally satisfy the requirements of the top-quality market, and although there are some notable exceptions for highly specialised users, e.g. tweed wools and mattress stuffing, most of our home-bred wool is sold on a low-grade market and commands a low price when compared with fine quality worsted wool like that of the Merino.

Weight of fleece is the most important single factor affecting wool output per ewe, and while affected by feeding and management, this is primarily a function of breed and will range from about 2 to 2·5 lb for a Scottish Blackface ewe in her native habitat, to 12 to 14 lb for some of the long-wool and close-wool breeds on good quality feed.

Handling and presentation of the fleece both affect price, and although presentation and final marketing of the wool is now the responsibility of the British Wool Marketing Board, much can be done on the farm to ensure that the fleece is kept free from contamination and is properly shorn, rolled and stored. Heavy penalties are deducted by the British Wool Marketing Board where careless handling or storage might result in a reduction in the market value of the clip.

C. *Replacement costs*

On the debit side of the gross output calculation must be considered the flock depreciation.

With an orthodox breeding flock, this simply entails the cost of new ewes and rams joining the flock, set against the cull value of those which are no longer suitable and are sold.

Replacement costs depend on:

1. Rate of replacement.
2. Cost of replacement.
3. Value of culls.

Rate of replacement. Female replacements usually join the flock at about 18 months of age as 'gimmers' or 'Two-tooths'. This is by no means a standard practice and the age at which ewes join the flock will vary according to system and area. On good lowland conditions and with early maturing breeds, it may be possible to tup ewe lambs in their first autumn and still get a fair crop, thereby saving the cost of a year's unproductive keep. Other systems rely entirely upon cast ewes to provide their replacements, and since these will have a shorter breeding life ahead of them, a much larger proportion of the flock will need to be replaced each year.

Under lowland conditions and with good management an average breeding life of 4–5 years should be possible for a ewe. Full-mouthed ewes which are cast for age from hill country will usually last for a further two to three seasons when brought down to better conditions. (The degree of culling practised in any livestock enterprise is governed by the principles discussed in the section on dairy replacements.)

Cost of replacement. The price paid for replacement ewes is extremely variable but basically will depend on the likely productive life of the animal and its suitability for immediate production. Gimmers from the north usually fetch £10 to £12 a head in the fat lamb producing areas.

Rams will usually have an active life of 4–5 seasons and their rate of inclusion in the flock varies from 2 per cent to 3 per cent depending upon their age, virility and the type of country in which they are running. (Smaller enclosed areas require less rams than when mating under open-range conditions.) Ram prices are again extremely variable, but sound commercial crossing rams for fat lamb production are available in the £15 to £25 range.

Value of culls. The price paid for a cull ewe will depend upon the possible alternative uses of the animal. A cast-for-age hill ewe will still have a value as a breeding animal whereas a cull ewe from a lowland flock is usually only assessed on her carcase value, which will depend upon weight and degree of finish and will also vary according to the time of year.

As a very rough yardstick for budgeting (cigarette-packet style) the annual depreciation of a ewe is approximately equalled by the value of the fleece she provides.

Example

	£
Cost of gimmer	10·50
less value of cull ewe	4·00
∴ *Depreciation*	6·50
Depreciation per year over 5 years	1·30
Value of wool clip 6·5 lb at £0·2	1·30

Variable costs

The principal variable costs affecting the sheep enterprise are:

(*a*) Concentrate costs;
(*b*) Other purchased feed costs and agistment charges;
(*c*) Vet., medicines and sundries.

These are best illustrated by the gross margin accounts which follow.

Stress has already been given to the widely varying systems of sheep production that occur in this country and no single set of standards is universally applicable.

The following three hypothetical gross margin accounts attempt to illustrate the likely levels of costs and outputs that will occur in average situations under three completely different systems of sheep farming in the British Isles.

Case I. A true hill flock (see Table 6.19)

A full rate of subsidy is payable on flocks of certain breeds in specified hill and moorland areas. This would be a pure breeding flock and since the ewes are cast-for-age when full mouthed and a lambing percentage of only 80 per cent is likely to be achieved, most of the females bred are needed for flock replacements.

The outputs from the flock consist of wool sales from the breeding flock and replacements, sales of cast ewes, cast rams, all wether lambs and occasionally a few surplus ewe lambs or gimmers.

Livestock replacement costs are minimal, consisting only of bought-in replacement rams. At a low stocking density, vet. and medicine costs are kept fairly low and so also are concentrate costs, since only a very small amount of concentrates will be fed, 10–14 lb per ewe being given in the last few weeks before lambing. A little hay will probably have to be bought in for late winter feeding.

Table 6.19   Typical gross margin account for a hill flock expressed per 100 ewes
         5% Mortality   80% Lambs reared

VARIABLE COSTS			RETURNS	£	£
(a) Vet., medicines and sundries, incl. shearing at £0·625		62·50	(a) *Wool* 97 ewe fleeces at £0·75	73	
(b) *Concentrates* 10 cwt at £25/ton		12·50	34 ewe lambs at £0·75	26	99·00
(c) *Bought hay* 2 tons at £10		20·00	(b) *Store lambs* 44 at £4		176·00
(d) *Agistment* Away-wintering 36 ewe lambs at £1·75/head		63·00	(c) *Draft ewes* 31 at £4·50		140·00
Margin without subsidy		242·00	(d) 1 cast ram		5·00
					420·00
			Less Replacement ram 3% for 3 years: 1 ram		20·00
		400·00	*Gross output without subsidy*		400·00

PLUS SUBSIDIES

	£	
1. Hill sheep subsidy: 100 ewes at £1·05	105	
2. Supplementary winter keep allowance: 100 ewes at £0·175	17·50	
		122·50

Gross margin including subsidy	364·50	*Gross output including subsidy*	522·50

Gross output/ewe without subsidies	£4.0
Gross output/ewe including subsidies	£5.2
Gross margin/ewe without subsidies	£2.4
Gross margin/ewe including subsidies	£3.6

N.B. Gross margins before deducting forage costs

The major item of costs incurred is that of away-wintering the replacement ewe lambs in their first winter. This is a recognised practice in the hills in order to give maximum attention to the ewe flock and to give the ewe lambs the chance of making better growth than would be possible at home.

The account shows that under normal conditions the margin left to cover forage and all fixed costs is extremely slim and that the contribution of the Hill Sheep Subsidy is very considerable (it increases the gross margin per ewe by 50 per cent).

Case II. Marginal upland flock (see Table 6.20)
This represents an intermediate situation between the true hill farm and the lowland unit producing fat lamb.

Table 6.20   Typical gross margin account for a marginal upland flock expressed per 100 ewes

VARIABLE COSTS	£	RETURNS	£
(a) Vet., medicines and sundries, incl. shearing at £0·625	63	(a) *Wool* 97 fleeces at £0·85	82
(b) *Foods:* Concentrates 35 cwt at £25/ton	44	(b) *Store lambs* 120 at £5·50	660
Hay 2½ tons at £10/ton	25	(c) *36 draft ewes* at £1·50	54
		(d) *Cast ram* ⅔ at £6	4
			800
		Less Replacements (a) ⅔ ram at £21 14 (b) 40 ewes at £4·50 180	194
Gross margin	474		
	606	*Gross output*	606

Gross output/ewe   £6.06
Gross margin/ewe before deducting Forage costs   £4.74

The flock in this case is situated on poor-quality marginal grazing but does not qualify for hill sheep subsidy. A cross-breeding policy is followed using cast-for-age hill ewes as replacements and mating these to long-wool rams to produce half-bred females (e.g. Scotch half-bred, Greyface and Masham) for sale as breeders and wethers for fattening as stores.

Ewes stay in the flock for 2–3 years and produce slightly more wool and a rather better lambing percentage when kept under slightly softer conditions. Concentrates are fed for the last 6–8 weeks of pregnancy and hay will be made for the flock or bought in. Ewe mortality is higher at about 10 per cent due to the high average age of the flock, but a lambing percentage of 120 is achieved.

Output consists primarily of store lamb sales plus cull ewes, rams and the wool cheque.

The main cost item is replacement ewes with 40 per cent of the flock replaced annually; also replacement rams.

Feedingstuffs and sundries costs are higher than on the hill unit, but there is no heavy charge for away wintering of replacements.

Table 6.20 shows that due to a higher gross output, a better gross margin is achieved per ewe than on her native hill.

No allowance has been made for hill sheep subsidy though some farms in marginal areas, adopting this sort of system might be eligible for Hill Subsidy at half-rate, leaving a gross margin per ewe of £5·25 to £5·50 (excluding forage costs).

Case III. Typical lowland flock (See Table 6.21)

A typical lowland flock producing summer fat lamb. In this case it is assumed that replacements are bought in as gimmers and last for an average of four productive years in the flock. Rams also last for four years and are used at 2 per cent.

Hybrid ewes, e.g. Scotch half-bred, are mated with a Down ram, e.g. Dorset Down, to produce a three-way cross intended for slaughter.

The main output will be the sale of fat lambs. There will also be a few store lambs at the end of the season, along with cull ewes, rams and the wool cheque.

Expenditure on feedingstuffs will be higher as more concentrates are used in the period immediately before and after lambing.

Table 6.21 Typical gross margin account for a lowland flock producing summer fat lamb expressed per 100 ewes

VARIABLE COSTS		£	RETURNS		£
(a) Vet., medicines and sundries, incl. shearing at £0·75		75	(a) *Wool* 97 fleeces at 6½ lb at £0·225		137
(b) *Foods:*	£		(b) *Lambs* 140 lambs at £6·50		910
Hay 3 tons at £10	30		(c) *Cull ewes* 22 culls at £2·50		55
Concentrates Steaming up 0–1·5 lb × 8 wk 37·5 cwt at £25/ton	47		(d) *Cull rams* ½ cull ram at £6		3
After lambing 0·5 lb × 4 wk 12·5 cwt at £25/ton	15				1 105
		92	*Less* Replacements	£	
			(a) 25 gimmers at £10	250	
			(b) ½ ram at £16	8	
					258
Gross margin		680			
		847	*Gross output*		847

Gross output/per ewe £8.47 approx.
Gross margin/per ewe £6.80
(before deducting forage costs)

At an average lambing percentage of 140, the gross margin per ewe, before deducting forage costs, is £6 to £7. If one accepts an average stocking density of 2·5–3 ewes per acre, this leaves a gross margin of £15 to £21 per acre before deducting forage costs, or in the order of £12 to £16 per acre after allowing for forage costs appropriate to these levels of stocking density.

This presents a rather dismal picture and with levels of fixed costs rising annually by about £1 an acre on most lowland farms, a traditional sheep enterprise does not appear to be a viable proposition, and unless it can be justified by its contribution to other more profitable sections of the farm economy, then there may be a strong case for replacing sheep with a grazing enterprise having a higher financial potential.

Statistics indicate that this has recently happened on a large number of farms, for sheep numbers and flock numbers are dwindling, particularly on better quality land carrying high levels of fixed costs.

But must the sheep go?

The national economy clearly needs home produced sheep meat. Short of a miraculous increase in the price of mutton and lamb, how can the sheep enterprise be made to stand on its own feet, under modern conditions?

In order to make the sheep enterprise more competitive, it is necessary to raise both its net output and its gross margin in relation to the land it uses. This means that output per acre must be raised or a significant reduction made in variable costs.

Variable cost levels are already low and clearly any increase in gross margin must come from an improvement in gross and net output per acre, which may be achieved in two ways:

(*a*) by increasing net output per ewe;
(*b*) by increasing numbers of ewes per acre.

Reference to the cost structure diagram (Figure 6.*k*, p. 189) shows numerous possible avenues for increasing the gross output per ewe. These factors have already been discussed in detail, and if one examines each in turn it is clear that improvements in wool sales, replacements costs and prices obtained per lamb under existing price structure are likely to produce only marginal improvements in output per ewe. Significant improvement can only therefore arise from an increase in lambing percentage.

Scientists and research workers have endeavoured with great enthusiasm to bring about this increase in prolificacy. Strange breeds with incredible names and even more incredible appearance have been resurrected to form a mysterious 'gene pool' from which the 'wonder sheep' of the future is supposed eventually to emerge. The ovine female has been subjected to varying light patterns and intensities and her reproductive cycle has been violated by numerous hormone potions administered from either end.

The result: it is now technically possible under research conditions to produce litters of three to five lambs and to obtain three lamb crops in two years. Technically possible – just. But few ewes are able to rear successfully more than two lambs, so what does one do with lamb nos. 3, 4, 5, etc.? They must be artificially reared, and further research shows that this is again technically possible, though an exacting business. Unfortunately, very few of these developments have proved financially worth while under farm conditions. New breeds have shown an improved lambing percentage, but only where improved environment and attention have allowed it to be expressed. Under large-scale flock management, the so-called 'new breeds' have proved disappointing and a growing scepticism exists as to their value.

Hormone treatments have produced litters of five, but the average number of lambs produced per ewe is still nearer three, even under experimental conditions and the extra lambs are costly to rear to a sensible slaughter weight. At £4 feed cost to rear a lamb to slaughter there is very little margin to cover the remaining costs incurred.

Raising the lambing percentage beyond reasonable levels is fraught with difficulties and does not appear to give sufficient return to justify the extra trouble involved. Under conditions of large flock management an overall lambing of 170–180 per cent can be obtained by good management and husbandry without recourse to gimmickry or to the adoption of practices as yet unproven in the field.

Any dramatic improvement to be achieved in the gross margin per acre obtained from sheep must, therefore, in the foreseeable future, arise from an increase in stocking density.

Traditional stocking rates of 2·5–3 ewes per acre are typical of a set stocking pattern on grassland of only moderate quality. Surely then, if dairy cows can be kept on less than an acre for the year by heavy manuring and by controlled grazing techniques, then it should be possible by adopting similar practices to obtain a similar increase in stocking density with sheep. On well-managed leys, 6–8 ewes with their lambs can be carried per acre during the growing season, but to maintain this level of stocking during the winter months is another matter altogether, and in order to avoid excessive poaching, it is usually necessary to ease stocking density, either by scattering the sheep over a larger area or by getting the sheep off the land by housing them. The latter development has become an essential feature of many intensive systems of sheep management.

What level of gross margin could one expect to achieve per acre from intensive fat lamb production if the technical problems of high density stocking could be overcome?

The graph (Figure 6.*l*) attempts to illustrate the levels of gross margin that should be obtainable as a result of increasing stocking density and lambing percentage. Certain basic assumptions have been necessary in drawing up this graph which is based on Table 6.22. Lamb sales have been taken as £6·5 per head, wool sales have been assumed to equal replacement costs and the food cost of artificially rearing the third lamb has been taken as £4 per head (this latter assumption is primarily responsible for the downward trend in gross margins after two lambs per ewe are achieved and prevents a straight-line relationship existing between gross margin per acre and lambing percentage.

If standard gross margins for other grazing livestock enterprises are now superimposed on to this graph, the basic weakness of the sheep enterprise becomes very apparent. For example, in order to achieve what would be a very moderate gross margin of £45 per acre from dairy cows, one needs five ewes per acre at 200 per cent or seven ewes per acre at 160 per cent or ten ewes per acre at 120 per cent.

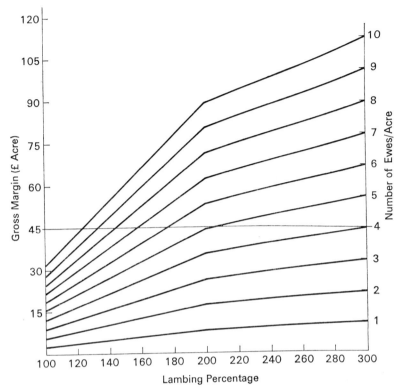

Figure 6.1 Fat lamb production: The effect of stocking density and lambing percentage on gross margin per acre

The graph (Figure 6.*1*) also indicated that at a given level of lamb production or Total Sales per acre, there is an optimum level of lambing percentage beyond which gross margin per acre is likely to fall.

For example, if one aims at producing six fat lambs per acre, this can be achieved by:

6 ewes per acre at 1 lamb per ewe, giving a G.M. of £18·5 per acre

3 ewes per acre at 2 lambs per ewe, giving a G.M. of £26·0 per acre

2 ewes per acre at 3 lambs per ewe, giving a G.M. of £22·0 per acre.

Similarly, nine fat lambs per acre can be achieved by:

9 ewes per acre at 1 lamb per ewe giving a G.M. of £28·5 per acre

4½ ewes per acre at 2 lambs per ewe giving a G.M. of £39·5 per acre

3 ewes per acre at 3 lambs per ewe giving a G.M. of £33·5 per acre

or 12 fat lambs per acre can be achieved by:

12 ewes per acre at 1 lamb per ewe giving a G.M. of £38·0 per acre

6 ewes per acre at 2 lambs per ewe giving a G.M. of £53·0 per acre

4 ewes per acre at 3 lambs per ewe giving a G.M. of £45·0 per acre.

Table 6.22 Fat lamb production: The effect of stocking density and lambing percentage on gross margin per acre

Lambing Percentage

Ewes per acre	100						200						300					
	Vet.	Concs.	Forage	V. Costs	Output	G.M.	Vet.	Concs.	Forage	V. Costs	Output	G.M.	Vet.	Concs.	Forage	V. Costs	Output	G.M.
	£	£	£	£	£	£	£	£	£	£	£	£	£	£	£	£	£	£
1	0·75	1	2·5	4·25	6·5	2·25	1	1·5	2·5	5·0	13	8·0	1	5·5	2·5	9	19·5	10·5
2	1·50	2	4·0	7·50	13·0	5·50	2	3·0	4·0	9·0	26	17·0	2	11·0	4·0	17	39·0	22·0
3	2·25	3	5·5	10·75	19·5	8·75	3	4·5	5·5	13·0	39	26·0	3	16·5	5·5	25	58·5	33·5
4	3·00	4	7·0	14·00	26·0	12·00	4	6·0	7·0	17·0	52	35·0	4	22·0	7·0	33	78·0	45·0
5	3·75	5	8·5	17·25	32·5	15·25	5	7·5	8·5	21·0	65	44·0	5	27·5	8·5	41	97·5	56·5
6	4·50	6	10·0	20·50	39·0	18·50	6	9·0	10·0	25·0	78	53·0	6	33·0	10·0	49	117·0	68·0
7	5·25	7	11·5	23·75	45·5	21·75	7	10·5	11·5	29·0	81	62·0	7	38·5	11·5	57	136·5	79·5
8	6·00	8	13·0	27·00	52·0	25·00	8	12·0	13·0	33·0	104	71·0	8	44·0	13·0	65	156·0	91·0
9	6·75	9	14·5	30·25	58·5	28·25	9	13·5	14·5	37·0	117	80·0	9	49·5	14·5	73	175·5	102·5
10	7·50	10	16·0	33·50	65·0	31·50	10	15·0	16·0	41·0	130	89·0	10	55·0	16·0	81	195·0	114·0

The reduction in gross margin per acre at the higher levels of lambing per acreage is due entirely to the extra concentrates which are necessary for rearing the third lamb artificially.

Further systems of lowland sheep production
Lowland sheep farming is not restricted to the production of fat lamb, and other systems deserve consideration.

1. Keeper sheep
A valuable contribution to the income of many farmers with winter grazing to spare is the provision of agistment for 'keeper sheep'. These are usually ewe lambs or store sheep and realise about £0·075 per head per week, while often benefiting pasture by removing surplus growth.

The remaining sheep enterprises all depend very heavily upon skill at buying and selling and consequently no reliable standards can be calculated for them.

2. Store fattening
This enterprise can be subdivided as winter fattening and summer fattening.

Winter store fattening involves the purchase of store lambs in late summer and early autumn and then taking them on to finish during the winter usually on roots or green crop with some hay and concentrates. A gross output of £2 to £3 per lamb is possible but concentrate costs are likely to be between £0·05 and £0·10 a week.

Summer store fattening involves the purchase of hoggets in late winter – early spring and running these on pasture till fat. Gross output in this case amounts to increase in carcase value plus the value of the fleece which is usually taken before this type of lamb is sold fat. A heavy carcase is produced at this age (15–18 months) and the popularity of this system has decreased since fatstock guarantee is now only payable on the first 60 lb dead carcase weight.

3. Couples
Draft ewes purchased in the autumn are mated and then sold in the wool with their lambs early in the following summer. Couples usually realise £9 to £11. The ewe is shorn and then sold after weaning the lamb which is fattened. This system is well suited to farms with surplus winter grazing but where sheep would compete with more valuable stock if kept all the year.

Comparisons on the basis of gross margins alone can be extremely misleading. In all the cases demonstrated, the gross margins quoted fail to illustrate one of the great advantages of the sheep enterprise, namely its extremely low fixed capital requirement.

Return on capital invested in the sheep enterprise must always be given due consideration in assessing its contribution to the farm business.

The pigs enterprise

Pigmeat in its various forms accounts for approximately 11 per cent of our national agricultural output. Home consumption of pork and bacon is rising slowly but is only partly supplied by home production. One-third of our total consumption of all pigmeat and two-thirds of our total bacon requirements are imported, with Denmark supplying about 75 per cent of this quantity.

In spite of increasingly severe grading and tighter prices, pig production in the U.K. expanded remarkably up to the summer of 1965. Then it took a turn for the worse, production and breeding stock numbers fell off sharply, reaching a very low point at the end of 1966. A substantial price increase (equivalent to £0·10 per score) at the 1967 Annual Price Review has eventually led to a slow recovery in home pigmeat production and total numbers of breeding stock are at the time of writing increasing slowly but steadily.

Average herd sizes are tending to increase, while numbers of pig herds are diminishing, indicating that pig production is tending to become more specialised. The larger units tend to be more concentrated in the Eastern Counties.

Pig production, while becoming more specialised, has also become far more competitive in recent years. Labour costs and overheads have increased steadily but there is evidence of a slight improvement in the relationship between producers' returns and feedingstuffs costs, due primarily to the lower market price of feeding cereals.

The margin from pig production is extremely finely balanced and a high standard of managerial efficiency is absolutely essential if a satisfactory return on capital is to be achieved. In examining costings, there is always a very noticeable difference between the results of the 'average' and 'premium' farms – probably more so than with any other enterprise. This is because a large number of factors are involved and attention to detail is extremely important since the effect of small improvements in efficiency tends to be accumulative. In the examples which follow, the sensitivity of ultimate profitability to small changes in production efficiency is amply illustrated. In the past, pig prices have been notorious for their instability and pigs have had the reputation of being either 'copper' or 'gold' – never 'silver'. Prices have tended to follow a cyclic pattern with a frequency of approximately four years, increased output leading to over production–low prices–falling numbers–increased prices–increased output–over production, etc., etc.

Stability of pig prices has improved in recent years due to the following reasons:

1. *Pig herds have become larger*

The small marginal producer has tended to disappear and be replaced by the more specialised unit having a high capital investment in pig housing and equipment. The small man, keeping a few sows as a side line, could quickly get in or out of pigs as it suited him. The specialist is committed to stay in pig production and must stay in business by improving his efficiency.

2. *The flexible guarantee scheme*

The basic guaranteed price for pigmeat is directly related to the number of pigs certified. If the forecast certifications increase then price per score falls automatically, conversely, if production falls then the price per score will automatically rise.

3. *Feed price formulae*

Guaranteed prices are also related to current feed prices, thereby stabilising margins even though feed prices may fluctuate.

4. *Vertical integration*

Feedingstuffs compounders are taking an increasing interest in the production of the finished article. Advantages of scale may lead to tolerance of finer margins and steadier and more stable production.

Prosperity of the pig industry is closely related to the prevailing price of cereals and in an era of falling prices for home grown cereals, pig production may become an attractive proposition on the arable farm.

Pigs are capable of converting cereals into meat and into cash more efficiently than cattle as Table 6.23 indicates.

Table 6.23   Comparison between cattle and pigs as converters of cereals

	Conversion rate (lb cereals/ lb l.w.g.)	Price/pound D.W.	Killing out percentage	Price/pound L.W.	Output/pound of cereals
		£		£	£
Pork	3·4	0·135	70	0·0945	0·027
Bacon	3·7	0·125	73	0·0913	0·025
Heavy hogs	4·0	0·110	78	0·0858	0·021
Barley beef	5·0	0·175	56	0·098	0·0195
Barley beef	5·2	0·175	56	0·098	0·0189
Barley beef	5·4	0·175	56	0·098	0·0182

Production economics and profitability

When dealing with crops and with grazing livestock, land use has always been a major factor to consider, since land is usually the most limited factor of production. Efficiency of such enterprises has always been assessed primarily on the basis of land use (gross margin per acre, etc.), while always bearing in mind the importance of an adequate overall return on capital. In these cases return on capital was often closely linked with efficiency of land use and except in cases of excessive capital investment the two factors were more or less synonymous.

In assessing the profitability and viability of the 'concrete' enterprises, i.e. pigs and poultry, a completely different approach is called for. Land is not a serious limiting factor of production where these enterprises are concerned, consequently output and margins per acre are virtually useless in assessing profitability.

Efficiency of production is more suitably assessed according to the use made of the remaining resources, i.e. labour and capital.

Capital is the major limiting factor of production in the case of the pigs enterprise and return on capital must be given top priority in assessing and comparing the efficiency of pig production.

Outline efficiency factors

While the importance of assessing efficiency in relation to capital is acceptable in theory, it may not always be possible to evaluate the capital involved, particularly when sorting out a farm trading account which includes pigs along with other farm enterprises.

If capital cannot be assessed, how then can one attempt to evaluate the productivity of the pigs enterprise?

The following simple measures can be calculated from a basic trading account and will give outline pointers to efficiency when compared with figures for other farms or with standards:

A. *Output factors*

1. *Gross output from pigs* – per pig sold or per sow.

B. *Feed economy factors*

Feedingstuffs are the major cost item in pig production, therefore feed economy and profitability are closely related.

1. *Net output from pigs* – Total – per pig sold – per sow. Net output (i.e. gross output less purchased feeds costs) is an extremely useful factor in assessing the efficiency of the enterprise since it represents the actual output generated by the pigs themselves. It could otherwise be called 'margin over purchased feeds costs'.

2. *Feeds costs per £100 gross output.* The standards in Table 6.24, based on average ratios of feeds costs to output, give a quick measure of feed efficiency

for any form of pig production. A combined standard can easily be constructed where both breeding and fattening occur simultaneously.

Table 6.24   Output: feed cost ratios for pig production

	Feed cost/£100 gross output	Gross output/£100 feeds costs
Weaner production	58	171
Bacon	69	142
Pork	74	136
Cutters	75	134
Heavy hogs	76	132

Sophisticated efficiency factors

Detailed records of feedingstuffs used, together with information on births, deaths, sales, purchases, transfers and miscellaneous costs will enable a wide range of sophisticated efficiency factors to be calculated. These can then be compared with standards such as those in Table 6·25 which were originally introduced by the Pig Industry Development Authority in 1966. (P.I.D.A. is now incorporated into the Meat and Livestock Commission.)

Table 6.25   P.I.D.A. efficiency factors

	Good	Average	Poor
No. of litters/sow or gilt/6 months	1·0	0·9	0·7
Pigs born alive/litter	12·0	10·0	8·0
Av. no. pigs reared/litter	11·0	8·0	6·0
Av. weight pigs weaned (lb – 8 wk)	40·0	35·0	30·0
Meal equivalent/pig reared to weaning (lb)	180·0	230·0	270·0
Feed cost/pig reared to weaning	£3·0	£3·5	£4·0
Feed cost/lb weaner production	0.079	0.104	0.129
Feed consumption/lb weaner production	5·0	6·5	8·0
Conversion rate (lb ME/lb l.w.g.)			
Porkers	3·25	3·50	3·75
Baconers	3·50	3·75	4·00
Heavy hogs	3·75	4·00	4·25
Cost/lb l.w.g.			
Porkers ⎫			
Baconers ⎬	£0·045	£0·054	£0·062
Heavy hogs ⎭			

N.B. 1 lb meal equivalent = 4 lb potatoes
                          = 5 lb fodder beet
                          = 1·2 gallons whey
                          = 0·8 gallons skimmed milk

Comparative profitability of alternative outputs

Systems of pig production can be broadly classified as under:

1. Breeding.
2. Meat production (pork, cutters, bacon, heavy hogs).
3. Combination of both.

In order to assess and compare profitability the following factors must be considered:

(*a*) Gross margin per pig;
(*b*) Net margin per pig;
(*c*) Gross margin per unit house space per year;
(*d*) Net margin per unit house space per year;
(*e*) Net margin per unit of capital per year, i.e. percentage return on capital.

Return on capital is the most important single factor, and since much of the capital invested will be tied up in housing and equipment, the margin per unit of house space is a closely related factor. This involves another dimension namely *Time* or rate of throughput and this must be given full consideration when judging the relative importance of margin per pig and margin per unit.

Example

	Pork	Bacon	Heavy Hog
Net margin per pig (£)	1·0	1·54	1·81
Fattening time	13 weeks	20 weeks	23 weeks
Batches per year	4·0	2·6	2·2
Net margin per pig space per year	£4·0	£4·0	£4·0

Net margins per pig vary considerably on the three cases cited, but the ultimate margin per unit of house space is the same in each case.

Calculation of return on capital

This is basically net margin per £100 capital invested.

Capital invested in the pig enterprise will be in the following forms:

A = Fixed capital in housing and equipment and breeding stock
plus B = Trading capital in the growing pigs
plus C = Working capital to cover running expenses, i.e.:
Food costs
Labour
Miscellaneous costs and overheads.

Evaluation of A and B is straight-forward and can be taken as the average of valuations.

Working capital (C) is more difficult to evaluate since this form of expenditure is a continuous process. One needs to assess the average amount of capital tied up during a production cycle, e.g. fattening a batch of pigs.

Example
To find the working capital employed in food for a batch of fattening pigs:

Average capital in food = half total foods cost.

This calculation is adequate if foods are paid for as they are consumed, but if merchants' credit is given, and the producer is allowed a month's grace in which to pay for his foodstuffs, then correspondingly less working capital will be tied up on this item.

The new formula for calculating the amount of capital invested in food thus becomes:

$$\text{Average capital in food} = \text{half cost} \times \frac{\text{fattening time} - \text{credit time}}{\text{fattening time}}$$

Miscellaneous costs and all other costs for which credit time is available can be treated in the same way.

The above procedure has been adopted in assessing percentage return on capital in all the examples quoted in this enterprise study.

Weaner production

The factors affecting profitability are set out in Figure 6.*m*.

Variable costs per sow are partly constant and partly proportional to the number of pigs produced per year. The constant portion of these costs, however, is by far the greater and the extra cost incurred by creep feeding additional piglets represents a very small fraction of the cost of keeping a sow for a year.

An increase in output per sow per year then represents a disproportionate increase in gross margin as Table 6.26 illustrates.

Table 6.26   Relationship between numbers weaned and gross margin per sow

Pigs weaned/annum	Output at £5·75/pig	Variable costs	Gross margin	Cumulative increase in G.M.
	£	£	£	£
13	74·75	52·3	22·45	—
14	80·50	52·8	27·70	5·25
15	86·25	53·3	32·59	10·50
16	92·00	53·8	38·20	15·75
17	97·75	54·3	43·45	21·00
18	103·50	54·8	48·70	26·25

Figure 6.m.   Factors affecting the profitability of weaner pig production

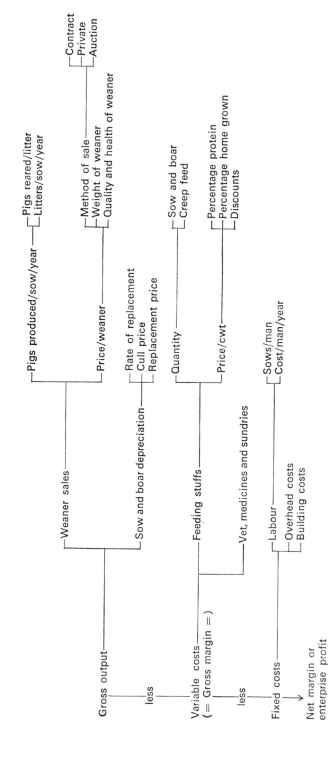

Output per sow is a function of pigs produced per sow per year and price obtained per weaner.

At a constant price per weaner, gross output will depend on numbers of weaners sold per sow per year and this in turn upon numbers of weaners sold per litter and Farrowing Index or litters per sow per year. Ability to produce and rear large litters is partly genetic and partly controlled by nutrition and management. Both these characteristics are of low heritability and apart from exploiting heterosis by cross breeding, more progress in increasing piglets per sow per year has been made by improving the farrowing index than by raising numbers weaned per litter. Increasing the number of litters per sow per year has only been possible by early weaning techniques and with three week weaning, five litters every two years can be obtained, giving an output of 20 weaners per sow per year.

The adoption of such practices is demanding not only of labour and management skills but also of capital.

A higher capital investment per sow will be required on an early weaning system, since the sow will spend more of her time in the maternity quarters.

Price obtained per weaner will depend on the type of pig and its suitability for a given market when finished. It will also depend on the way in which the weaner is sold.

Auction markets are notoriously unreliable for this class of stock and the advantages of producing under contract are well worth considering. This gives a guaranteed outlet either direct to a fattener or through an agency or weaner pool.

Points to be agreed in drawing up such a contract are:

(*a*) Forward scale of prices per pound liveweight;
(*b*) Health standards – approved farms, disinfected vehicles, etc.;
(*c*) Numbers supplied per month or quarter with acceptable degree of variation, e.g. 10 per cent;
(*d*) Period of agreement (usually six months);
(*e*) Period of credit (usually very short, agents will not give credit);
(*f*) Transport and delivery charges;
(*g*) Agent's commission;
(*h*) Arbitration in case of dispute.

Sow and boar depreciation can be calculated as follows:

Average herd life of sow	3 years
Average herd life of boar	3 years
Average number sows per boar	20
Average price gilt	£40
Average price young boar	£60
Average cull price sow	£15
Average cull price boar	£15

$$\text{Annual depreciation sow} = \frac{40-15}{3} = £8\cdot3$$

$$\text{Annual depreciation boar} = \frac{60-15}{3} = £15$$

$$\text{Sows annual share of boar depreciation} = \frac{£15}{20} = £0\cdot75$$

∴ Total annual depreci-
ation expressed per sow = £9·05.

Food costs per sow and boar are controllable within limits. Table 6.27 shows the effect of reducing the ration of the pregnant sow upon annual consumption and feed costs at a constant price of £30 per ton.

Table 6.27   Effect of level of feeding during pregnancy on annual food cost of sow

Level of feeding	Food/year	Cost/year*	Food cost saved
lb/day	cwt	£	£
6	25	37·50	—
5·5	24	36·00	1·50
5	23	34·50	3·00
4·5	22	33·00	4·50

* Sow and weaner ration at £30 per ton

Cost per ton of food may be reduced slightly by bulk buying and the use of home-grown cereals charged at 'on farm' prices. Buying in small lots could lead to a considerable increase on this figure.

Sensitivity to changes in output costs

Profitability is finely balanced in this enterprise and small changes in basic input–output ratios can have very considerable effects upon final percentage return on capital. The figures in Table 6.29 are calculated from Table 6.28 and illustrate this point.

Meat production

This term is chosen in preference to 'fattening', since lean meat is at a premium and fattening is now to be avoided rather than encouraged. The main outlets for finished pigs will be considered as follows:

(a) Pork;
(b) Bacon;
(c) Heavy hogs.

Table 6.28   Example of costs and outputs for a sow producing weaners for sale

	6–8 week weaning		3 week weaning
	£		£
SALES			
Weaners	16 at £5·75	92·0	20 at £5·75	115·0
$\frac{1}{3}$ cull sow at £15		5·0		5·0
$\frac{1}{60}$ cull boar at £15		0·25		0·25
Total sales		97·25		120·25
Less purchases				
$\frac{1}{3}$ in pig gilt at £40		13·3		13·3
$\frac{1}{60}$ boar at £60		1·0		1·0
Gross output		82·95		105·95
VARIABLE COSTS				
Foods: Sow 25 cwt at £30/ton		37·50		37·50
Boar 1·25 cwt at £30/ton		1·87		1·87
Creep 16 × 28 lb = 4 cwt at £45/ton	}	9·00	20 × 40 lb = 7 cwt at £45/ton }	15·75
Total food		48·37		55·12
Vet. and medicines		3·60		3·60
Other miscellaneous		1·80		1·80
Total variable costs		53·77		60·52
Gross margin		29·18		45·43
FIXED COSTS				
Labour £1 000/70 sows		14·3	£1 000/60 sows	16·6
Depreciation on buildings 10% of £50		5·0	10% of £60	6·0
Overheads		5·0		5·0
Total fixed costs		24·3		27·6
Net margin		4·88		17·83
AVERAGE CAPITAL INVESTMENT/SOW				
Sow		40·0		40·0
$\frac{1}{20}$ boar		3·0		3·0
Buildings $\frac{1}{2}$ (£50)		25·0		30·0
Food $\frac{1}{2} \times \frac{5}{6} \times 24\cdot2$		10·0	$\frac{1}{2} \times \frac{4}{5} \times 22$	8·8
Misc. $\frac{1}{2} \times \frac{5}{6} \times 5\cdot4 \times \frac{1}{2}$		1·1		1·1
Labour $\frac{1}{2} \times 14\cdot3 \times \frac{1}{2}$		3·6		4·2
Overheads $\frac{1}{2} \times \frac{1}{2} \times 5$		1·2		1·2
		83·9		88·3
Return on average capital		5·8%		20·2%
Feed cost/£100 gross output		58·0		52·0
Time to complete production cycle		6 months		5 months

Table 6.29   Eight week weaning: effect of changes in basic data upon return on average capital invested

Factors	Effect on net margin/sow	Effect on average capital/sow	Effect on % return on average capital
± 1 pig/sow/year	± £5·25	nil	± 6·2
± £0·25/pig	± £4·00	nil	± 4·8
± 1 cwt food/sow	± £1·50	negligible	± 1·8
± £1/ton on food	± £1·50	negligible	± 1·8
± 10 sows/man	{ +£1·80 −£2·30 }	{ negligible }	{ +2·1 −2·7 }
± £10/sow on buildings	± £1·00	± 5	+1·3 −1·1

While various intermediate stages, e.g. heavy and light cutters, all find a market the meat production enterprises are best illustrated by these three distinctly different products. Each of these products requires a different carcase weight. The pigs are, therefore, slaughtered at appropriately different ages, involving a different rate of turnover for each enterprise and also different building space requirements. It must also be remembered that food conversion efficiency tends to decrease with increasing weight of carcase, while this is to some extent compensated by a lower protein requirement and consequently a cheaper ration.

The essential physical differences between these three products are summarised in Table 6.30.

Table 6.30   Basic data for pigmeat production enterprises

	Pork	Bacon	Heavy hogs
Relative space requirements pigs/unit space	100	90	80
Fattening time (weeks)	13	20	23
Batches/pig space/year	$\frac{52}{13} = 4$	$\frac{52}{20} = 2·6$	$\frac{52}{23} = 2·2$
Pigs/year/100 pork pig spaces	400	234	176
Average conversion rate lb meal/lb l.w.g.	3·4	3·7	4·0
Cost/cwt of food	£1·55	£1·45	£1·40
Liveweight at slaughter	140 lb	200 lb	260 lb

Apparent advantages in one direction are usually offset by disadvantages in another, consequently there is no 'best' system for all circumstances, one can only aim to select the system best suited to an individual set of farm conditions.

The factors affecting profitability of pigmeat production are basically the same whichever product is chosen. These are summarised diagrammatically in Figure 6.*n* (p. 213).

Figure 6.n. Factors affecting the profitability of pigmeat production

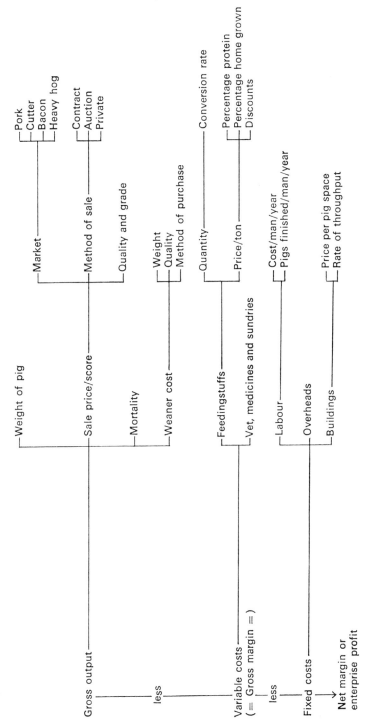

H

The examples which follow are based upon the data summarised in Table 6.30 in an attempt to show the likely margins and capital investment and yield in an average set of circumstances. Small changes in basic input–output relationships can have a very significant effect upon final return on capital and because of this 'sensitivity' factors have been calculated to show the effect of changing any one item of output or cost, while others remain constant.

Pork (see Table 6.31)

This term can be applied loosely to pigmeat from a wide range of carcase weights, when sold in a fresh uncured state. The lighter carcase usually 120–130 lb liveweight invariably demands the higher price per pound, but many producers favour a slightly heavier animal (130–150 lb) since this will realise a higher gross price and will gain the additional weight at an economic conversion rate. Carcase grading, at one time restricted to bacon pigs, is now becoming more widely applied to pork, quality premiums being paid on carcases with a high proportion of lean and minimum fat.

Slaughter at these lighter weights allows for rapid turnover of working capital and a very efficient output–feed costs ratio. At lower weights, however, gross output is reduced along with margin per pig. Annual margin per pig space and return on capital can only be maintained by rapid throughput of at least four batches per year.

Bacon (see Table 6.32)

Increasing competition from imports, particularly from Denmark has subjected the U.K. bacon industry to tighter and tighter grading requirements. The differential between Grade I and II becomes wider every year, necessitating an increasing percentage of Grade I pigs in order to maintain level of gross output. Where breeding, feeding and management are of sufficiently high standard to maintain a high proportion of Grade I pigs then the return on capital from bacon production is greater than that obtained from alternative products. Inferior stock, however, cannot hope to compete with what is now recognised as a very high quality product and such animals are usually better suited to the cutter or heavy hog market.

Heavy hogs (see Table 6.33)

A growing interest has been shown in this type of pig, both by manufacturers and producers. Recent developments in breeding a manufacturing or meat pig, with a high percentage of lean and a high genetic capacity for turning a cereal-based diet into meat, have made heavy hog production an attractive proposition.

Table 6.31   Examples of outputs and costs per pig: pork

	£
SALES	
140 lb liveweight = 5 sc. deadweight at £2·55/score	12·75
Less marketing cost and M.L.C. levy	0·30
	12·45
Less 3% mortality	0·36
Net receipts/pig	12·09
Less price of weaner	5·75
Feeders margin or gross output	6·34

VARIABLE COSTS
Foodstuffs:

	£
100 lb l.w.g. at C.R. of 3·4 = 340 lb food at £31/ton	4·70
Miscellaneous variable costs	0·10
Total variable costs	4·80
Gross margin	1·54

FIXED COSTS
Labour:

Assume 500 pigs space house/man $\dfrac{\text{£1 000/man/year}}{2\,000 \text{ porkers produced/year}}$ 0·50

Buildings:
£12·5/pork pig space, depreciation over 10 years

4 pigs/space/year $= \dfrac{\text{£12·5}}{10} \times \tfrac{1}{4}$ 0·31

	£
Miscellaneous fixed costs	0·20
Total fixed costs	1·01
Net margin: (a) per pig	0·53
(b) per pig space	2·12

AVERAGE CAPITAL INVESTMENT/PIG SPACE	£
Buildings $\frac{1}{2}$ (12·5)	6·25
Weaner	5·75
Food $\frac{1}{2} \times \frac{9}{13} \times 4·65$	1·60
Miscellaneous $\frac{1}{2} \times 0·35$	0·18
Labour $\frac{1}{2} \times 0·5$	0·25
	14·03

Return on average capital $= \dfrac{2·12 \times 100}{14·03}$ $=$ 15·1%

Sensitivity of pork production to changes in basic data

Factor	Margin/pig	Margin/pig space	Av. capital/pig space	Return on av. capital
	£	£		%
± £0·5 G.O./pig	±0·5	±2·0	nil	±14·3
± £1 food costs/ton	±0·15	±0·6	negligible	±4·3
± £5 buildings costs/pig space	} ±0·12	±0·5	±2·5	{ +4·3 / −3·0
± 100 pig spaces/man	{ +0·08 / −0·13	{ +0·33 / −0·50 }	negligible	{ +2·4 / −3·55
± 0·1 conversion rate (≡ 10 lb food)	±0·14	±0·55	negligible	±3·9

Table 6.32   Examples of outputs and costs per pig: bacon

	£
SALES	
195 lb liveweight = 7 sc. deadweight at £2·5/score	17·50
Less marketing costs and M.L.C. levy	0·40
	17·10
Less 3% mortality	0·52
Net receipts/pig	16·58
Less price of weaner	5·75
Feeders margin or gross output	10·83

VARIABLE COSTS	
Foodstuffs:	
155 lb l.w.g. at C.R. of 3·7 = 574 lb at £29/ton	7·47
Miscellaneous variable costs	0·10
Total variable costs	7·57
Gross margin	3·26

FIXED COSTS
Labour:

At 500 pig spaces/man $\dfrac{£1\,000/\text{man/year}}{1\,300\ \text{baconers/year}}$ 0·77

Buildings:

$£12·5 \times \dfrac{10}{9} \times \dfrac{1}{10} \times \dfrac{1}{2·6}$ depreciation/pig 0·50

Miscellaneous fixed costs	0·25
Total fixed costs	1·52
Net margin: (a) per pig	1·74
(b) per pig space	4·52

AVERAGE CAPITAL INVESTMENT/PIG SPACE	£
Buildings $\frac{1}{2}$ (£12·5 × $\frac{16}{9}$)	6·95
Weaner	5·75
Food $\frac{1}{2} \times \frac{16}{20} \times 7·47$	2·98
Miscellaneous $\frac{1}{2} \times 0·35$	0·18
Labour $\frac{1}{2} \times 0·77$	0·38
Average capital invested/pig space	16·24

$Return\ on\ average\ capital = \dfrac{4·52 \times 100}{16·24}$ $= 27·8\%$

Sensitivity of bacon production to changes in basic data

Factor	Margin/pig	Margin/pig space	Av. capital/pig space	Return on av. capital
	£	£		%
±£0·5 G.O./pig	±0·5	±1·3	nil	±8·0
±£1 food costs/ton	±0·26	±0·67	negligible	±4·2
±£5 buildings costs/ pig space	±0·2	±0·5	±£2·5	{ +3·6 / −2·7
±100 pig spaces/man	{ +0·13 / −0·19	+0·34 / −0·50 }	negligible	{ +2·1 / −3·1
±0·1 conversion rate (≡ 16 lb food)	±0·2	±0·52	negligible	±3·2

Table 6.33   Examples of outputs and costs per pig: heavy hogs

	£
SALES	
260 lb liveweight = 10 sc. deadweight at £2·15/score	21·50
Less marketing costs and M.L.C. levy	0·40
	21·10
Less 4% mortality	0·84
Net receipts/pig	20·26
Less price of weaner	5·75
Feeders margin or gross output	14·51

VARIABLE COSTS

Foodstuffs:

220 lb l.w.g. at C.R. of 4·0 = 880 lb at £28/ton	11·00
Miscellaneous variable costs	0·10
Total variable costs	11·10
Gross margin	3·41

FIXED COSTS

Labour:

At 500 pig space/man $\dfrac{£1\,000/\text{man/year}}{1\,100\text{ heavy hogs/year}}$ 0·90

Buildings:

$£12\cdot5 \times \dfrac{10}{8} \times \dfrac{1}{10\text{ yrs}} \times \dfrac{1}{2\cdot2\text{ batches}}$ 0·71

Miscellaneous fixed costs	0·25
Total fixed costs	1·86
Net margin: (*a*) per pig	1·55
(*b*) per pig space	3·41

AVERAGE CAPITAL INVESTMENT/PIG SPACE	£
Buildings $\frac{1}{2}(12\cdot5 \times \frac{10}{8})$	7·8
Weaner	5·75
Food $\frac{1}{2} \times 11 \times \frac{19}{23}$	4·54
Miscellaneous $\frac{1}{2} \times 0\cdot35$	0·18
Labour $\frac{1}{2} \times 0\cdot90$	0·45
Average capital invested/pig space	18·72

Return on average capital $= \dfrac{3\cdot41 \times 100}{18\cdot72}$ $= 18\cdot2\%$

Sensitivity of heavy hogs production to changes in basic data

Factor	Margin/pig	Margin/pig space	Av. capital/pig space	Return on av. capital
	£	£		%
±£0·5 G.O./pig	±0·5	±1·1	nil	±5·9
±£1 food costs/ton	±0·4	±1·0	negligible	±5·4
±£5 buildings costs/ pig space	} ±0·23	±0·5	±£2·5	{ +3·1 −2·3
±100 pig spaces/man	{ +0·15 −0·23	+0·34 } −0·50	negligible	{ +1·8 −2·7
±0·1 conversion rate (≡ 22 lb food)	±0·25	±0·55	negligible	±2·9

Heavy carcases of 200 lb deadweight are cut to produce a wide variety of products, rather than a single product, as in the case of the pure pork and bacon pig. Joints of pork or bacon are made with the knife and all surplus meat and offcuts are used for manufacturing purposes, e.g. sausages and pies. This produces a range of pigmeat products particularly well suited to supermarket requirements and the demand for this type of pig has increased considerably in recent years.

From the producer's point of view the heavy hog has the following advantages:

1. With less emphasis on a lean carcase, *ad-libitum* feeding can be safely used, thus reducing labour requirements.
2. A cheaper, less elaborate type of housing, e.g. straw yards or pole barns can be effectively used.
3. A cheaper ration consisting almost entirely of cereals is adequate particularly in the later stages of growth.
4. Faster growth rates can be obtained where it is not necessary to restrict feed intake.
5. Attractive contract terms are available when selling to some of the larger companies specialising in this type of product.

The main disadvantage is the slower rate of throughput in terms of pigs produced per pig space per year and the resulting slower turnover of working capital.

In the examples given, labour and buildings costs have been based on the requirements for pork and adjusted to the greater space requirement and slower turnover of heavy hogs. In practice, however, cheaper housing might well be employed and by using *ad-libitum* feeding a larger number of pigs might be looked after by each man. The fixed cost and capital requirement could thus be reduced. The sensitivity tables show the effect of such reduction on margin per pig and on percentage return on capital.

Conclusions

Provided that a high standard of managerial efficiency and stockmanship can be maintained, then pigs offer an excellent opportunity for a high gross margin to be obtained on a minimal acreage.

Ultimate profitability will depend on the level of fixed costs incurred and the amount of capital invested, and it is here that careful planning and organisation will really pay dividends, in evolving systems which will enable labour to be as productive as possible without necessitating an excessively high initial capital investment in buildings and equipment.

The sensitivity tables in the foregoing examples clearly illustrate the disastrous effect of over-capitalising the pigs enterprise by rapidly reducing return on capital invested even though gross margin levels may be comparatively high.

The poultry enterprise: egg production

Poultry enterprises are often referred to as 'concrete' enterprises, since they require only a very small area. Therefore, as with the pigs enterprise, efficiency measures calculated on a per acre basis provide no useful guide to efficiency. There are, however, certain specific efficiency measures applicable to this enterprise which is well known for its finely balanced profit margins. Margins per bird are often calculated and these do provide a useful efficiency measure when compared alongside appropriate standards, but the most significant efficiency measure for poultry enterprises is that of return on capital invested in the enterprise.

Post-war developments in the poultry industry have probably been more rapid than those in any other branch of farming. The days of the 'farm yard' hen have gone; even a poultry unit of 500 to 1000 birds as a farm enterprise is made to look small nowadays when units of 10000 birds are commonplace, and several units of 100000 birds exist. In addition to the establishment of larger and larger egg production units during the 25 years following the Second World War, very specialised units, usually on a large scale, have been developed for meat production (broilers), hatching eggs and for rearing stock which have been carefully bred, often with the aid of a computer.

The formation of larger units in the poultry field undoubtedly results from the impact of economic pressures which have left poultry enterprises with smaller and smaller profit margins. Poultry producers have, therefore, moved towards larger units in order to gain advantages of scale.

The poultry industry today has many facets, most of which are highly specialised, ranging from commercial egg production on general farms, to highly specialised units producing table meat or hatching-eggs. Since a high degree of specialisation is inevitably involved in the latter, it is likely that few general farmers will carry any other poultry enterprise than an egg production unit and, therefore, this chapter will be confined to this subject.

Nowadays, it is generally agreed that the most profitable systems of egg production can be classified under three headings: deep litter, battery and wire or slatted floor systems – all under controlled environment.

Capital costs for different egg production systems

Capital costs of housing and equipment, assuming a reasonably level site, road access and electricity and water supply, usually fall within the following range:

Deep litter	£1·75–£2·0 per bird
Wire or slatted floor	£1·25–£1·35 per bird
Battery	£1·25–£1·75 per bird, depending on the number of birds in a cage.

The amount of capital invested in laying houses and equipment will vary and depends largely on the following factors – size of unit, standards of ventilation, the amount of automatic equipment, stocking density and any extra equipment needed.

The importance of return on capital as a measure of efficiency in an egg production unit has already been mentioned. However, before any attempt can be made to calculate return on capital invested in an enterprise, the factors influencing the profitability of the enterprise will be considered. A summary of these factors is given in Figure 6.*o*.

Factors influencing gross output in egg production units

Number of eggs produced

Assuming a high standard of housing, feeding and general management, the following factors will influence levels of gross output in egg production units.

1. *Strain of bird.* The effect of strain of bird is probably the greatest of all the factors influencing gross output. Therefore, probably the biggest decision the poultry farmer has to make is choosing the right strain of bird. Since feed costs account for about 70 per cent of the cost of egg production, food conversion rate or the number of eggs produced for the food consumed is a most important ratio. This varies with strain of bird and generally speaking high yielding birds usually show good returns for food consumed, and the high yielding bird generally turns out to be more profitable in the end.

Light strains of birds produce more eggs than heavy strains, but the price realised per dozen is generally lower. Light strains consume less food, which is usually of a higher price than that fed to heavy-strain birds. The light-strain bird commands a lower cull price than the heavy-strain bird. The net effect of this is that a poultry-farmer must select the strain that will give him the best output under his particular circumstances.

In a 52-week laying period the following levels of egg output provide a guide to average levels of performance that may be expected:

Strain	Egg output – 52-week laying period
Light	20 dozen (240)
Medium	19 dozen (228)
Heavy	18 dozen (216)

In addition to strain of bird, light patterns may influence the number of eggs laid per bird. Also, stresses that may occur may depress the number of eggs produced, as well as a low house temperature and a poor level of nutrition. The number of eggs laid varies with the season of the year and also fewer eggs are laid in the second year if birds are kept through a moult.

2. *The size of eggs laid.* Since there is a premium for larger eggs, egg size will have an influence on gross output. Heavy strains tend to produce larger,

Figure 6.0. Factors affecting the profitability of egg production

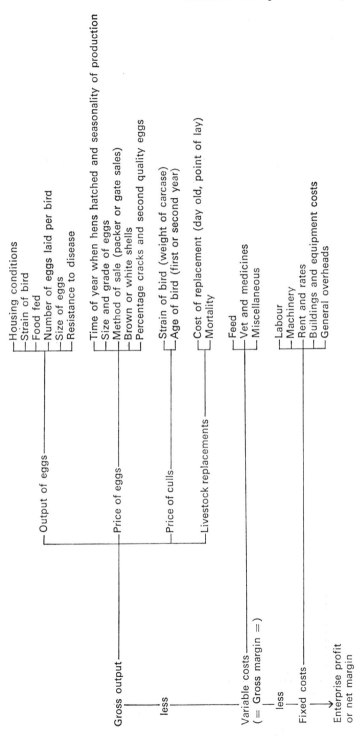

but fewer, eggs than do lighter strains and also the older the hen the larger the egg that will be laid. Hens kept through a moult into their second year will generally produce larger eggs but unfortunately production in the second year will be lower.

3. *Incidence of disease.* Obviously incidence of disease will influence egg output and all precautions including medication of a preventative nature should be taken wherever possible.

Factors influencing price of eggs

1. *Time of year when birds are hatched*

Egg prices follow a definite pattern through the year. In winter, spring and early summer the price differential between large and standard eggs is lower than during the late summer and early autumn, see Figure 6.*p*. It will be

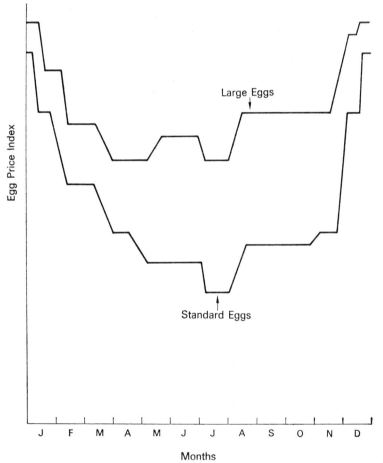

Figure 6.p Seasonal variations in egg prices

beneficial therefore to have flocks hatched in the late summer/early autumn, so that birds come into lay between December and February, i.e. when they are approximately 20 weeks old, so that the maximum number of large and standard eggs will be laid when the price for those grades is greatest. As the bird gets older more large eggs are produced which command the highest price per dozen.

2. *Size and grade of egg*

The proportion of large and standard eggs produced will influence the overall price realised since seconds, cracks, etc., receive a much lower price.

3. *Method of sale*

Considerably higher prices can be obtained by selling eggs at the farm gate than by selling to packing stations. Eggs sold privately tend to attract a premium, especially if they can be acclaimed to be 'free range' eggs.

4. *Shell colour*

Brown-shelled eggs always command a better price than white ones, although, in fact, the egg inside the shell is exactly the same.

5. *External and internal egg quality*

The price obtained for 'seconds' is much lower than that obtained for other eggs and so the proportion of seconds will obviously have a considerable influence on final profit margins. Different strains of hybrid layers vary considerably in respect of the internal quality of eggs produced by them, although much emphasis is placed on this aspect in the selection of breeding stock. Egg quality can also be influenced considerably by the way in which eggs are handled, cleaned, collected and stored. Quality in eggs is likely to be a more important factor in the future than it has been in the past.

Livestock replacement costs

When considering the gross output of a laying flock it must be remembered that livestock depreciation must be included as well as output and prices of eggs. Livestock depreciation covers the cull prices obtained for hens at the end of their production period as well as the cost of replacements brought in to replace them in the flock. Cull prices will be greatest for the heavier strains of bird and lowest for the lighter strains. Carcase value will also vary somewhat with the age of the bird when culled and also the time of the year when sold.

When it comes to replacing stock the poultry farmer must consider whether to buy his stock as day-old chicks, 3–4-week-old chicks, 8-week-old stock or birds at point of lay (18–20 weeks of age). If rearing facilities and labour are available the day-old chick may be the best proposition since purchase price is low and this, together with the cost of its rearing to point of lay, will come to less than the cost of a point of lay bird. An advantage of buying in 3–4-week-old birds is that mortality will be lower than for day-old chicks but, of course, brooder equipment will still be needed. Eight-week-old birds are quite popular; risks of mortality are mostly over, and brooder equipment is no longer necessary. Buying point-of-lay pullets means that the capital invested begins to produce almost immediately and the problems associated with rearing do not arise.

There are various arguments for, and against, keeping laying stock for a second year. In summary, the advantages are that larger eggs will be produced and little extra livestock depreciation costs will be incurred. However, fewer eggs (about 20 per cent) will be produced and a lower percentage of these comes in the winter months, and of course feed costs will be incurred during the moult period.

At the present time most poultry farmers do, in fact, cull their laying stock completely at the end of one year's production.

Variable costs

1. *Feed costs*

Feed accounts for approximately 70 per cent of the costs of egg production. The actual amount of food consumed will depend on the strain of bird, type of ration fed and the temperature of the environment. Since food is a major cost item in egg production, poultrymen should pay particular attention to wastage: 5 per cent wastage of food increases the feed cost of a light hybrid by £0·062 per bird per year. Common causes of wastage are badly designed troughs, incorrect adjustment and overfilling of feeders.

The actual cost of the feed itself is more important. Purchases of bulk quantities may lower price, but, of course, the installation of a bulk bin will be necessary and the feasibility of purchasing feed in bulk quantities will depend on the size of the egg production unit and the distance from the supplying mill.

2. *Vet., medicines and other miscellaneous variable costs*

These will not be very great per bird, but nevertheless are very important despite the fact that these are often applied as a preventative measure, since the consequence of disease outbreak in a poultry unit can be devastating.

Fixed costs

Labour represents about 5–10 per cent of costs of production. It comprises only a small proportion of the total, but it can prove to be false economy to reduce it too much. Stockmanship is most important especially where large numbers of birds are being looked after by one man. An extra £0·05 per bird spent on labour is covered by 4–5 eggs per bird per year. While it may be difficult to actually get these extra eggs per bird, it is very easy to lose them if the poultryman neglects certain aspects of his work.

It may be possible to reduce labour costs by mechanising certain jobs. Of course, any labour saved must be profitably employed in some other way otherwise there is no financial gain to the business. At the same time the extra costs (both capital and operational) relating to the extra machinery installed must not be forgotten. Furthermore, certain fixed costs can easily be overlooked with intensive enterprises like pigs and poultry, e.g. fixed cost items like electricity can be quite high for such enterprises and therefore should be watched carefully.

Measures of efficiency in egg production

The main efficiency measures are:

1. Egg returns per bird
   - (a) price per egg
   - (b) yield of eggs per bird
2. Food cost per bird
   - (c) quantity fed per bird
   - (d) price per ton of feed
3. Flock depreciation
   - (e) replacement cost at point of lay less cull price
4. Food cost per dozen eggs — encompassing *a*, *b*, *c* and *d* above
5. Food cost per £100 output — encompassing *a*, *b*, *c*, *d* and *e* above
6. Profit margin per bird — either gross margin or net margin per bird.

When dealing with an enterprise like poultry it is most important to look beyond the profit margin per bird and to consider the capital invested per bird and the return obtained on that capital.

7. Return on capital.
   This may be either gross margin or net margin expressed as a percentage over the average capital invested in the hen, hen housed space, equipment and working capital – *see* Table 6.34, where net margin per bird and percentage return on average capital are given for two flocks, one buying in point of lay pullets and the other rearing replacements from day-old chicks.

The figures in Table 6.34 show that the flock B, rearing its own replacements, finishes up with the better net margin per 100 birds, and also a better return on average capital.

Table 6.34 Egg production: gross margin and net margin per 100 birds and percentage return on capital

	Flock A (buying in point of lay pullets)	Flock B (rearing own replacement stock from day-old chicks)
Period:	12 months in lay	5 months rearing 12 months laying
GROSS OUTPUT	£	£
Egg returns:		
20 dozen at £0·1375/dozen	275	275·0
Livestock depreciation* (footnote on opposite page)	70	47·5
Gross output/100 birds	205	227·5
VARIABLE COSTS		
Feed: 100 lb/bird at £28/ton	125	125
Miscellaneous, inc. meds. at £0·1/bird	10	10
Total variable costs/100 birds	135	135·0
Gross margin/100 birds	70	92·5
FIXED COSTS		
Labour at £0·1625/bird	16·25	16·25
Overhead costs:		
Depreciation on house and equipment, electricity and running costs at £0·2/bird	20·0	20·0
Total fixed costs	36·25	36·25
∴ Net margin/100 birds	33·75	56·25

CAPITAL INVESTED

Housing and equipment (£1·375/hen space) = £137·5/100 birds

∴ average capital = $\frac{1}{2}$(137·5)   =   68·75   =   68·75

Capital/100 birds (at £0·875/bird)   87·50

Working capital = $\frac{1}{12}\left\{\begin{array}{ll}\text{Feed} & 125 \\ \text{Labour} & 16\cdot25 \\ \text{O/hds.} & 20\end{array}\right\}$ 13·44   13·44

                                $\overline{161\cdot25}$

Capital in rearing stock:

Housing and equipment (at £0·5/bird), average capital = $\frac{1}{2}$(50)   —   25·00

Capital/100 birds (£0·15 at day old)   —   15·00

Working capital = $\left\{\begin{array}{l}\text{Feed} \\ \text{Labour} \\ \text{O/hds.}\end{array}\right\}$ £50   —   50·00

                                169·69   172·19

∴ % return on average capital = $\dfrac{33\cdot75 \times 100}{169\cdot69}$ = $\dfrac{56\cdot25}{172\cdot19} \times \dfrac{12}{17}$

                    = 19·9%   = 23·05%

Scale of enterprise in egg production

There are a number of arguments for smaller units and various reasons that support large ones. In summary these are:

In favour of small farm units

1. Certain facilities and services are already on the farm and can be used, e.g. roads, concrete, cottages, buildings, machinery (e.g. tractors) and milling, mixing and possibly bulk storage equipment for feedingstuffs.
2. Family or supplementary labour may be available and labour peaks created by the poultry enterprise can be integrated with other farm work.
3. The fact that the poultry enterprise is based on a farm may facilitate manure disposal.
4. The rest period after depopulation can be more easily borne since some income will probably be coming in from other enterprises.
5. Risks generally are lower – disease risk is less fatal if it occurs.
6. There may be scope for farm gate sales because of location and limited production.
7. Egg production may be higher per bird from the smaller unit.

In favour of large, specialised units

1. Because of scale of enterprise, the capital cost per bird for housing and equipment may be lower.
2. Feed can be purchased in large quantities and will therefore be cheaper per ton.
3. Specialist labour can be employed and the cost per bird can be minimised. Also specialist management can be engaged.
4. Mechanisation, on a large scale, can be justified.
5. In a large unit certain costs may be saved by rearing replacements and even hatching day-old chicks for replacements.

Conclusions

Post-war developments in the poultry industry have brought about decreases in egg producers' profit margins and this has led to the setting up of larger

---

* *Livestock depreciation*

	Flock A		Flock B
Cost of point of lay 100 pullets (£0·875/bird)	£87·5	Cost of chick and rearing to point of lay (£0·65/bird inc. mortality)	£65·0
Mortality in laying year	12½%		12½%
Cull value at end of year (£0·2/bird)	£20·0		£20·0
Depreciation = 87·5−17·5 =	£70·0	65−17·5 =	£47·5

units with the inevitable demands on capital to try to maintain profits. This increase in specialisation has meant that greater skills and attention to detail has been required of poultrymen and a more astute business approach and degree of expertise has been necessary at managerial levels. Whatever is the future of the poultry industry it is certain that considerably more emphasis will be placed on quality rather than quantity in egg production, and so this high degree of operational and managerial skill is likely to continue to be necessary if poultry enterprises are to be profitable and weather the economic storms of the future.

Crops enterprise studies

The cereals enterprise

Technically speaking, cereal crops are fairly easy to grow and indeed are grown on a high proportion of farms in the British Isles. Some farmers have been able to grow cereals very profitably in the past, but in recent years both variable and fixed cost items have increased, resulting in reductions in cereal growers' profit margins. Surveys of levels of outputs and inputs in cereal production show a very wide range in levels between cereal growers and at the same time confirm that it costs almost as much to produce a poor crop as it does a good one. There is, in fact, a close correlation between cereal yields and final profit margins in most cases.

The acreages of the various types of cereals have changed in the 1960s and figures are given in Table 7.1, indicating the nature of these changes.

Table 7.1 Cereal acreages in England and Wales

All figures in thousands

Enterprise/year	1959	1960	1961	1962	1963	1964	1965	1966	1967	1968	1969
Wheat	1843	2004	1731	2144	1837	2111	2433	2171	2223	2326	1961
Barley	2803	3059	3396	3501	4148	4385	4652	5287	5221	5083	5138
Oats	1113	1091	917	787	616	530	485	426	522	526	566
Mixed corn (for threshing)	224	195	142	120	94	75	68	67	80	98	137
Rye (for threshing)	13	17	17	17	21	21	18	10	11	11	8
Total	5996	6366	6203	6569	6716	7122	7656	7961	8057	8044	7810

(Source Agricultural Statistics. 1959–68. H.M.S.O.)

The total acreage of cereals in England and Wales was about eight million acres between 1966 and 1969 – the highest actual total cereal acreage being 8 057 000 acres in 1967. During the eleven-year period 1959–69 covered by Table 7.1 wheat acreages increased slightly, reaching nearly 2·5 million acres in 1965, but fell again in the following four years. Obviously seasonal factors influence this; a poor autumn may well result in more spring wheat or even spring barley being sown in place of winter wheat. In the 1960s barley acreages increased, but the oat crop decreased, reaching an 'all time low' of under 0·5 million acres in 1966, although the years immediately following show a slight 'come back'. Acres of mixed cereals varied a lot over the period, obviously influenced to a large extent by seasonal factors. The small acreage of rye for threshing decreased during the latter years of the 1960s.

Reasons for changes in acreages of cereals: England and Wales – 1960s

There are a number of reasons that may explain the changes that have occurred in the acreages of cereals grown in the 1960s:

1. Taking the country as a whole the yield of barley is likely to be greater than that of oats. Figures of national average yields of oats and barley are given in Table 7.2. The ten-year national average yield figure for 1956–65 shows a differential between oats and barley of 3·5 cwt per acre. In 1968 this was 2·3 cwt per acre, whereas over the ten-year period 1934–43 (when the acreage of oats sown in England and Wales was much greater) the differential was only 0·5 cwt per acre.

Table 7.2 National average yields of cereals (England and Wales)

Cereal	Ten-year avg. 1956–65 cwt/acre	1968 cwt/acre	Ten-year avg. 1934–43 cwt/acre
Wheat	28·6	29·1	18·5
Barley	25·8 } 3·5	27·9 } 2·3	16·7 } 0·5
Oats	22·3	25·6	16·2

(*Source: Agricultural Statistics U.K.* H.M.S.O.)

2. In the period since the Second World War, and especially in the late 1950s and the 1960s, a greater number of new varieties of barley than oats were bred and brought on to the market. Obviously this introduction of new genetic material with higher yielding potential has helped favour the increase in barley acreage to the detriment of oats.

3. The yield of S.E. (Starch Equivalent) of barley is higher than that of oats (S.E. of barley = 71, S.E. of oats = 60). Therefore the yield per acre of feeding value measured as Starch Equivalent per acre will be considerably greater from barley than from oats. Taking the national average yields for

barley and oats in 1968 (see Table 7.2) the following yields of S.E. per acre can be calculated:

Barley: National Average Yield = 27·9 cwts per acre × 71 (S.E.)
= 19·8 cwt S.E. per acre

Oats: National Average Yield = 25·6 cwt per acre × 60 (S.E.)
= 15·4 cwt S.E. per acre.

4. Since the national average yield per acre is likely to be higher for barley, then profit margins from barley will often prove to be greater than those of oats since the price for barley and oats, relative to each other, do not vary very much.

5. The Cereal Deficiency Payment on oats in the latter years of the 1960s was greater than for barley, thus helping to compensate for the generally lower yield of oats. This higher C.D.P. for oats may help to explain the slight increase in oat acreages between 1966 and 1969. In addition, oats are being used as a break crop.

6. Some farmers are able to grow a sample of barley that is suitable for malting and this will command a premium over and above the price realised by feeding barley. There is no such scope for oat producers other than a small acreage nationally which is grown for porridge oats.

7. Winter barley varieties may have proved to have been more hardy than winter oat varieties in some areas. Unfortunately, winter barleys are notorious as hosts for the overwintering of cereal foliar diseases.

Some of these reasons may well have influenced farmers and, therefore, help to explain the changes in acreages of cereals grown in the 1960s.

Factors affecting the profitability of the cereal enterprise

A summary of the main factors affecting the profitability of cereal enterprises is presented in Figure 7.*a*. Gross output is mainly influenced by yield and price, and the costs have been grouped as variable and fixed costs which, when deducted from the gross output, leave the final enterprise profit or net margin.

Factors affecting cereal yields

A number of factors will influence cereal yields, and these will be considered in turn:

1. *Natural factors*

Cereals, like all farm crops, are influenced by a number of natural factors, e.g. rainfall, soil type, aspect, etc. These factors cause variations in cereal yields from year to year and area to area in any one year, and the farmer has no control over them. The combined effect of these factors

Figure 7.a. Factors affecting the profitability of the cereal enterprise

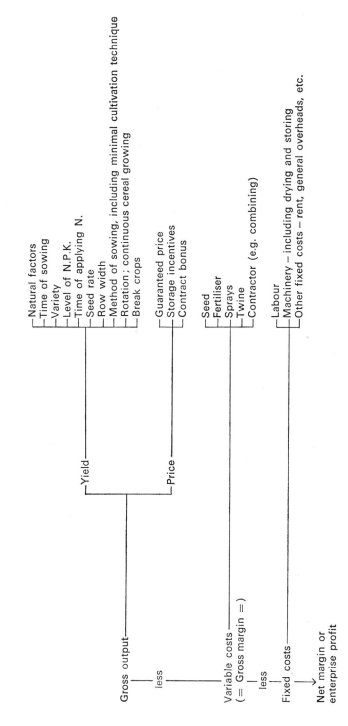

was most noticeable in the 1960s since one or two particular years were bad both in the autumn and spring at drilling time and in the summer at harvesting.

2. *Time of sowing cereals*

Broadly speaking, crops sown late and crops sown very early in a season tend to yield less than those sown at about the optimum time. Results of trials on date of drilling generally confirm this and one set of results is given in Table 7.3. In these particular trials at Bridgets Experimental Husbandry Farm in Hampshire, drilling in March gave better yields than drilling earlier, in February, or much later, in April. Obviously, the optimum date will vary from year to year and from place to place, but it is important that farmers realise the basic principles underlying the results of these trials and aim to drill at the right time.

3. *Variety*

Variety of cereal grown will influence yields obtained since each variety differs in its yield potential. Information on the performance of cereal varieties in different parts of the country is available in the Recommended List of Cereal Varieties published annually by the N.I.A.B. (National Institute of Agricultural Botany, Cambridge). Information should be sought by the cereal grower from the latest list available since varieties do vary from year to year – older ones become outclassed in terms of yields as new ones are introduced, and also some new varieties may break down in resistance to a particular disease and therefore produce lower yields after being 'on the market' for a few years.

Table 7.3 *Influence of date of sowing on yield of grain in cwt per acre at 15 per cent M.C.*

Results 1967

		Sowing date		
Nitrogen units/acre		8 February	14 March	19 April
60	Proctor	(−10·6) 24·5 ÷	35·1	17·8 (−17·3)
	Impala	(−8·8) 25·0	33·8	14·2 (−19·6)
90	Proctor	(−2·3) 31·6	33·9	18·1 (−15·8)
	Impala	(−0·4) 34·6	35·0	13·6 (−21·4)

Note: Figures in brackets indicate difference compared with yield obtained by drilling 14 March

(*Source:* Bridgets Experimental Husbundry Farm, Hampshire, *Farm Guide*, 1968, p. 20).

4. Fertiliser application

Nitrogen fertiliser applied in the autumn to winter cereals is important to encourage tillering of the cereal plants. Nitrogen fertiliser applied in the spring to either winter or spring cereals does lead to increased yields, but the extent depends on the time of the application of the nitrogen fertiliser.

The basic principles of economics underlying nitrogen application to cereals were covered in Chapter 2, where the law of diminishing returns was explained and also the technique of marginal analysis was used to locate the point of optimum level of input of a resource so as to maximise profits.

The effect of date of nitrogen fertiliser application upon final yield of cereals is in general terms as follows. Nitrogen fertiliser applied early in the spring will cause leaf and straw growth and consequently higher grain yields, whereas that applied later will not only increase yield of grain but will also cause the nitrogen content of the grain to be higher – which may be desirable for feeding grain or for wheat to be used in breadmaking, but is most undesirable for malting barley, since a high protein content causes poor fermentation in the brewing process. Some figures, indicating the effect of date of application of nitrogen fertiliser on the nitrogen content of barley grain are given in Table 7.4.

Table 7.4 Effect of time of applying nitrogen fertiliser on the nitrogen content of barley and yield of grain

Amount of N	Yield of grain	% N in grain
No N	20·2	1·50
50 units/acre applied:		
Combine drill	32·3	1·58
Broadcast on seedbed	29·9	1·59
Broadcast in May	29·4	1·70
50 units/acre combine drilled *plus* 50		
units broadcast in May	33·0	1·88

(*Source:* Cooke, G. W., *Fertilisers and Profitable Farming*, 2nd Edition, p. 49)

5. Seed rate and row width

The basic principle to bear in mind when considering seed rates and row widths for cereals is that the overall objective should be an optimum plant population per unit area (see Table 7.5). Too high a seed rate will produce too many plants which will compete with each other for light, space and nutrients, while too low a seed rate will produce fewer plants and although each plant may produce a larger number of ears of grain than usual, the total yield per acre will be lower due to fewer total ears per acre.

Table 7.5   Influence of row width and seed rate on spring barley yields (Impala barley). Yield of grain at 85 per cent D.M. – cwt/acre.

	Method of sowing			
Seed rates	7 in. rows	4·75 in. rows	Broadcast	Mean
84 lb/acre	37·6	40·7	37·8	38·7
112 lb/acre	40·5	39·2	34·6	38·1
140 lb/acre	40·0	42·5	37·2	39·9
168 lb/acre	38·4	41·3	37·5	39·1

(*Source:* High Mowthorpe Experimental Husbandry Farm. *Farm Guide*, 1965, pp. 38–39)

If cereals are drilled in rows narrower than the usual 7 inches, then an increase in yield can be expected. The results of investigations into drilling cereals in narrow rows tend to indicate an average increase of about 5 per cent in yield, when the row width is reduced by half, i.e. to 3·5 inches. There are, however, certain technical problems associated with the operation of narrow coulter drills; generally speaking, it may be worth while for a farmer to consider a 'narrow row' drill if he is buying a new drill anyway, but since only a slight increase in yield can be expected, this alone is unlikely to be sufficient incentive to justify purchasing such a machine.

6. Method of sowing

Some farmers, in recent years, have broadcast their cereal seed and fertiliser rather than use the traditional drilling in rows technique. The results of broadcasting, in terms of yields, have been quite satisfactory; the chief advantage of the operation is that it is completed more quickly than drilling – a factor that is most important in an autumn or spring when weather conditions are 'catchy'. Trials carried out at M.A.F.F. Experimental Husbandry farms suggest that seedrates should be increased somewhat where cereal seed is being broadcast, if yields comparable with those from drilling are to be obtained.

7. Seedbed preparation and minimal cultivations

Since the introduction of certain herbicides that will kill off all green material, including grasses, some farmers have tried cereal growing using 'minimal cultivation' techniques. The basic plan is to kill all green material by spraying with a herbicide and then to drill the cereal seed into a slit in the ground cut by a special coulter drill. Some success has been achieved, but a number of problems have been encountered, one of which has been slug damage caused by slugs feeding down the rows cut by the drill coulter. This technique is still very much in the trial stage. The importance of a good, well-prepared seedbed cannot be overemphasised, where normal cultivations, all well done, have been thoroughly carried out.

8. *Weed control*

In any survey of factors influencing cereal yields, brief mention should be made of weed control. Most farmers spray their cereals nowadays as a matter of routine and therefore weed problems are not very great. Nevertheless, it should be remembered that weeds not killed by herbicides will compete with the cereal crop and so result in lower cereal yields. Also, the importance of selecting the right herbicide must be emphasised since resistant weeds will be left growing to compete with the cereal crop. Obviously, the actual application of a herbicide may cause some loss of yield as a result of wheel damage; if a crop is free of weeds in the spring it may turn out to be more profitable not to spray it at all. The basic requirement is a clean crop not only during the growing season but also at harvest time, especially in a bad season.

9. *Continuous cereal growing*

In the late 1950s and 1960s some farmers have grown cereals on the same land fairly frequently, and some fields have been cropped 'continuously' with cereals. In some instances yield levels have been maintained year after year, but in others yields have deteriorated with the consequent build up of pests and disease, weeds and a lowering of both soil fertility and general soil condition. Figures indicating the decline experienced when growing Spring Barley continuously over six years at the Bridgets Experimental Husbandry farm in Hampshire, at three levels of nitrogen fertiliser 30, 60 and 90 units per acre are given in Table 7.6 and the average yields obtained shown in Figure 7.*b* indicating a decline in yield in subsequent years, with some

Table 7.6   Figures showing declining yield of spring barley when grown 'continuously' on the same field for six years – cwts/acre.

Units of nitrogen fertiliser/acre	Number of successive barley crops					
	1	*2*	*3*	*4*	*5*	*6*
30	27·5	21·2	20·9	18·8	19·9	19·3
60	32·7	31·2	27·2	26·0	27·4	24·5
90	30·2	30·5	29·1	29·6	30·0	26·1
Mean	30·1	27·6	25·7	24·8	25·8	23·3

(*Source:* Bridgets Experimental Husbandry Farm, Hampshire. *Farm Guide*, 1969, p. 10)

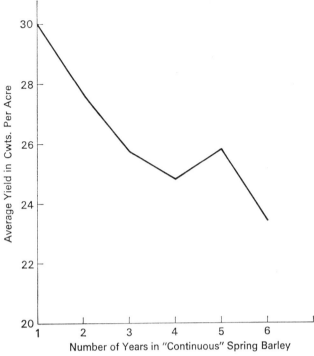

Figure 7.b   The declining yield of spring barley when grown 'continuously' on the same field for six years (average yields from 3 levels of nitrogen fertilizer applied at 30, 60 and 90 units per acre)

seasonal variation. Where such a decline in yield has occurred, farmers have looked for break crops to solve their problems – see Breakcrops Enterprise (p. 243).

The factors discussed above are the main ones influencing cereal yields. Since there is a close correlation between final profit margins and yields the impact of these factors must be considered carefully. If these factors are within the farmer's control then he should try to organise them in such a way as to achieve the greatest possible profit margins from cereals.

Factors influencing price obtained for cereals

The factors influencing price obtained for cereals will fall under two headings, i.e. the purpose for which the grain is sold and the time of the year when it is sold.

The purpose for which grain is sold

Cereals may be grown for seed and depending on the quality of the seed sample, and the husbandry and hygiene standards under which the seed was produced, a premium of £5·0–£7·5 or more per ton may be obtained, especially if grown under contract.

Barley samples that are suitable may be sold for malting purposes and may command a premium of £3·0–£5·0 per ton over feeding barley prices. The chief requirements of a malting sample are a low protein content of the grain which should be plump and thin skinned.

Payment for quality in wheat samples has not been very common in the past, but certain varieties are now receiving a slightly higher price, e.g. Maris Widgeon winter wheat for its bread-making quality.

Time of the year when sold

The market price of cereals normally increases throughout the cereal year (1 July to 30 June). Although the increase in actual market price that occurs may vary somewhat from year to year, the trend is generally upwards during the period. In addition, there is the storage incentive scheme for barley and wheat coupled with the guaranteed price system of increasing increments for wheat and barley which are designed to encourage farmers to store grain and await higher prices (see Tables 7.11 and 7.12). Furthermore, there is the forward contract scheme operated by the Home Grown Cereals Authority which pays a bonus (in 1970 this was £0·4 per ton for wheat and barley) on forward contract grain for sale after at least a two-month contract period.

Levels of costs in cereal production

The fact that costs in cereal production have increased in recent years has already been pointed out. The main variable cost items are seed, fertiliser, sprays (herbicides), contract work, e.g. combining and casual labour if employed as well as certain miscellaneous costs, e.g. twine. Fixed cost items, which are difficult to allocate to specific enterprises, also increased considerably during the 1960s – in many areas by as much as £1 per acre per year. Figures of average levels of outputs, variable costs and gross margins for cereals are given in Table 7.7.

Table 7.7   Average levels of outputs, variable costs and gross margins for cereals (per acre)

	Winter wheat	Spring wheat	Barley	Oats
Yield – cwt/acre	33	29	30	30
Output/acre (£)	47·8	42·0	37·5	39·2
Variable costs:				
Seed	3·4	3·7	2·7	3·8
Fertiliser	5·1	4·5	4·5	3·8
Sprays	1·0	0·8	0·8	0·8
Total variable costs	9·5	9·0	8·0	8·4
Gross margin £/acre	38·3	33·0	29·5	30·8

(*Source:* Nix, J., *op. cit.*)

Economics of grain storage

When trying to estimate the worthwhileness of storing grain, it must be remembered that in addition to the annual costs of the grain store itself other factors must be costed. If the grain itself had been sold rather than stored it would have realised capital that could have brought in some return in the form of interest. Therefore, interest on the value of grain in store, over the store period, should be considered. During the store period grain will actually lose weight and there will also be extra handling and drying charges. All these items have been included in the calculation in Table 7.8 (*i*), where the cost of storage per ton of grain for the eight-month period September to May has been calculated. The annual buildings costs of the grain store are shown in Table 7.8 (*ii*), and the total annual costs given in Table 7.8 (*iii*), calculated by adding together the cost of the grain in store and the annual cost of grain storage.

These figures in Table 7.8 indicate the increase in grain price necessary to justify storage facilities at the different capital cost levels.

The cereal deficiency payment scheme

In the Annual Review and determination of guaranteed prices, guaranteed prices for cereals are fixed each year. The guaranteed price levels for 1969–70 and 1970–71 are given in Table 7.9.

The determination of the amount of cereal deficiency that is to be paid is, in essence, the difference between the excess of the guaranteed price over the average 'at farm' price, and this is adjusted according to whether the average 'at farm' price falls short of, or exceeds, a target indicator price which is set each year. Target indicator prices are determined by reference to minimum import prices which are fixed by agreement with the major overseas suppliers so as to prevent low-priced imports from disrupting the market in this country. Target indicator prices for wheat and barley for 1969–70 and 1970–71 are given in Table 7.10.

If the 'at farm' average price is above the target indicator price, then the difference between the guaranteed price and the average farm price is paid as cereal deficiency payment (see Figure 7.c – case (*i*)). If, however, the average farm price is lower than the target indicator price, then the cereal deficiency payment is paid on the difference between the guaranteed price and the target indicator price (see Figure 7.c – case (*ii*)).

A seasonal scale of premiums is arranged for both wheat and barley (see Tables 7.11 and 7.12). This is to encourage storage, thereby promoting a distribution of marketing throughout the season and is an attempt to dissuade farmers from marketing their grain during the harvest peak period.

In some years the amount of cereal deficiency payment on wheat and barley has been limited to specific quantities produced called 'standard quantities'. These were abolished for wheat in 1968–69 and barley in 1969–70.

Table 7.8   Economics of grain storage

(i) *Cost of storage/ton for eight months* (*September to May*)

		£
Interest on grain at £22/ton at 10% = £22 at 10% = £2·2 ÷ $\frac{8}{12}$		1·465
Loss in weight = $\frac{1}{2}$ cwt/ton at £22/ton		0·550
Extra drying and handling – say £0·5/ton		0·500
Storage cost		2·515

(ii) *Annual buildings cost/ton*

Capital cost/ton storage space	10-year life	15-year life
£5/ton	£0·75	£0·583
£10/ton	£1·50*	£1·166
£15/ton	£2·25	£1·75

* Example of above calculation:

£10/ton capital cost spread over 10 years

= £1/ton capital cost spread over 1 year (straight-line depreciation calculation)

Plus 10% on $\frac{1}{2}$ capital invested

i.e. $\frac{£10}{2}$ at 10% = £0·5

Therefore, the total buildings cost = annual capital cost	£1·0
interest on $\frac{1}{2}$ capital	£0·5
	£1·5

(iii) *Annual costs/ton stored*

	10-year life			15-year life		
	£	£	£	£	£	£
Capital cost/ton storage space	5	10	15	5	10	15
Annual buildings cost	0·750	1·500	2·250	0·583	1·166	1·750
Storage cost (8 months)	2·515	2·515	2·515	2·515	2·515	2·515
Total annual cost	3·265	4·015	4·765	3·098	3·681	4·265

Table 7.9   Guaranteed prices for cereals (*price per cwt*)

	1969–70	1970–71
	£	£
Wheat	1·45	1·5125
Rye	1·079	1·079
Barley	1·30	1·35
Oats	1·392	1·392

Table 7.10   Target indicator prices for wheat and barley (price per cwt)

	1969–70	1970–71
	£	£
Wheat	1·083	1·062
Barley	1·041	1·016

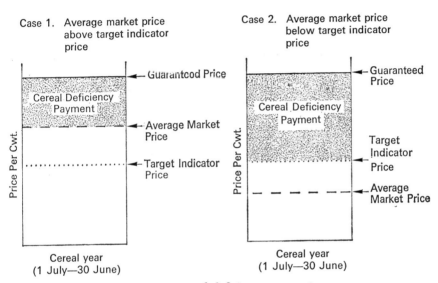

Figure 7.c   Determination of cereal deficiency payments

Table 7.11   Storage incentive: seasonal scale for wheat

	1969–70
Guaranteed price/cwt	£1·45
Seasonal scale	Steps
Delivery in month of:	(£)
July to September	—
October	+0·066
November	0·02
December	0·02
January	0·02
February	0·02
March	0·02
April	0·16
May and June	0·12

Table 7.12   Storage incentive: seasonal scale for barley

	1969–70
Guaranteed price/cwt	£1·30
Seasonal scale	Steps
Delivery in month of:	(£)
July to September	−0·025
October	−0·012
November and December	+0·012
January	+0·018
February	+0·025
March	+0·031
April	+0·037
May and June	+0·047

Cereal deficiency payments for wheat and rye are paid on the millable quantity of grain sold and delivered for which a certificate has been issued by an authorised merchant. For barley, oats and mixed corn, payment is made on the acreage declared to be harvested. The rate of payment per acre for barley and oats is calculated by multiplying the appropriate deficiency payment by the average yield per acre of merchantable grain over the previous three years.

It should be noted that the Cereal Deficiency Payment Scheme provides scope for individual farmers to sell their grain for as high a price as they can get; since the cereal deficiency payment farmers receive will have been based on the national average market price.

Conclusions

The 1960s saw many changes in cereal production. In the earlier years acreages increased; throughout the decade cereal producers' margins decreased considerably. Latterly, haulage costs have increased enormously and it now costs as much to transport a ton of grain from Hull to Liverpool by road as it does to ship a ton of grain from North America to Liverpool. It is likely that cereal growers of the future will be confronted with further problems of both a husbandry and an economic nature at home and with sharp competition from producers overseas. The situation at home may be helped somewhat by the use of break crops though there is little promise in the range of break crops available at the moment. On the foreign front there is little that the cereal producer can do to help himself since this is a problem that involves political rather than production and marketing affairs.

In the final analysis, success from the individual farmer's point of view in cereal production results largely from marginal efficiency. The result of attention to detail all along the line is accumulative and the outcome is quite enormous in terms of effect on final profitability.

Break crop enterprise

The annual acreage of cereals increased during the 1960s and therefore some fields were cropped with cereals more frequently, often resulting in 'continuous' cereal growing, on some land for several years. This created various problems of both a husbandry and an economic nature and therefore many cereal growers searched in earnest for an ideal arable break crop which could be grown to help overcome these husbandry problems and at the same time produce a reasonable gross margin per acre.

Some farmers who went in for 'continuous' cereal growing consistently obtained good yields but many other cereal growers were not so fortunate. Several problems have been encountered such as the spread of wild oats and certain grass weeds (e.g. *Agrostis sp.* and couch) as well as a build-up of soil-borne fungus diseases such as take-all (whiteheads) and eyespot, and also a spread of foliar diseases, e.g. rhyncosporium (leaf blotch), mildew and yellow rust, whose spread was favoured by the increased cereal acreage. Furthermore, there has been a deterioration in soil structure and fertility on many fields as a result of over-cropping with cereals.

In addition to these husbandry problems there have been economic consequences. Cereal yields during the latter years of the 1960s remained rather static and over the same period both wheat and barley suffered a number of reductions in guaranteed prices and 'standard quantities' were also applied to each commodity. The overall effect was that levels of cereal gross output per acre did not increase very much in the 1960s. During the same period, however, levels of cereal variable costs and farmer's fixed costs did increase so that the final outcome was an inevitable lowering of net margins for cereal producers.

In an attempt to overcome both the husbandry and financial problems resulting from the increased cereal acreages, farmers looked for arable break crops that would solve all their husbandry problems and at the same time yield a high gross margin per acre, without upsetting fixed cost structures. Unfortunately, no single break crop exists that fulfils all these requirements. However, farmers have grown various break crops and a few brief comments on a number of them will now be made, together with a guide to the average levels of gross margins per acre that can be obtained from these break crops (see Table 7.13).

Beans

Beans are a legume crop and therefore supply nitrogen to the soil which can be utilised by the following crop. Beans also provide a break against soil-borne fungus diseases of cereals. While some weeds are controlled by using herbicides on the bean crop, grass weeds may continue to increase.

Table 7.13   Average levels of yields, prices and variable costs for some arable break crops

Arable break crop	Winter beans	Spring beans	Dried peas	Vining peas	Oil seed rape	Maize for grain*
Yield – cwt/acre	26–30	22–26	23–28	—	12–16†	27–36
Price/cwt (£)	1·375	1·375	2·35	—	1·9	1·25
Gross output/acre (£)	37·75–41·25	30·25–35·75	54–65·8	70–80	22·8–30·4†	33·75–45·0
Variable costs:						
Seed (£)	5·0	4·3	10·0	14·5	1·8	3·3
Fertiliser (£)	2·2	2·7	3·0	3·0	7·2	8·7
Sprays (£)	3·3	4·5	4·0	3·5	2·5	}5·5
Misc. (£)	—	—	1·0	—	—	
Total variable costs (£)	10·5	11·5	18·0	21·0	11·5	17·5
Gross margin/acre (£)	27·25–30·75	18·75–24·25	36–47·8	49–59	11·3–18·9†	16·25–27·5

* Assumed drying is done on farm. If drying is done by contract this may be £4 per ton at 35 per cent moisture content

† The higher outputs generally apply to the winter sown crop

(*Source:* Nix, J., *op. cit.*)

Winter beans

Varieties are susceptible to chocolate spot, but because of their forward growth in the summer may avoid aphid attack. The protein content of different varieties is fairly consistent.

Spring beans

Spring beans are not so susceptible to chocolate spot, but are very likely to be attacked by aphids and in a bad season insecticide costs can be considerably more than those quoted in Table 7.13. Varieties do vary somewhat in protein content.

A grant of £5 per acre was paid for three years up to 1970 to encourage farmers to grow beans as a break crop.

Peas

Like beans, peas are also legumes and, therefore, improve soil fertility by fixing nitrogen in the soil. Peas provide a good break crop against soil-borne cereal diseases, but grass weeds and wild oats may continue to build up in the pea crop.

Dried peas (Marrowfat peas for processing)

Harvesting of the dried pea crop can be quite a problem, especially in a poor summer when the peas may be shed from the pods before being harvested.

Vining peas (for freezing and dehydration)

Vining peas are usually grown on contract and therefore the farmer wishing to grow this crop will need to be fairly near a processing factory. The capital involved in growing and harvesting vining peas can be high since either a mobile viner or access to a static vining machine is necessary. Labour costs are also high. Although the crop produces a good gross margin per acre, associated fixed costs are high.

Oil seed rape

Whilst this crop provides a break against soil-borne diseases of cereals, it does little to improve soil fertility or condition. Problems may be encountered with the seed shedding at harvest time, as well as the crop lodging. The very small seeds have to be dried down to 10 per cent moisture content for storage in bulk, and this, together with the problem of marketing the crop, may limit its usefulness to many farmers.

Maize

Maize can be grown for silage in England, south of a line from the rivers Humber to Mersey, with reasonable success. Maize for grain is rather limited to more southerly areas, mainly near the south and south-east coast. This crop affords a break against some soil-borne diseases of cereals; grass weeds and wild oats may be encouraged under maize. The growing of maize will do little to improve either soil condition or fertility.

Maize for silage

A yield of 15–20 tons per acre or more of settled silage can be obtained. When measured in terms of yield and starch equivalent per acre it is questionable whether maize is better than Italian or perennial ryegrasses whose aftermath can be used for further grazing or conservation, whereas maize produces only the one cut per year. It should be noted from Table 7.13 that the variable costs will be about £17 per acre as for maize grain.

Maize for grain

Maize for grain is limited to those areas where late spring frosts do not occur since frost damage can be serious in the spring and may also affect

I

yields in the autumn. Birds feeding on maize grain may be a real problem after drilling and also when the grain is ripening in the cob. Young maize plants are very susceptible to weed competition, especially in the early stages of growth, but this can be overcome by the use of pre-emergence herbicides. Unfortunately, both weed grasses and wild oats may increase where maize is grown.

Herbage seeds

For those farmers who can produce good crops of herbage seeds this is a very good break crop. Soil conditions and fertility is improved; some soil-borne fungus diseases tend to break down while land is down to grass (although certain grasses do act as host to take-all), and wild oats may be overcome to some extent. A range of average levels of gross margins that can be obtained is given in Table 7.14.

Table 7.14   Levels of gross margin per acre from herbage seeds crops

	Gross margin	Yield of seed
	(£/acre)	(cwt/acre)
S.22 Italian ryegrass	26–44	6·5–9·7
S.24 Perennial ryegrass	31–51	6·6–9·9
S.48 Timothy	36–58	2·1–3·1
S.215 Meadow fescue	33–53	4·1–6·1
S.143 Cocksfoot	27–45	4·0–6·0
S.123 Red clover	33–51	1·6–2·4
S.100 White clover	10–18	0·5–0·75
Kent indigenous perennial ryegrass and wild white clover	19–30	0·25 (WWC)–0·35 (WWC)* 2·0 (PRG)–3·0 (PRG)

* These are usually together in the same cut
(*Source:* Nix, J., *op. cit.*)

Broadly speaking, herbage seed production is a very specialised job and those who can do it well can obtain very good financial results. Crops grown for herbage seed can often be utilised by livestock, e.g. sheep, so the total gross margin for the crop will be greater than that of just the seeds harvested.

Other seed crops

Various other crops can be grown for seed production as a break in the cropping sequence where cereals predominate. Such crops are sugar beet seed, mustard seed and coriander seed. Production of crop seed is usually done on contract and the financial results are very variable; technically these seed crops may help to overcome some of the husbandry problems that arise from 'continuous' cereal growing.

Field scale vegetables

On the right type of soil, field scale vegetables make a good break crop and yield a good gross margin per acre. Since supply can easily exceed demand, growers should seek a contract to ensure a satisfactory price. A guide to likely average levels of gross margin per acre is given in Table 7.15.

Table 7.15   Field scale vegetables: likely gross margins

Crop	Likely average gross margin/acre
Brussels sprouts	£80–90 (allowing £40/acre for casual labour)
Brussels sprouts (quick freezing)	£90–100
Autumn cabbage	£65–75
French beans (for processing)	£45–55
Beetroot – main crop	£55–65
Carrots – main crop	£105–115
Onions	£80–90

(*Source:* Kerr, H. W. T., *Farm Planning Handbook*, University of Nottingham)

Root crops

Where root crops such as potatoes and sugar beet can be incorporated into a rotation these provide an excellent break against cereal disease; the residual value of fertilisers left for the following crop is quite high and these root crops afford the farmer a chance to combat both wild oats and weed grasses by inter-row cultivations or spraying. In addition, the gross margin per acre is likely to be fairly high. Further details of these root crops are given in the Potato and Sugar Beet Enterprise Studies.

Leys

Short leys are often used as a break crop in cereal production. Unfortunately, however, certain soil-borne fungus diseases, e.g. take-all, can live on the roots of certain grasses, e.g. perennial ryegrass and then attack cereals when the grass is ploughed up. Soil condition and fertility is improved under a ley and wild oats may be decreased by putting land down to grass. The gross margin which finally results depends upon the method of utilisation of the grass, and if this involves grazing livestock the density of stocking will be a most important factor. One- or two-year leys may be cut for hay and sold as a cash crop. Lucerne may be grown; it does especially well on light dry soils where it can be grazed or conserved but is usually left down for several years owing to the high cost of establishment.

Fallows

Some cereal growers may feel that where husbandry problems are particularly bad a field should be completely rested from cropping for a season – this is called fallowing. Fallowing a field should provide a farmer with opportunities to kill off grass weeds by cultivations and/or chemicals. Since no crop is grown there are no host plants for soil-borne fungus disease and, therefore, their life cycle is broken. Soil conditions may also be improved by fallowing.

Fallowing offers many advantages but unfortunately there is no direct output from it apart from the increased yield in subsequent crops. The cost involved in fallowing a field can be quite considerable. If an amount of fallowing is done on a farm in a year the overall farm gross margin will be tremendously 'diluted' by the fallowed acres that make no contribution.

General conclusions on break crops

When trying to decide whether or not to grow a break crop and when choosing the type of break crop, the following points should be considered:

1. The effect that the break crop may have on the labour on the farm – Will the present labour force cope with the break crop; can there be a reduction in the present number of workers or will more labour be needed to cope with the break crop?
2. What effect will the break crop have on machinery? Will extra specialist machinery be needed, or will the machinery already available on a farm be better used, e.g. peak demands for machinery might be spread?
3. Will the break crop have any effect on the variable costs of the following cereal crop, i.e. it may be possible to use less expensive sprays if certain weeds have been eradicated in the break crop year; fertiliser costs for the cereal following the break crop may be lower, e.g. where a cereal follows a legume break crop?
4. Will a cereal crop grown after a break crop produce higher yields as a result of the break crop?
5. What effect will the break crop have on the rotation of the farm, i.e. will the break crop fit into the present farm system or will a new cropping sequence have to be planned?
6. What effect will the introduction of a break crop have on the fixed costs of the farm business? While a break crop may produce a good gross margin per acre, e.g. vining peas, any subsequent increase in fixed costs must be carefully considered and the likely effect on the net farm income of the farm budgeted.

One of the problems of trying to evaluate the usefulness of a break crop is that beneficial effects may result over a number of years. A useful guide can be obtained by calculating a rotation or cropping sequence gross margin and comparing this with the gross margin that would result from a cropping sequence which did not contain a break crop over the same period of time. This has been done in Table 7.16.

Table 7.16   Rotation or cropping sequence gross margin

(*i*) *Cropping sequence gross margin (no break crop)*

Year	Crop	Gross margin (£)/acre
1	Spring barley	33
2	Spring barley	31
3	Spring barley	29
4	Spring barley	28
5	Spring barley	28
	Total	149

Average/year = 29·8

(*ii*) *Cropping sequence gross margin (break crop – spring beans)*

Year	Crop	Gross margin (£)/acre
1	Beans	25
2	Spring barley	35
3	Spring barley	33
4	Spring barley	31
5	Spring barley	29
	Total	153

Average/year = 30·6

(*iii*) *Cropping sequence gross margin (break 'crop' – fallow)*

Year	Crop	Gross margin (£)/acre
1	Fallow	0
2	Spring barley	35
3	Spring barley	33
4	Spring barley	31
5	Spring barley	29
	Total	128

Average/year = 25·6

Assuming that the level of fixed costs is not altered on the farm in Table 7.16, which could well be the case where beans are grown since the same machinery can be used for both barley and beans, and also for a fallow if a break is to be achieved by fallowing, then the better net margin over the five years came from the cropping sequence which included the beans break crop.

The potato enterprise

Most housewives regard potatoes as a daily necessity and therefore national demand remains fairly constant irrespective of price – i.e. there is an inelastic demand for potatoes. Although demand is fairly consistent, yields of potatoes are affected considerably by natural factors, e.g. rainfall, blight, etc., so supplies fluctuate and, therefore, the price the producer receives varies considerably from year to year. In the earlier years of this century fluctuation in price gave rise to the 'potato cycle' where acres planted were influenced by prices obtained in the preceding year or two. In more recent years there has come between the producer on the one hand and the consumer on the other the Potato Marketing Board, which attempts to ensure an adequate supply of potatoes each year by regulating acreages planted and absorbing, if necessary, excess potatoes in years of overproduction.

Human consumption of potatoes per person has altered very little in recent years – as shown by the figures in Table 7.17. Annual demand for potatoes is, therefore, fairly predictable, but supplies are variable from one season to another. The data in Table 7.18 indicates the variations in national average yields over recent years and it can be seen that these have been considerable. Even a small variation in yield per acre can have a substantial effect nationally, e.g. if the national acreage of potatoes is 650000 acres and a variation of 0·25 tons per acre (5 cwt per acre) occurs this would mean a change in national output of 162500 tons of potatoes.

The influence of seasonal factors on yields obviously creates an almost insurmountable obstacle to any attempt at the regulation of national output. However, the Potato Marketing Board set up in 1955 (under the 1931 and 1933 Agricultural Marketing Acts) tries to regulate the national output of potatoes, and makes this one of its main objectives.

The main functions of the Potato Marketing Board

1. Acreage control

In an attempt to prevent overproduction of potatoes in one year and scarcity in another, every potato grower who grows more than one acre of potatoes must register with the Board. Each grower is allocated a basic acreage each year. This has usually been based on the average acreage of the previous three years' plantings made by the producer. New growers can apply to the Board for a basic acreage allocation.

In certain years the Board may reduce, or increase, each registered producer's acreage – and this is called his quota acreage. Basic acreages have been reduced by certain percentages in the following years:

> 1961 – quota acreage was 90 per cent of the basic acreage
> 1968 – quota acreage was 85 per cent of the basic acreage
> 1970 – quota acreage was 95 per cent of the basic acreage.

Table 7.17   Human consumption of potatoes

Year	Pounds of potatoes/head consumed
1957–58	201
1958–59	195
1959–60	187
1960–61	198
1961–62	195
1962–63	198
1963–64	198
1964–65	195
1965–66	201
1966–67	199
1967–68	195
1968–69	199

(*Source:* Potato Marketing Board, *Potato Statistics Bulletin,* December 1968, and Annual Report, 1969)

Table 7.18   Potato producer and production statistics

Crop year (July–June)	1955	1957	1959	1961	1963	1965	1967	1968	1969
No. of registered producers (P.M.B.)	86 843	81 685	76 446	74 933	66 380	57 726	50 310	48 239	45 130
Basic acreage* ('000)	725	748	760	810	758	708	709	700	700
Acreage planted by regd. producers† ('000)	689	660	671	592	653	649	613	608	536
Total acreage planted in Gt. Britain‡ ('000)	757	709	719	628	687	679	651	640	571
Average yield (tons/acre)	7·3	7·1	8·6	9·0	8·6	10·2	10·1	9·8	n/a

* In 1967 and 1968 a registered producers' basic acreage was the average of the plantings in the three previous seasons
† 1967 and 1968 were 100 per cent quota years
‡ Different from line above due to small producers who are not registered with the P.M.B.
n/a = Not available
(*Source;* as for Table 7.17 for each year)

Each producer growing more than one acre of potatoes is charged a levy which is payable to the Board, on each acre planted. If a producer plants more than his quota acreage, then the rate of levy for the 'extra quota acres' is much higher. (In 1969 the levy rates were £3 per quota acre and £25 per 'extra quota' acre planted.)

About 95 per cent of the acreage of potatoes planted in 1968 was controlled by the Potato Marketing Board (see Table 7.18). The distribution of potato acreages between producers is such that a large number of 'small acreage' producers still produce a large proportion of the total crop, e.g. in 1968 89·3 per cent of the producers grew crops of under 30 acres and these, together, accounted for 44·4 per cent of the total national acreage.

2. *Control of the ware size*

The Potato Marketing Board can also regulate the amount of ware potatoes coming on to the market by regulating riddle size. Usually only bottom riddle sizes are stipulated, but top riddle size can also be set so that very large mis-shapen potatoes are removed, thereby further reducing the amount of potatoes coming on to the market.

3. *Market control*

In years when there is a surplus of potatoes, the Potato Marketing Board can enter the market and buy up any excess potatoes which farmers may wish to offer to the Board. These are purchased by the Board and usually dyed violet/blue in colour and are sold by the Board for stock feed, the loss being financed primarily by a deficiency payment made by the Exchequer to the P.M.B.

4. *Research*

The Potato Marketing Board conducts research into certain aspects of the potato crop. A research farm at Sutton Bridge in Lincolnshire is currently investigating various production, handling and storage techniques for potatoes.

5. *Publicity*

The Potato Marketing Board also undertakes certain publicity campaigns and general advertising of potatoes to promote various ways in which potatoes can be used by the consumer.

Factors affecting the profitability of the potato enterprise

Potato producers should be concerned with more than just the husbandry of potato growing; they should make it their business to be aware of factors which influence the net margin (or enterprise profit) of the crop. Of course, many factors do influence this final net margin. Some of these are outside the control of the farmer, but there are several others which are clearly within the farmer's control so he can influence considerably final profit margins derived from his potato crop. Recent surveys[1, 2] of potato production clearly show a wide range in final net margins from the potato producers covered by the surveys. A range of figures of gross output and variable costs for potatoes with the resulting gross margins is given in Table 7.19.

A summary of the most important factors affecting the net margin of the potato enterprise is given in Figure 7.d.

Table 7.19   Range of gross output, variable costs, and gross margins for potatoes

	Main crop		
	Low	Average	High
Yield (tons/acre)	8	10·5	13
Output (£)	120	158	195
Variable costs:			
Seed		28	
Fertiliser		13·5	
Sprays		5	
Casual labour		18	
Miscellaneous		5·5	
Total		70	
Gross margin	50	88	125

(Based on figures in Nix, J., *op. cit.*)

Factors affecting gross output of potatoes

The two chief factors influencing gross output are yield and price obtained for the potato crop. The influence of certain natural factors such as rainfall, soil type, etc., will cause variations in yields from year to year, but this must be accepted by the farmer. Many other factors that influence yields are, nowadays, within the control of the farmer. For example, incidence of pest and disease attack can be controlled to a large extent by the judicial application of fungicides and insecticides. Many other factors such as levels of nitrogen, phosphate and potash fertiliser applied to the crop, the variety planted, use of irrigation, date of planting and the seed rate (or seed

1 Dawson, E., *Potato Production in Yorkshire* – An Economic Study, University of Leeds, 1967, p. 15
2 Middleton, A. M. and Webster, J. P. G., *The Potato Crop in Kent*. Wye College (Department of Economics), 1967

Figure 7.d. Factors affecting the profitability of the potato enterprise

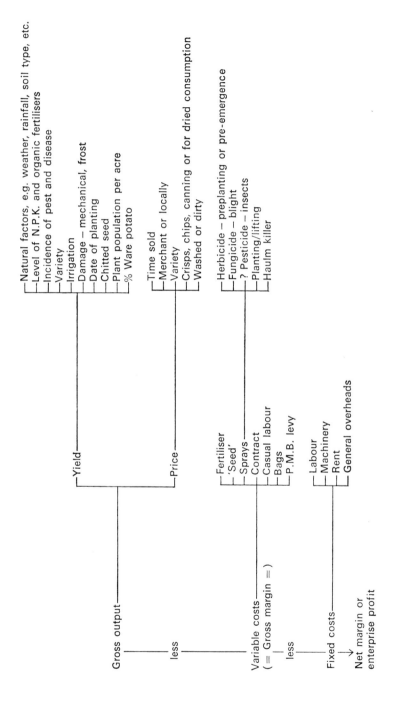

weight planted per acre), sprouting of seed before planting and also any crop damage, will influence final yields and are all controllable by the farmer.

Having produced the crop and even having got the sample of potatoes ready to sell, the farmer should remember that price as well as actual yield go together in the calculation of gross output. The actual price that will be obtained for potatoes in a particular year depends to a large extent upon the variety that was grown. Certain pink varieties, e.g. King Edward and Desiree, usually sell at a premium over white-skinned varieties. The size and the shape of the potatoes as well as flesh colour and the proportion of mis-shapen, cracked and damaged tubers in the sample will also influence price received, as will the selling of potatoes loose or pre-packed. In addition, the farmer's own bargaining ability should not be overlooked together with the natural variations in potato prices that occur in most seasons. A further important factor is the purpose for which the potatoes are sold – whether for 'seed' or human consumption, or perhaps in a glut year to the Potato Marketing Board to finally finish up as stock feed. The price actually realised for potatoes can also vary considerably, depending on whether they are sold to a merchant, direct to a retailer or at the farm gate direct to the consumer.

Levels of costs in potato production

Variable costs

From Table 7.19 it can be seen that the variable costs per acre incurred in the growing of potatoes is quite high. 'Seed' planted at a ton to the acre for maincrop varieties and up to 25 cwt per acre for earlies may well cost £30–£40 per ton or even more. Fertiliser applied to supply something of the order of 100 units nitrogen, 100 units phosphate and 150–180 units potash, may cost £13–£20 per acre. In addition there are various chemical sprays that are used – pre-emergence or pre-planting herbicides, fungicides mainly against potato blight, possibly pesticides against insects and also haulm killers; these together may cost £5–£10 per acre. Each grower, growing more than one acre of potatoes, must pay the Potato Marketing Board levy. Further variable costs are casual labour and contract work if used, as well as other smaller cost items, e.g. sacks or paper bags.

Fixed costs

The potato crop is an expensive crop to produce; in addition to the high level of variable costs, high fixed costs can be incurred when the crop is fully mechanised for planting and harvesting. Furthermore, this crop creates a substantial demand for labour even where a high degree of mechanisation is employed.

The guaranteed price arrangement for potatoes

When the average market price exceeds the guaranteed price of potatoes, then no deficiency payment is made. In fact, in most years the average market price has been higher than the guaranteed price and Table 7.20 shows that during the 1960s a deficiency payment was only paid in two years. In conclusion it must be reiterated that potatoes can be a very profitable crop but a fairly large amount of capital is involved in its production. Despite the far ranging effects of certain natural factors in some years on crop yields, the potato grower is, nevertheless, himself responsible to a large extent for the final financial success or failure of his crop. The fact that survey data shows a wide range in final profit margins suggests that many producers could achieve better financial results if they paid greater attention to the factors influencing potato production that are within their control.

Table 7.20   Guaranteed and average market price/ton of potatoes

	Guaranteed price	Average market price	Deficiency payment
	£	£	£
1960–61	13·0	11·708	1·291
1961–62	13·25	18·175	—
1962–63	13·25	17·904	—
1963–64	13·75	17·804	—
1964–65	14·0	14·070	—
1965–66	14·25	14·216	0·033
1966–67	14·5	19·350	—
1967–68	14·5	14·654	—
1968–69	14·875	15·50	—
1969–70	15·125	—	—
1970–71	15·875	—	—

The sugar beet enterprise

After the first World War, the Government encouraged the introduction of sugar beet growing into England by the payment of a subsidy. Therefore, during the 1920s and '30s sugar beet factories were built, mainly in the eastern part of the country, and sugar beet growing became established in those areas.

Today there are eighteen sugar beet factories under the control of the British Sugar Corporation and the annual acreage of beet grown is about 450000 acres. Each sugar beet grower must have a contract with the British Sugar Corporation's factory which covers his area. This contract contains a number of stipulations covering the price that will be paid for the beet, which is an 'annual review' commodity, crop rotation control so as to limit the spread of sugar beet root eelworm, arrangements for the delivery of beet to the factory and provisions for the growers' representative to verify weights, sugar contents, etc.

Any farmer in any part of the country, who considers his soil suitable for sugar beet growing, can approach the British Sugar Corporation for a contract to grow the crop. Obviously, proximity to a factory is an important consideration, especially since haulage costs will be incurred. After a contract has been drawn up, the factory will provide the seed, although the farmer chooses the variety and type of seed that he would like.

Undoubtedly the beet crop is a useful root crop in a rotation and provides an opportunity for the control of certain weeds, deeper ploughing, etc. When first introduced in the 1920s it was very demanding on labour for chopping out and singling, as well as keeping the crop clean and harvesting by hand. Nowadays, with precision drilling of monogerm seed, mechanical thinning of the crop, the use of herbicides and the mechanical harvesting of the crop the demand for labour is much less, but the cost of production is, nevertheless, still high. However, on soils where a good yield and a reasonable percentage sugar content can be achieved a good profit margin can result.

The British Sugar Corporation base payment for the crop on the weight of washed (clean) beet delivered to the factory and the percentage sugar content of that beet. In the 1970 Annual Price Review the price for sugar beet was £6·825 per ton at 16 per cent sugar content. This basic price is, however, adjusted with the percentage sugar content of the beet:

For each 0·1 per cent sugar content above 16·0 per cent the price per ton of washed beet is increased by £0·05.

For each 0·1 per cent sugar content below 16·0 per cent the price per ton of washed beet is decreased by £0·05.

This modification of the basic price for sugar beet according to the percentage sugar content means that sugar content will considerably influence final profit margins. Unfortunately, there is little that a sugar beet producer can do to influence the sugar content of his beet. Broadly speaking, soil type and weather conditions, especially hours of sunshine, are the main influencing factors, all of which are outside the control of the farmer. This being the case, most farmers will set out to produce as high a yield as possible and hope for the best as far as sugar content is concerned. The effect of this 'weighting' of the basic price for sugar and the compensating effect of yields are shown in Table 7.21, where the different yields necessary to produce the same gross output at varying sugar contents have been calculated.

Clearly the implications of the figures in Table 7.21 are that increases in yields do compensate for low sugar content, but the extra yield required is quite considerable.

It should be noted that farmers are paid only for the amount of washed (clean) beet delivered to the factory. Deductions are made for dirt and top tare sent to the factory although haulage costs will have been incurred for this dirt and top tare.

Table 7.21   Examples of growers' returns for sugar beet at different percentages of sugar content

Yield/acre (tons)	% Sugar content of beet	Price/ton of washed beet received by grower	Gross output/acre
10·0	16·0	£6·80	68·0
8·718	18·0	£7·8	68·0
12·83	13·0	£5·3	68·0

Factors affecting the profitability of the sugar beet crop

Yield and price of beet are the main factors influencing gross output of the crop. Variable costs may be high where casual labour and contract work is involved. A range of output and variable cost figures is given in Table 7.22.

Table 7.22   Levels of output, variable costs and gross margins for sugar beet

	Low	Average	High
Yield (tons/acre)	10	13	15
Output (at 15·4% sugar, i.e. £6·5/ton)	65·0	84·5	97·5
Variable costs:			
Seed		3·0	
Fertiliser		11·5	
Sprays		2·5	
Casual labour		14·0	
Haulage (contract)	7	9	11
Total variable costs	38	40	42
Gross margin	27	44·5	55·5

Harvesting date will have an effect on final gross margin of the sugar beet crop. The later the crop is harvested the higher will be the yield of beet in most years. The percentage sugar content also increases as the autumn progresses, especially if the days are sunny, but falls somewhat in December and January time.

A systematic presentation of the factors influencing the profitability of the sugar beet crop is given in Figure 7.*e*. It has already been pointed out for other farm enterprises that comparison of gross margins must be done carefully, making sure that the same range of variable cost items is being

Figure 7.e.   Factors affecting the profitability of the sugar beet enterprise

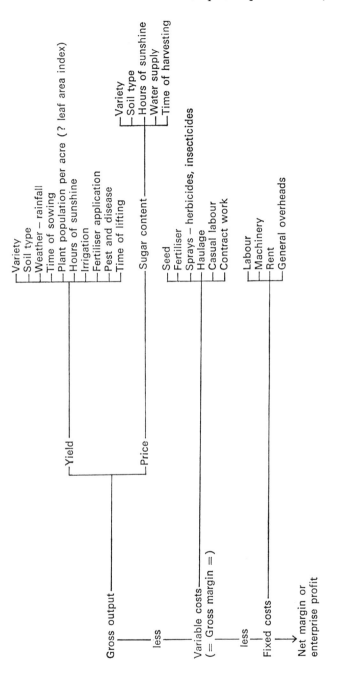

compared. In the case of sugar beet, casual labour and contract work may be involved in some cases and the inclusion of these costs will considerably influence the final gross margin figure.

For those farmers near a beet factory with suitable soil, the sugar beet crop can be quite profitable in most years. But for those farmers who have to pay high transport costs because of distance to a factory, their profit margins will be that much smaller. From the husbandry point of view beet provides a good root break and also affords opportunities for cleaning ground. The capital involved in mechanising the crop can be quite considerable, so the relevant fixed costs will therefore be correspondingly high. The result of this, of course, is a lower net margin.

The forage crop enterprise

Some farmers have changed their outlook on grass in more recent years, but the potential of the nation's grassland remains largely unexploited in many areas. At first this may seem to be a sad state of affairs since the total acreage of leys and permanent pasture (excluding rough grazing) is greater than that of arable crops, but on reflection the potential in terms of national production from grass is enormous. Indeed, those grass farmers who wish to maximise profits from their farm business must come to regard grass as a crop in the same way as they do barley or potatoes, rather than natural vegetation which just grows. The importance of a right outlook or philosophy on grass and forage crops cannot be overemphasised and the reasons for this will now be discussed.

1. *National acreage of grass*

The acreages of leys, permanent pasture and rough grazings in England and Wales in 1969 are given in Table 7.23, where leys and permanent pasture (excluding rough grazings) accounted for 47 per cent of the total area of farmed land in England and Wales. The area covered by rough grazings was a further 16·5 per cent, leaving 36·5 per cent of the total farm land in arable crops. If figures for the United Kingdom are examined, a large area

Table 7.23   *Acreages of arable crops and grass in England and Wales 1969*

	acres	%
Arable crops	10 519 000	36·5
Clovers and rotational grasses	3 552 000	12·3
Permanent grass	9 996 000	34·7
Rough grazings	4 764 000	16·5
Total arable crops, grass and rough grazings	28 831 000	100·0

of rough grazing in Scotland (about 12 million acres) considerably increases the percentage of land in rough grazings. In England and Wales, therefore, the total farmed area devoted to grass is greater than that covered by arable crops, and this reason alone should stimulate farmers to look upon grass as a crop of some importance, since it will occupy a large proportion, if not all, of the acreage of many farms.

2. *Forage crops – a cheap feed?*

Forage crops, especially grass, are a cheap source of feed for ruminant animals when compared with the cost of other feeds. Calculations of the cost per ton of Starch Equivalent from grass and other feeds indicate that in broad terms, purchased cake is four to five times the cost of grass grazed when compared on a cost per ton of S.E. basis. Even when conserved, grass still compares well with other forms of feed although the costs involved in its conservation will obviously make it more expensive per ton of S.E. than grass consumed by a grazing animal.

3. *Grass production and the level of sward management*

Perhaps one of the reasons why grass has been a 'neglected' crop in the past is that certain species will grow under almost any conditions found in the British Isles, whether managed intensively, extensively or given no attention at all. Obviously low yields result where little or no attention is given; if high levels of production are required, then very careful management will be necessary, and furthermore this will need to be coupled with a high degree of managerial skill so as to ensure good utilisation of the grass produced.

4. *National potential in grassland*

Figures from survey data show that the average level of nitrogen applied to grassland in recent years is still extremely low (see Table 7.24).

Table 7.24   Use of nitrogen fertiliser on grassland in England and Wales 1966 (units/acre)

	Overall average rate	*Average actual rate*	*Area treated*
			%
Temporary grass	53	71	75
Permanent pasture	25	54	46

(*Source: Fertiliser Statistics*, Fertiliser Manufacturers Association. 1967 Edition)

From Table 7.24 it can be seen that in 1966 only 75 per cent of the temporary (ley) grass area and 46 per cent of the permanent grass area received nitrogen fertilisers. Of those acres that did, only 71 units of nitrogen fertiliser per acre were applied to leys and 54 units of nitrogen fertiliser per acre to permanent pasture – indicating obvious scope on many farms for an increase in production from grassland.

Forage crops: efficiency of utilisation

Forage production techniques are fairly straight-forward and technically relatively simple. What is perhaps more important than its actual production is the efficiency of its utilisation. By the simple application of high levels of fertilisers, especially nitrogen, to any reasonable grass sward, high yields of forage output will result. Unless the utilisation of this is carefully planned – by using a high stocking rate per acre and an appropriate grazing system, or a carefully planned conservation scheme, a lot of grass produced can go unused – either soiled by dung or urine, trampled underfoot or just left as stemmy grass which animals refuse to eat. Utilisation by means of conservation is, of course, likely to be less efficient than by grazing animals, but the importance of defoliation of grass at the optimum stage of growth must be borne in mind, i.e. when the digestibility (or 'D' value) has not fallen lower than about 65.

It is essential, then, that those concerned with forage production are quite clear in their minds on these two aspects of forage cropping, i.e. production of the crop and its utilisation, and that they plan utilisation of forage as thoughtfully and thoroughly as they do the production and harvesting techniques for their other farm crops.

The economics of forage production

In considering the economics of forage production, it is necessary to survey the various factors that will influence yields of forage crops. These will now be considered:

1. *Type of forage crop*

Grass swards containing vigorous strains of grasses and clovers will respond well to high levels of nitrogen fertiliser and will produce high yields per acre – up to 1·5 tons or more of utilised starch equivalent. Certain crops, other than grasses and clovers, are also grown specifically for forage. Kale provides a useful 'green feed' in the autumn/early winter. Marrow stem kale usually produces the highest total yield per acre; thousand-head kale produces a good yield of leaf per acre and hungry-gap kale (curled leaf kale), although producing a lower total yield, can be grazed later in the winter since it is fairly frost resistant. Rape, which is a quick-growing brassica crop, is often grown for sheep grazing in the autumn. Because it grows quickly it rapidly covers the ground and is often sown on a field that has been fallowed during a summer. Certain legume crops, e.g. lucerne, produce high yields of forage and grow very well on dry soils, e.g. chalk, and are useful crops for conservation.

A guide to costs of production of various forage crops is given in Table 7.25. Although grass is in most cases a cheap form of feed, the use of expensive short-term ley mixtures, together with heavy fertiliser treatment, can easily result in a cost of more than £15 per acre, or over £20 per cow.

Table 7.25   Annual variable costs of production for some forage crops

	1-year ley (Italian ryegrass)	4-year ley (timothy, meadow fescue, white clover)	Intensive paddock grazing perennial ryegrass	Permanent pasture	Kale	Lucerne
Seed	30lb at £0·15/lb = £4·5	20 lb/acre at £0·25 ÷4 years = £1·25	25 lb at £0·25 ÷4 years = £1·56	Nil	4 lb/acre at £0·4/lb = £1·6	20 lb/acre at £0·4/lb ÷4 years = £2·0
Fertiliser*	5·0	5·0	17·00†	5·0	8·0	4·0
Sprays	—	—	—	—	3·0	—
Total	9·5	6·25	18·56	5·0	12·6	6·0

* On grassland this can obviously vary – £5·0 per acre is taken as an average figure
† Heavier fertiliser applications to paddocks

2. Level of fertiliser application

Fertiliser applications, especially nitrogen, can boost yields of forage crops and also influence the natural growth patterns of grasses, depending on the time applied. Obviously, as the level of nitrogen fertiliser applied to a sward is increased, diminishing returns set in, but the limited amount of experimental results available indicate that with efficient livestock utilisation, up to at least 400–500 units of nitrogen per acre can be applied over a season and marginal return still exceeds the marginal cost.

3. Natural factors

Many natural factors will influence forage production and the extent of their influence will vary from place to place and from year to year. Such factors as soil type, aspect of fields, rainfall, sunshine and degree of exposure to cold winds are all relevant factors here. There is little that a farmer can do to alter the influence of these factors on crop growth, but their combined effect may mean the difference between being able to begin grazing pastures in March as opposed to the end of April; to have an intensive rather than an extensive stocking density and to be able to produce late season bite 'foggage' and thereby delay the beginning of inwintering.

4. *The use of clovers in grass swards*

The inclusion of some clover in a grass sward is traditional; even nowadays very few farmers grow swards of grass which contain no clover at all. Undoubtedly clover can be useful in a sward in that it 'fixes' nitrogen in the soil and the companion plants in the sward benefit. Furthermore, the forage produced is higher in protein content because of the clover. However, when high levels of nitrogen fertiliser are applied the clover is crowded out of the sward. It is important therefore that farmers really ought to consider, when selecting a seeds mixture, the function of the sward that is to be established; if it is to be grazed extensively at a low stocking density, then clovers will be very useful and should be included in the seeds mixture. If, on the other hand, the sward is to be grazed intensively or conservation cuts taken several times during the year, high levels of fertiliser – especially nitrogen – will be applied, and any clover included in the seeds mixture will be simply a waste of money since very soon after establishment it will be killed out.

Utilisation of grass by grazing

Likely forage variable costs at different levels of stocking density for grazing livestock were given in the appropriate enterprise studies. When considering the intensification of stocking rates for any class of livestock it is essential to consider the financial effect of the proposed changes and their final effect on net farm income. By simply increasing the stocking rate on a farm from 2·0 forage acres per grazing livestock unit to 1·0, it does not mean that the gross margin per forage acre will be doubled. Some figures have been calculated in Table 7·26 to illustrate this point. Admittedly the gross margin per acre is much higher at the better stocking rate although the gross margin per cow is lower, but because of the higher forage costs per acre incurred at the more dense rate of stocking, the gross margin per acre is less than double that at the poorer stocking rate. The all-important factor of net farm income of the farm business must be remembered, and where intensification has occurred, considerably higher fixed costs may also result. This point must be watched carefully, otherwise the increase in fixed costs might be greater than the increase in gross margin.

The economics of forage conservation

Nutrient losses are inevitable whatever method of conservation is employed. Even the most efficient systems will incur a loss of about 5 per cent of the digestible nutrients in the material when cut. The actual loss of nutrients

Table 7.26   Levels of gross margin per acre for dairy cows at two stocking rates

	Extensive stocking rate (2·0 f.a./cow)	Intensive stocking rate (1·0 f.a./cow)
*Gross output/*cow	138	138
Variable costs:		
Feed	33	33
Vet. and medicines	7	7
Total variable costs (excluding forage)	40	40
*Gross margin/*cow (excluding forage)	98	98
Forage costs/cow at £4/acre	8 at £19/acre	19
*Gross margin/*cow after deducting forage costs	90	79
*Gross margin/*forage acre	45	79

will depend on the system of conservation employed and on the efficiency with which the work is carried out. Systems of fodder conservation which claim minimum losses of nutrients are generally those involving a very high investment of capital in buildings and equipment.

Any budgeting on forage conservation systems must consider the real cost (after allowing for charges on capital invested together with operational costs) of retaining these nutrients, in relation to the cost of providing the nutrients in another form, e.g. purchased feedingstuffs.

Sophisticated conservation systems are, in the final analysis, only justified if the material conserved is efficiently utilised by livestock.

Conclusions

Forage crops, especially grass, probably present the greatest challenge of all farm crops to farmers and managers, since different species are involved together with many other factors that influence productive levels. Within the broad compass of forage cropping, planning of the utilisation of forage crops is also involved and this is complex in that it needs to be geared to production which varies seasonally and from year to year. Utilisation of grass by livestock means the employment of capital, and shortage of capital may well be one of the reasons why there is under employment and poor utilisation of grass both nationally and on many farms.

8 | Past questions and some worked answers

A selection of past questions set in the City and Guilds of London Institute Examination in Farm Organisation and Management (No. 278), Stage III, is given below. Questions have been selected as representative of the types of questions set in past years and some worked examples of some of these questions (those marked*) follow later in this chapter. The year that the question was set and its number on the paper is given at the end of each question. In presenting this selection of past questions permission is acknowledged for their publication from the City and Guilds of London Institute, but the worked answers remain our own work and no responsibility for the accuracy or otherwise of these can be attributed to the Institute.

1970

1. Show how you might assess the effect of the change on your total net farm income, assuming you are a farmer in ONE of the following situations:

   *(a) Increasing the dairy herd by buying 20 cows and home rearing 12 young stock, whilst reducing the sheep flock by 130 ewes. Capital expenditure on buildings will be £1 600.

   *(b) You have lost your contract for growing 40 acres of sugar beet. You will increase your cereal acreage, and be able to sell some sugar beet equipment for £300.　　　　　　　　　　　　　(1970　No. 2)

2. Write notes on TWO of the following:

   (a) Agricultural Wages Board.

   (b) 'Standard quantities' for certain agricultural commodities in the February Price Review.

   (c) Agricultural Mortgage Corporation.　　　　　　　(1970　No. 4)

3. (a) What are the main economic and husbandry factors in your district which influence the most usual system of EITHER (i) beef production OR (ii) cash root production?

   (b) Give reasons that would justify further capital investment in the enterprise you have described.　　　　　　　　　(1970　No. 5)

4. *Comment on the methods used in assessing how efficiently labour and machinery are used on a farm. *(1970 No. 6)*

5. For what farm business purposes are the following most suitable and likely to be available:
   (*a*) Merchants' credit
   (*b*) Bank overdraft
   (*c*) Bank loan?
   Give your reasons. *(1970 No. 7)*

6. How can a farmer seek to reduce the risks in his farming business? *(1970 No. 8)*

1969

7. The following figures were obtained from a 200-acre lowland farm. What further information would you require before considering any changes in the cropping or stocking of the farm?

	The farm	Regional standard
	£	£
Gross margin per acre from wheat	35	32
Gross margin per acre from barley	31	28
Gross margin per forage acre from beef	20	15
Gross margin per acre from potatoes	50	60

(1969 No. 9)

8. Write notes on TWO of the following:
   (*a*) Agricultural Mortgage Corporation
   (*b*) Central Council for Agricultural and Horticultural Co-operation
   (*c*) National Agricultural Advisory Service. *(1969 No. 6)*

1968

9. *(*a*) How can you calculate 'return on capital employed' for a complete farm business?
   (*b*) What are the difficulties in doing this for a single enterprise on a mixed farm? *(1968 No. 1)*

10. Show how you would decide whether to have any ONE of the following types of work done by a contractor or with your own labour and equipment:
    EITHER (*a*) harvesting of 80 acres of cereals
    OR (*b*) planting 30 acres of potatoes
    OR (*c*) rearing replacements for a livestock enterprise of your choice. *(1968 No. 2)*

1967

11. *A farmer employs two men, grows 70 acres of cereals and keeps 45 dairy cows and 35 followers on his 200-acre farm. He wonders whether he should put the whole farm down to grass, spend £4000 on new

buildings and equipment for the dairy herd and increase the herd to 80 cows and 50 followers.

If you were in his position what factors would you consider important in coming to a decision? *(1967 No. 3)*

12. Write notes on TWO of the following:
    (*a*) Pig Industry Development Authority
    (*b*) Egg Marketing Board
    (*c*) County Council Smallholdings *(1967 No. 7)*

1966

13. *Prepare a budget to help a farmer decide whether to have his 50 acres of cereals harvested by contract or to buy his own combine harvester.
    (1966 No. 3)

14. A farmer has 100 acres of cereals and also 240 ewes on 100 acres of grass. His grain storage is already used to capacity. He is thinking of intensifying his sheep stocking rate to about four ewes per acre. Do you consider the farmer should keep his present flock on a smaller acreage or increase his flock? Give your reasons. *(1966 No. 4)*

15. Write notes on TWO of the following:
    (*a*) Machinery syndicates
    (*b*) The Small Farm (Business Management) Scheme (1965)
    (*c*) N.A.A.S. experimental husbandry farms.
    (*d*) Government aid for hill farming *(1966 No. 5)*

16. *The following information was collected from a 120 acre lowland farm:

	The farm £	Regional standard £
Margin of milk sales over concentrate feed cost per cow	90	95
Milk yield per cow (gallons)	770	840
Average per cent dry cows	28	20
Gross margin per forage acre from the dairy herd	40	33

What do these figures suggest to you?
What further investigations, if any, would you make before deciding whether the management of this dairy herd should be changed?
(1966 No. 6)

1965

17. What factors should the farmer consider when planning investment in machinery for his farm? Give reasons for your answer. *(1965 No. 4)*

18. Describe how the application of method study has affected the way in which any ONE farm product is produced. *(1965 No. 8)*

19. Answer EITHER (*a*) or (*b*).
    *(*a*) A farmer is considering purchasing and farming a 120-acre heavy-land farm equipped with a cowshed for 40 cows. The price of the land

and buildings is £15 000. He has £10 000 in cash, his bank overdraft is limited to £4000 at 6 per cent per annum, and he can obtain a mortgage for £8000 at 7 per cent per annum. Would you advise the farmer to complete the purchase? Give reasons for your advice.

20. *(b) A farmer is considering purchasing and farming a 200-acre light-land arable farm with no grain storage facilities. The freehold price is £36 000. He has £15 000 of his own capital, and can obtain a mortgage of £18 000 at 7 per cent per annum and a bank overdraft of £8000 at 6 per cent per annum. Would you advise the farmer to complete the purchase? Give reasons for your advice. (*1965   No. 9*)

1964

21. In what ways might a farmer overcome seasonal labour 'bottle-necks' on his farm? (*1964   No. 3*)

22. The following information was collected from 150-acre lowland dairy farm:

	The farm	Regional standard
Milk yield per cow (gallons)	650	820
Calving Index (days)	380	370
Average per cent dry cows	30	20
Concentrates per cow (cwt)	26	19
Forage acres per cow	1·6	1·9

What further investigations would this information lead you to make in relation to this herd? (*1964   No. 8*)

1963

23. What are the main economic and husbandry factors a farmer should bear in mind when deciding upon the system which is most suitable for his farm of EITHER (a) sheep production OR (b) beef production? (*1963   No. 3*)

24. What information is required by a farmer to check the efficiency of his pig enterprise? He has a herd of 40 sows and fattens their progeny to bacon. (*1963   No. 7*)

25. *A pig farmer has enough accommodation for 40 sows and their progeny reared to pork. He now receives an extra £2000 capital. Show how he would decide whether to increase his herd or to put up grain storage for home milling and mixing of his food stuffs. (*1963   No. 9*)

1962

26. *(a) What are the main economic and husbandry factors which a dairy farmer should bear in mind when deciding whether to buy or rear replacement heifers? (*1962   No. 2a*)

*(b) What are the main economic and husbandry factors which a sheep farmer should bear in mind when deciding whether to buy or rear re-placement ewes? (*1962   No. 2b*)

27. A dairy farmer with 100 acres carrying 40 cows and their followers has bought an additional 15 acres of land. Show how he might decide whether it would be more profitable to increase his dairy herd or grow cereals on the extra acreage.   (*1962   No. 7b*)

1961

28. A 30-acre lowland dairy farm carried 10 cows and 11 followers in 1958. The present stocking is 20 cows. Explain how this change in stocking may have affected the net farm income.   (*1961   No. 2*)

29. Owing to cereal disease, a farmer must put an extra 40 acres down to grass on his 280-acre farm. Demonstrate how the farmer might assess the effect of this change upon his total net farm income.

(*1961   No. 4b*)

30. The following data were collected for the year 1960–61 on a 150-acre farm:

Stock	*Average number*	*Feed used*	*tons*
Cows	40	Home grown cereals and	
Other cattle	24	purchased concentrates:	
Sows	8	Cows	60
Poultry	50	Other cattle	4
		Sows	10
		Poultry	2·5
			76·5

Milk sales for the year	£5100
Milk produced	36200 gallons
Kale	15 acres
Grass	108 acres

Comment on the feed economy of this farm and suggest any changes you would make.   (*1961   No. 5*)

Farm organisation and management (Stage III) No. 278/2

Set problem: for the practical/oral examinations

The candidate will be expected to present an economic analysis of any data provided and compare the respective merits of the suggestions he makes in answering the question.

1963

Assume that the farm staff is reduced by one man. Draw up a comprehensive farm plan (including both annual income and expenditure and capital budgets) with the objective of minimising any reduction in present net farm income which this event might cause.

1964
Suggest ways in which the farmer might try to maintain or improve his present net farm income in the light of a 10 per cent increase in rent (or rental value), a 10 per cent increase in agricultural wages rates, and a 10 per cent reduction in the guaranteed price for the major sale product.

1965
You are asked to prepare a tender for the tenancy of the farm. Give details of the farming system you would carry out on this farm and present capital and income/expenditure budgets for the first three years of the tenancy.

1966
Assume that you occupy the larger of two farms, and that the smaller nearby farm becomes available for purchase.

Prepare a report upon the problems and profitability of amalgamating the two farms. Give details of proposed livestock, cropping and mechanisation and fixed equipment programmes. State the additional capital required, and also the effect upon the total profitability of the business together with income and expenditure budgets for the first three years of the new arrangement.

1967
Draw up a managerial report upon a proposed establishment of a machinery syndicate for three farms.

Details of the type of machinery and of the three farms involved will be given to you by your examination centre.

The management report should contain, among other things, recommendations concerning the provision and servicing of the capital, the procedure for allocating the machine to participants, and the economic effect of the scheme on any ONE of the participating farms.

1968
Assume that further capital has become available equivalent to 25 per cent of present live and deadstock valuation (at current prices).

Prepare a report in which you consider and evaluate three alternative ways of investing this money in order to increase farm family income. State which investment you would select and give your reasons. Investment outside the farm is excluded.

1969
Assume that you are the farmer. The prices of your main products are assumed to fall at the rate of 3 per cent per annum. Wage rates and the cost of living are assumed to rise by 3 per cent per annum.

Prepare a report how you would maintain your real income. Give details of changes in stocking and cropping and prepare capital and income and expenditure budgets for each of the next three years.

1970

Assume that the farm staff, already fully employed, is reduced by one man. Draw up a comprehensive farm plan (including income and expenditure, and capital budgets) with the objective of maintaining, or increasing, the present net farm income, with the reduced labour force. Assume that any new capital required is borrowed at 10 per cent per annum.

Worked examples for some of the questions from the list 1–30

1970 No. 2 – 1(a)

Show how you might assess the effect of the change on your total net farm income, assuming you are a farmer in the following situation:

Increasing the dairy herd by buying 20 cows and home-rearing 12 young stock, whilst reducing the sheep flock by 130 ewes. Capital expenditure on buildings will be £1600.

Introduction

This question asks for an assessment of the effect of the change on net farm income. This can be done by calculating and preparing a partial budget. In so doing it should be remembered that net farm income is the income to the farm for the year's trading and completely ignores any family labour. Since this question asks for the effect on net farm income, interest charges on capital should not be included in the partial budget.

In preparing a partial budget certain assumptions must be made:

1. The land that has been used by the sheep is suitable for the dairy cows, i.e. access, nearness to milking facilities, etc.

2. The capital expenditure of £1600 is sufficient to cover all the buildings and equipment necessary for the extra cows and dairy young stock.

3. The labour costs of the farm will not alter, i.e. that employed on the 130 sheep can be used on the extra cows and dairy young stock.

4. Other than the sale of sheep themselves, no other capital will be realised.

5. The farmer has access to the capital required to purchase the building and equipment (£1600) plus the extra cows: some capital will be generated by the sale of the sheep.

6. The stocking rate will be the same with the 20 extra cows and 12 Dairy Young Stock as it was for the 120 ewes:

$$130 \text{ ewes} \times 0 \cdot 2 = 26 \cdot 0 \text{ livestock units}$$
$$\left.\begin{array}{l} 20 \text{ cows} \times 0 \cdot 1 = 20 \cdot 0 \\ 12 \text{ D.Y.S.} \times 0 \cdot 5 = 6 \cdot 0 \end{array}\right\} 26 \cdot 0 \text{ livestock units}$$

Although the number of livestock units will be the same (26·0), the forage costs per acre might be greater for cows than sheep.

7. When the change has become effective all the necessary dairy young stock replacements will be reared at home (12 D.Y.S. = 5 heifers reared per year and these will replace 5 culled cows each year).

8. The 130 ewes would normally have been replaced with 30 gimmers and 1 ram per year.

9. Five heifer calves will be kept each year from the 20 extra cows, and these will be reared as replacements. This will leave 5 other heifer calves to be sold and 10 bull calves to be sold (assuming 20 calves (10 bull, 10 heifers) from these 20 cows). This has assumed that 20 calves will be reared from the 20 cows, where mortality can be estimated it should be allowed for.

PARTIAL BUDGET

20 extra cows + 12 D.Y.S. v 130 ewes + 4 rams

Extra costs	£	*Costs saved*	£
20 cows:		130 ewes + 4 rams:	
Feed – 20 tons at £30/ton	600	Feed at £1/head	134
Vet., med. and sundries at £7/cow	140	Vet. med. and sundries at £0·8/head	107
12 D.Y.S.:		Replacements:	
Feed – 5 heifers/year at £25	125	30 gimmers at £10	300
Vet., med. and sundries – 5 heifers/year at £3	15	1 ram	20
Annual costs on £1 600 building:			
depreciation $= \dfrac{1\,600}{10\,\text{yr}}$	160		
repairs and insurance $= 1\cdot5\%$	24		
? Extra forage cost to cows + D.Y.S. although stocking rate is the same as for sheep			
	1 064		561

Revenue foregone		*Extra revenue*	
Lambs: $130 \times 1\cdot5 = 195$ at £7	1 365	20 cows: milk at £140/cow	2 800
Wool: 125 fleeces at £1·5	188	Calves: 10 bull at £18	180
Culls: 28 cull ewes at £3	84	5 heifers at £12	60
1 cull ram at £5	5	Cull cows: $5 \times £60$	300
	1 642		3 340
Margin in favour of cows	1 195		
	3 901		3 901

Conclusions on the partial budget

Using the above levels of prices and performances, a margin in favour of the 20 extra cows and 12 D.Y.S. of £1 195 would result. The capital required for the 20 extra cows would be

	£
20 cows at £120	2 400
Buildings	1 600
	4 000

and the capital realised by the sale of the 130 ewes might be

		£
	130 at £6	780
plus	4 rams at £15	60
		840

So that the outlay for initial capital would be £3 160.

1970 No. 2 – 1(*b*)

Show how you might assess the effect of the change on your total net farm income, assuming you are a farmer in the following situation:

You have lost your contract for growing 40 acres of sugar beet. You will increase your cereal acreage, and be able to sell some sugar beet equipment for £300.

Introduction

This question asks for an assessment of the effect of the change on net farm income. This can be done by calculating and preparing a partial budget. When so doing it should be remembered that net farm income is the income to the farm for the year's trading and completely ignores any family labour.

In preparing a partial budget certain assumptions must be made:

1. The cereal to be grown, in place of the sugar beet, is winter wheat and the soil is suitable for this crop.

2. Since the farmer is increasing his cereal acreage, it is assumed that he already has a combine harvester which can deal with the extra 40 acres of winter wheat. Also, the farmer has cultivating, drilling and spraying machines for the extra acreage of cereals.

3. The farm labour is sufficient for the extra cereal acreage but there will be some saving in casual labour since beet is not being grown.

4. The beet tops were usually ploughed in as a source of green manure, and no financial value placed on them.

5. Extra initial capital will not be involved since the farmer already has sufficient equipment to cope with the extra cereals, unless he erects additional grain storage. Any interest yielded by the £300 capital realised by sale of beet equipment does not come into the calculation of net farm income.

6. Haulage of sugar beet is done by contractor and this cost will be saved when beet are no longer grown.

7. The machinery and power costs for both winter wheat and sugar beet are assumed to be the same.

8. The price of wheat grain is taken as £29 per ton including Cereal Deficiency Payment, Storage Bonus and Forward Contract Bonus.

PARTIAL BUDGET
40 acres winter wheat v. *40 acres sugar beet*

Extra costs	£	*Costs saved*	£
40 acres winter wheat		40 acres sugar beet:	
Seed: 1½ cwt/acre at £2·5/cwt	150	Seed: 6lb/acre at £0·5/lb	120
Fertilisers: at £5/acre	200	Fertiliser: at £12/acre	480
Sprays: at £1/acre	40	Insecticide: at £1·5/acre	60
		Casual labour: at £12/acre	480
		Contract haulage: at £10/acre	400
	390		1 540

Revenue foregone		*Extra revenue*	
Sugar beet:		Wheat:	
10 tons/acre – washed beet at £6·8/ton	2 720	Grain at 1·5 tons/acre at £29/ton	1 740
		Straw at 1 ton/acre at £5/ton	200
	2 720		1 940
Margin in favour of wheat	370		
	3 480		3 480

Conclusions

At these levels of costs, prices and performance the net farm income would increase by £370 if wheat were grown in place of sugar beet. Since £300 worth of beet equipment is sold, this capital sum could be invested in some other way so as to yield a return – say 10 per cent per annum = £30 per year; this sum would not, however, be included in the calculation of net farm income.

1970 No. 6 – 4

Comment on the methods used in assessing the efficiency with which labour and machinery are used on a farm.

Introduction

The various ways of assessing the efficiency of labour and machinery utilisation fall under the following headings:

1. *Labour and machinery efficiency measures for the farm business*

(*a*) *Technical efficiency.* Technical efficiency of labour utilisation is often considered to be the speed and thoroughness with which a worker does a particular job. Such criteria are rather intangible and therefore the calculation of a labour efficiency index is recommended. The total labour requirement (in standard man-days) is calculated for the whole farm, using average figures of labour requirement for each enterprise, and compared with the number of standard man-days actually available on that farm.

$$\text{e.g.} \quad \frac{\text{Number of standard man-days required}}{\text{Actual no. of standard man-days available}} \times 100$$

(*b*) *Economic efficiency.* The levels of labour and machinery costs per acre can be examined for the farm and compared with those for similar farms. Any comparisons must be made with great care since labour and machinery costs will be influenced by intensity of enterprise.

Measures of labour and machinery efficiency which overcome the weakness of the per acre measures, are labour cost per 100 standard man-days and machinery cost per 1000 tractor hours. These measures assess labour and machinery utilisation on a physical basis in relation to costs and although the 'standard' figures used in these calculations do not 'fit' all farms, the measures do, nevertheless, provide a useful comparison between similar farms.

The most important economic measure of labour and machinery utilisation will be their financial productivity in terms of net output per unit cost. It must be remembered that many factors do contribute towards the net output of a farm. If the net output of a farm is high enough, poor use of labour and machinery may be justified. If, on the other hand, there is a poor level of net output these measures will be low when compared with similar farms, yet the technical efficiency of labour and machinery use on the farm may be satisfactory. The reason for calculating net output per £100 labour and machinery together is that these are substitutionary resources, i.e. machines can replace men and costs on one may be high if costs on the other are low.

Each of these measures of economic efficiency of labour and machinery use has its limitations and deals with separate aspects of labour and machinery efficiency within the farm business. It is essential, therefore, that any conclusions drawn about labour and machinery efficiency on a farm should not be made until all the measures have been considered together. Any conclusions drawn from just one or two measures in isolation may give a false impression.

2. *Seasonal requirements of labour and machinery*

The seasonal labour requirements of a farm can be assessed by drawing a labour profile based upon average monthly labour requirements of each enterprise on the farm. These figures, when drawn as a histogram, will indicate when seasonal peaks are likely to occur and when general farm work can be fitted into the slacker periods.

Seasonal demands for specific machines can be determined by reference to average rates of working of various machines and correlating these with the acreages of particular crops being grown on a farm.

3. *Detailed examination of labour and machinery utilisation on farms*

A more detailed examination of labour and machinery utilisation can be made by the use of work-study techniques. These involve a detailed analysis of the way in which individual tasks are carried out and the time taken to do them. The chief function of work-study techniques is either to analyse farming jobs with a view to improving methods of work (method study) or to measure the time taken to carry out specific jobs which can be compared with average times (work measurement).

Work study techniques can lead to a better use of farm labour and machinery and better results should be achieved.

Many of these labour and machinery efficiency measures involve the use of average figures and care is necessary in interpreting such comparative measures in relation to particular circumstances of the farm in question.

Conclusions

Both labour and machinery are important resources on farms and comprise a large proportion of farmers' costs; therefore good utilisation of these resources is important and the measures described above should help to indicate whether or not good utilisation is being obtained.

1968 No. 1 – 9

(*a*) How can you calculate 'return on capital employed' for a complete farm business?

(*b*) What are the difficulties in doing this for a single enterprise on a mixed farm?

(*a*) Percentage return on capital can be broadly expressed as follows:

$$\frac{\text{Annual profit margin (excluding charges on borrowed capital)}}{\text{Capital employed}} \times 100$$

Since 'profit margin' can be expressed in many possible ways, e.g. net farm income; management and investment income; gross margin; net cash flow; and capital can also be considered in a number of possible forms, e.g. tenant's; landlord's; owner-occupier's; initial; average; marginal; there are numerous possible ways of expressing percentage return on capital employed. In management analysis the most commonly used measures are:

(*i*) *Percentage return on tenant's capital*

$$= \frac{\text{Management and investment income} \times 100}{\text{Tenant's capital}}$$

K

(ii) *Percentage return on landlord's capital*
$$= \frac{(\text{Rent less landlord's expenses}) \times 100}{\text{Landlord's capital}}$$

(iii) *Percentage return on owner-occupier's capital*
$$= \frac{\text{M.I.I.} + \text{rental value}}{\text{Owner-occupier's capital}}$$

(iv) *Discounted yield*

This is the rate of compound interest that equates the present value of the net cash flows of a business to that of the initial capital invested. This is approximately halfway between the rate of return on average capital and the rate of return on initial capital.

(b) The difficulties encountered in calculating a return on capital for a single enterprise are as follows:

1. Allocating a 'profit margin' to each enterprise. This involves accurate allocation of both outputs and costs to a single enterprise. Outputs are normally allocated by simple accounts analysis with suitable adjustments for valuation changes and transfers between enterprises. Costs are more difficult to allocate.

Variable costs can be allocated by means of careful and accurate recording. Fixed costs are less easily allocated since many of these items, e.g. rent, overheads, machinery costs, cannot be clearly divided between enterprises. Hence a system of arbitrary apportionment often has to be used, leading to difficulties in interpreting the results of enterprise costings.

Fluctuating incomes between different years and interrelationships between enterprises that cannot be expressed financially are further difficulties experienced in assessing a suitable profit margin for an individual enterprise.

2. Allocating 'capital employed' to each enterprise. This is difficult to allocate in many cases since 'capital employed' will be in two forms:

(i) Fixed capital – in breeding and production stock, buildings and equipment.

(ii) Working capital – Feeding stock, feeds, seeds, manure and running expenses.

The capital employed must firstly be assessed accurately by a reliable and realistic valuation of assets at any given time or for any given period. Capital requirements are likely to fluctuate where the enterprises are of a seasonal nature, in which case both 'peak' and 'average' levels of capital employment must be ascertained.

It is essential to state clearly the method of calculation used when expressing a percentage return on capital and great caution is necessary when interpreting such figures to ensure that like is compared with like.

1967 No. 3 – 11

A farmer employs two men, grows 70 acres of cereals and keeps 45 dairy cows and 35 followers on his 200-acre farm. He wonders whether he should put the whole farm down to grass, spend £4000 on new buildings and equipment for the dairy herd and increase the herd to 80 cows and 50 followers.

If you were in his position what factors would you consider important in coming to a decision?

Two considerations are most important:

1. Will the proposed change result in a better profit?
2. What extra capital will be required to make the change and is this available?

1. *The effect of the proposed change on profit*

This can be calculated by means of a partial budget in which it is assumed that:

(*a*) A slightly better stocking rate must be expected when compared with that already being achieved:

Present system		*Proposed system*	
45 cows × 1·0 L.U.s.	= 45	80 × 1·0 L.U.s. =	80·0
35 followers × 0·5 L.U.s.	= 17·5	50 × 0·6 L.U.s. =	30·0
	62·5		110·0
66 L.U.s. on 130 acres		110 L.U.s. on 200 acres grass	
= 2·0 FA/GLU		= 1·82 FA/GLU	

(*b*) The farmer has his own combine which is worth, say, £300 if sold.

(*c*) The farmer will do the same volume of manual work and therefore the present labour force will *not* be able to cope with the extra numbers of livestock.

This is shown by the following standard man-day figures:

	Present system S.M.D.		*Proposed system S.M.D.*	
70 acres cereals	2·0 S.M.D./acre =	140	None	—
45 dairy cows	10·0 S.M.D./head =	450	80 × 10·0 =	800
35 followers	0·5 S.M.D./head =	17·5	50 × 0·5 =	25
130 acres grassland	0·5 S.M.D./acre =	65	200 × 0·5 =	100
60 acres silage/hay	1·5 S.M.D./acre =	90	100 × 1·5 =	150
		762·5		1075
	plus 15% estate work	114·5	*plus* 15%	161
		877·0		1236
2 men + farmer × 292 man-days		= 876	3 men + farmer × 306 man-days	= 1236

(*d*) The acreage in barley is accessible to the dairy cows and the general farm layout will permit the proposed change.

PARTIAL BUDGET

To show the effect of the proposed change on profit

$$\left.\begin{array}{l}\text{200 acres grass}\\\text{80 cows}\\\text{50 followers}\end{array}\right\} \quad v. \quad \left\{\begin{array}{l}\text{70 acres cereals}\\\text{130 acres grass}\\\text{50 cows}\\\text{35 followers}\end{array}\right.$$

Extra costs

Cows: Feed 35 tons
     Vet. etc., $35 \times £7$
Followers ($= 8$ rep. units)
    Feed
    Vet. etc.
Forage: 70 acres fertiliser seed
Labour: 1 extra man
Buildings: Interest
$$\frac{£4\,000}{2} \times 8\%$$
Depn. $£4\,000 \div$ life
Interest on: extra cows
          extra replacements
? Annual cost of extra:
  Machinery
  Litter

Costs saved

70 acres cereals:
  Fertiliser
  Seed
  Sprays
  Miscellaneous

Revenue foregone

70 acres cereals
      grain
      C.D.P.

Extra revenue

from 35 cows
     milk sales
     calves
     culls
Interest on £300 combine

Note. The budget shows the items to be considered when the proposed change is completed. In effecting the change both extra cows and followers will have to be bought.

2. *Capital requirements*

Capital will be needed for:

      (*a*) 35 extra cows
      (*b*) 15 extra followers
      (*c*) £4000 for buildings
      (*d*) Any extra machinery needed
      (*e*) Seasonal working capital.

When the combine is sold some capital (say £300) will be generated.

Conclusions

If the capital is available, then the farmer can budget the likely effect of the change in profit as shown above, and may also estimate the marginal return on the marginal capital to be employed.

1966 No. 3 – 13

Prepare a budget to help a farmer decide whether to have his 50 acres of cereals harvested by contract or to buy his own combine harvester.

In preparing a partial budget to help a farmer decide whether to have his 50 acres of cereals harvested by contractor or to buy his own combine, the following assumptions are necessary:

Assumptions

(*i*) Secondhand combine harvester bought for £1000 to be kept for five years, and is worth £50 then.

(*ii*) Self-propelled, tanker-type, combine harvester.

(*iii*) Rate of working = 1 acre per hour (= 50 hr harvesting)

(*iv*) Repairs and spares – say 5 per cent of secondhand price.

(*v*) Assume farmer can operate combine himself.

(*vi*) Housing is available for combine.

EXAMPLE PARTIAL BUDGET: *50 acres cereals*
Secondhand combine at £1000 v. *Contractor*

Extra costs	£	*Costs saved*	£
Depreciation on combine = $\frac{£1000 - 50}{5 \text{ yr}}$	190	Contractor – 50 acres at £4/acre	200
		Contract drying costs, say – half crop dried at £2/ton (say 50 acres at 1·5 ton/acre = 75 tons)	75
Interest on $\frac{1}{2}$ capital = $\frac{£1000}{2} \times 10\%$	50		
Vehicle tax and insurance	10		
Fuel and oil, 50 hr at £0·125/hr	6·25		
Repairs at 5% of £1000	50		
	306·25		275

Revenue foregone		*Extra revenue*	
		Higher yield by combining cereals with own combine say – 0·2 cwt /acre extra = 10 cwt at £1/cwt	10
		Margin in favour of contractor	21·25
	306·25		306·25

Capital = £1000 for combine.

Conclusions

Under these conditions the margin in favour of using the contractor would be £21·25.

1966 No. 6 – 16

The following information was collected on a 120-acre lowland farm:

	The farm	Regional standard
	£	£
Margin of milk sales over concentrate feed cost per cow	90	95
Milk yield per cow (gallons)	770	840
Average per cent dry cows	28	20
Gross margin per forage acre from the dairy herd	40	33

What do these figures suggest to you?

What further investigations, if any, would you make before deciding whether the management of this dairy herd should be changed?

The most significant of these figures is the gross margin per forage acre. This measure of efficiency is the result of a number of contributory factors and, of the measures given, is the one most closely related to the net farm income.

The farm in question is superior to the regional standard in this respect in spite of a lower yield per cow and a low margin per cow of milk sales over concentrates.

The given material must therefore be examined closely.

Margin of milk sales over concentrates. This is low compared to the Standard. This could be due to either (*i*) low yield; or (*ii*) excessive use of concentrates.

Difference in yields is known. Must therefore try to calculate the difference in concentrates.

If the milk price per gallon is the same for the farm and for the regional standard, it is possible to calculate the amounts of concentrates fed in each case.

Therefore, if price/gallon = £0·15

	Farm			*Standard*		
Total receipts/gallon	$770 \times 0 \cdot 15 =$	£115·5		$840 \times £0 \cdot 15 =$	£126	
less margin/concs.		90·0			95	
Therefore value of concs. used/cow		£25·5			£31	
Concs. cost/gallon	$\dfrac{£25 \cdot 5 \times 100}{770} =$	3·31p		$\dfrac{£31 \times 100}{840} =$	3·69p	
lb. concs./gallon (if concs. are valued at £30/ton)	$\dfrac{£25 \cdot 5 \times 2240}{30 \times 770} =$	2·47		$\dfrac{£31 \times 2240}{30 \times 840} =$	2·8	

Then at the same milk prices the farm is using less concentrates per cow and per gallon than the regional standard.

Difference in margins over concentrates must therefore be due to low yield per cow rather than to poor concentrate usage.

The next figure of percentage dry cows gives an indication of the reason for low yield per cow per year since this is closely related to the calving index.

If Calving index is 365, cow dry for 8 weeks in 52.

Therefore average percentage dry $= \frac{8}{52} \times 100 = 16$ per cent approx.

If cows dry an extra month

Calving index is 395

and average percentage dry $= \frac{12}{52} \times 100 = 23$ per cent approx.

Therefore calving index on this farm is > 395

calving index on standard is < 395

and > 365

So difference in milk yields are largely due to calving index, i.e. low yield per cow per year rather than low yield per cow per lactation.

It is necessary now to decide why the farm has a better gross margin per forage acre than the regional standard.

This could be due to:

(*a*) Difference in cost of other purchased feeds.

(*b*) Difference in other variable costs, e.g. vet., medicines and sundries.

(*c*) Stocking rate on farm may be above average.

(*d*) Variable costs of forage production may be low on the farm.

(*e*) Replacement costs may be low on the farm.

This is however a comparison between a farm and a Regional Standard, and is not the same as comparing results of two separate farms.

Can therefore assume that the Regional Standard figures are not far from average figures and that any deviations from these averages are achieved by the farm in question and not by the regional standard.

Consequently the difference in results is unlikely to stem from changes in vet., medicines and sundries, or from purchased feeds other than concentrates, since the farm figures must be less than group in order to be significant and the average group figures for these costs are usually in the region of

	per cow
Vet. and medicines and sundries =	£7
Other purchased feed =	£5
i.e. max.	£12

This could, therefore, at maximum only cause a deviation of £10 per cow and is very unlikely to be as great.

Therefore differences are likely to be due to:

(*a*) Stocking rate

(*b*) Cost of forage

(*c*) Cost of replacement.

Must therefore know these in order to make a final decision.

Do these figures include young stock or not, as they refer to the total herd? If they do include young stock, then differences may be due to:

(*a*) Different proportions of milking cows and replacement stock.
(*b*) Valuation changes on young stock.
(*c*) Improved stocking rate on young stock.

1965 No. 9 (a) – 19

A farmer is considering purchasing and farming a 120-acre heavy-land farm equipped with a cowshed for 40 cows. The price of the land and buildings is £15000. He has £10000 in cash, his bank overdraft is limited to £4000 at 6 per cent per annum and he can obtain a mortgage for £8000 at 7 per cent per annum. Would you advise the farmer to complete the purchase? Give reasons for your advice.

		£
Capital required:	Land and buildings	15000
	50 cows at £100	5000
	Machinery, etc.	2000
		22000
Capital available:	Cash	10000
	Bank overdraft	4000
	Mortgage	8000
		22000

Capital is used to maximum in order to take on this farm.

Finance charge:
The business must generate sufficient income to provide the following:

	£
Living expenses	750
Bank interest	240
Mortgage interest	560
Capital repayment on mortgage over 20 years	400
	1950 (£16·25/acre)

N.B. No interest charge has been made on own capital since no actual payment will occur.

If the farm could carry 50 cows on 80 acres and grow a further 40 acres of winter wheat, the net farm income could be estimated as shown opposite.

Under these conditions sufficient margin is available to meet the finance charge and the investment would be viable. If the farm were unable to support this level of intensity, then the farmer would be ill advised to go ahead, unless he needed the land for its amenity value or as an investment with a view to capital gains.

	£
Gross margin	
50 cows at £80/cow	4 000
40 acres wheat at £30/acre	1 200
Total farm gross margin	5 200

	£	
less Fixed costs		
Machinery, fuel, repairs and depreciation at £8/acre	960	
Overheads at £5/acre	600	
Labour (1 man)	1 000	
	2 560	
Net farm income	2 640	(£22·0/acre)

1965 No. 9 (b) – 20

A farmer is considering purchasing and farming a 200-acre light-land arable farm with no grain storage facilities. The freehold price is £36 000. He has £15 000 of his own capital and can obtain a mortgage of £18 000 at 7 per cent per annum, and a bank overdraft of £8 000 at 6 per cent per annum. Would you advise the farmer to complete the purchase? Give reasons for your advice.

		£
Capital required:	Land and buildings	36 000
	Machinery	2 500
	Seed, ferts. and working capital	1 500
		40 000
Capital available:	Cash	15 000
	Mortgage	18 000
	Bank overdraft	8 000
		41 000

There is just sufficient capital to take on the farm.

Finance charge:

The business must generate sufficient income to provide the following

	£
Living expenses	750
Bank interest (£8 000 at 6%)	480
Mortgage interest (£18 000 at 7%)	1 260
Mortgage repayment over 20 years	900
	3 390

Plus taxation

N.B. No interest has been charged on own capital since this will not represent an actual payment.

This is equivalent to a net farm income of £16·95 per acre which would be extremely high for such land.

An estimate of likely Net Farm Income is as follows:

	£
Gross margin	
200 acres barley at £25/acre	5 000
Fixed costs	
Machinery (running costs of tractor and cultivation equipment)	1 000
Overheads	800
	1 800
Net farm income	3 200 (£16/acre)

At this level of gross margin the enterprise is not quite viable even though no labour is employed. Cereal growing on such a scale without grain storage would be extremely hazardous and a gross margin of £20 per acre would be more realistic, particularly since much of the work must be carried out by contract. At this level of profitability there is insufficient to cover the finance charge and the business would rapidly become insolvent, unless a suitable system could be evolved which would increase profitability without requiring further capital.

Unless the farmer has more of his own capital to invest, he would be ill advised to make this purchase, unless for amenity values or the possibility of future capital gains.

1963 No. 9 – 25

A pig farmer has enough accommodation for 40 sows and their progeny reared to pork. He how receives an extra £2000 capital. Show how he would decide whether to increase his herd or to put up grain storage for home milling and mixing of his foodstuffs.

Consider 1. Requirements of present system.
2. Storage requirements.
3. Cost of storage.
4. Number of sows rearing progeny to pork at same cost as storage.
5. Partial budget to show the better alternative.

1. *Requirements of present system*

$$40 \text{ sows at } 27 \text{ cwts} = 54 \text{ tons}$$
$$600 \text{ porkers at } 3\text{·}5 \text{ cwt} = \frac{105}{159} \text{ tons}$$

i.e. approx. 160 tons

2. *Storage requirements*

Assume following alternative ration:

70 per cent cereals;
15 per cent middlings;
15 per cent protein concentrates including minerals and vitamins.

∴ Grain storage requirement = 160 tons × 70 per cent
= 112 tons

Approx. 120 tons storage required

Assume middlings and concentrates can be bought when required and will not require storage for more than a few weeks.

3. *Cost of storage*

	£
120 tons at £12 per ton (bins in new building) =	1 440
Plus mill and mixing equipment and conveyors =	500
	1 940

4. *Number of sows rearing their progeny to pork that could be kept at same cost as storage entails*

Cost per sow: £

(*i*) Sow building   50

(*ii*) Fattening space – at 15 pigs per year at 3 batches per year, fattening space is $\frac{15}{3}$ space per sow
i.e. 5 spaces per sow at £12   60

(*iii*) Cost of sow   40

(*iv*) Capital in extra food and v. costs $27 \times 31 \times \frac{1}{2} \times \frac{1}{2}$ approx.   10

Total capital per sow   £160

Therefore number of sows kept instead of grain storage

$$= \frac{1\,940}{160} = approx.\ 12.$$

(5) PARTIAL BUDGET

120 tons grain storage v. *12 extra sows and progeny to pork*

Extra costs	£	*Costs saved*	£
Depn. grain storage, £1440 at 10%	144	Replacements on 12 extra sows,	
Depn. mixing equipt., £500 at £15%	75	3 sows at £40	120
Fuel and repairs, 120 tons at £0·10	12	Food costs at purchased prices:	
Loss of weight in grain, 2% = 0·5		1. on extra sows, $12 \times 27 \times £31$	502
cwt/ton at £20	60	2. on extra porkers, $12 \times 15 \times 3·5$	
Purchased concentrates:		cwt × £31/ton	976
24 tons protein, min. and vit. at		3. on present sows and porkers	
£60	1440	160 tons at £31	4960
24 tons middlings at £24	576	Other v. costs at £6/sow on extra	
Extra grain bought at harvest, say		sows	72
at £19 – 12 tons	228	Depn. on sow and fattening	
		buildings at 10% of (12 × 110)	132
	2535		6762

Revenue foregone		*Extra revenue*	
Sale home grown grain, 100 tons			
at £19	1900		
Sales: extra porkers, 12 × 15 × £12	2160		
Extra cull sows, 3 × £15	45		
	4105		
Margin (to cover extra labour			
costs and interest on capital in			
stored grain)	122		
	6762		6762

N.B. Physical considerations, e.g. labour, slurry, etc., may override these results

1962 No. 2 – 26(*a*)

What are the main economic and husbandry factors which a dairy farmer should bear in mind when deciding whether to buy or rear replacement heifers?

The main points to consider in answering this question are:

Numbers replacements required
    Level of culling – Yield obtained
                      Yield required
    Whether a constant or expanding herd
    Longevity and health of present stock.
Cost of rearing replacements
    Variable costs of rearing
    Alternative uses of land
        G.M. per acre rearing = £20–25
        G.M. per acre milk   = £45–60
    Replacements may utilise land which has no better alternative use.

Suitability of own breeding stock
  Breed
  Level of yield

Availability and price of suitable replacements if obtained elsewhere
  Age of replacements
  Time available to buy and negotiate for suitable stock. Good replacement stock usually scarce and expensive.

Possible alternatives, e.g. contract rearing

Disease
  Danger of buying-in disease, e.g. Salmonella, Johnes.
  Desirability of maintaining closed herd, e.g. Brucellosis eradication.
  Wastage rate usually higher with bought-in stock.

Availability of resources for either alternative:—
  For example, land, labour, capital.

Complementarity
  Scavengers after dairy cows.
  Use of by-products and second-quality fodder and grazing.

BUDGET

Rearing v. *Buying replacement heifers*

Extra costs	*Costs saved*
Cost of rearing:	Purchase of replacements
(*a*) Bought foods	
(*b*) Housing	
(*c*) Labour	
(*d*) Other variables, e.g. vet. and med.	

Revenue foregone	*Extra revenue*
Loss of income from reduced milking herd of land taken for rearing	Sale of spare replacements (if any)
Calf sales	

1962 No. 2 – 26(*b*)

What are the main economic and husbandry factors which a sheep farmer should bear in mind when deciding whether to buy or rear replacement ewes?

Numbers replacements required
  Level of culling and price of culls
  System of sheep farming
  Longevity of present stock
  Health of present stock
  Locality
  Age at first lambing
  Whether constant or expanding flock
  Breed.

Cost of rearing replacements
  Overwintering and agistment charges
  Value of fleece in first year
  Alternative uses of land – whether breeding stock the most profitable. Replacements will reduce size of main flock.
  Availability and cost of feed in winter
  Housing costs if necessary.

Suitability of own breeding stock
  Whether pure or cross bred flock
  Progeny may be unsuitable for breeding, e.g. fat lamb crosses.
  Selection from twins out of twins.

Availability and price of suitable replacements
  As ewe lambs
  As gimmers
  As ewes – cast for age
              culled
  Transport costs.

Need to be flexible and independent of market.

BUDGET

Rearing v. *Buying replacement ewes*

Extra costs	*Costs saved*
Wintering costs of replacements	Purchase of replacements
(*a*) Agistment	
(*b*) Bought foods	
(*c*) Housing	
(*d*) Other variable costs, e.g. vet. and med.	

Revenue foregone	*Extra revenue*
Loss of income from reduced breeding flock	Fleeces of lambs or hoggetts
Lamb sales	Lambs from ewe lambs

Appendix A

Capital budget for Littledown Farm for three years

A capital budget for Year 2 has been calculated on a quarterly basis and a further two years' trading, capital and personal requirements have been estimated on an annual basis.

In order to draw up these budgets additional physical information is required and Table 1.1 has been extended as follows to cover Years 4 and 5.

Table A.1   Littledown Farm: acres of crops – Years 1–5

Year	1	2	3	4	5
Winter wheat	25	20	30	40	45
Spring barley	60	65	65	60	60
Main crop potatoes	15	15	15	15	15
Leys	150	150	140	135	130
Permanent pasture	50	50	50	50	50
Total	300	300	300	300	300

During Years 3 and 4 it is intended that the following changes in the livestock enterprises should be made:

(*a*) Increase the dairy cows to 75.

(*b*) Increase the sows to 30.

(*c*) Reduce the ewe flock to 120.

Reconciliation of livestock numbers for Years 3 and 4 will be as shown in Tables A.2 and A.3.

The increase in numbers of milking cows requires no additional capital investment. The additional sows do however require extra accommodation which is provided as a tenant's fixture in Year 4.

The budget in Table A.5 shows the effect of three years' trading on the farm's cash position as reflected ultimately by the cumulative bank overdraft.

Table A.2   Littledown Farm: livestock numbers – Year 3

Enterprise	Opening number	Purchased	Trans-ferred in	Died	Sold	Trans-ferred out	Closing number	Average over year
Dairy cows	72	—	16	2	14	—	72	72
Ewes	152	30	—	6	36	—	140	146
Rams	4	1	—	—	1	—	4	4
Sows	18	8	—	1	5	—	20	19
Boars	1	—	—	—	—	—	1	1
Dairy young stock:								
0–1 year	16	—	18	—	—	16	18	17
1–2 years	16	—	16	—	—	16	16	16
2–2½ years	8	—	16	—	—	16	8	8

Table A.3   Littledown Farm: livestock numbers – Year 4

Enterprise	Opening number	Purchased	Trans-ferred in	Died	Sold	Trans-ferred out	Closing number	Average over year
Dairy cows	72	3	16	2	14	—	75	73·5
Ewes	140	20	—	5	35	—	120	130
Rams	4	1	—	—	1	—	4	4
Sows	20	18	—	—	8	—	30	25
Boars	1	1	—	—	—	—	2	1·5
Dairy young stock:								
0–1 year	18	—	18	—	—	18	18	18
1–2 years	16	—	18	—	—	16	18	17
2–2½ years	8	—	16	—	—	16	8	8

Table A.4   Littledown Farm: Cereals sales – Years 3 and 4

	o.v.	Grown		Fed	Sold	o.v.
	£		£	£	£	£
Year 3						
Wheat	945	30 acres × 35 cwt at £24/ton	1260	—	960*	1260
Barley	1440	65 acres × 30 cwt at £20/ton	1950	1200	700	1490
Year 4						
Wheat	1260	40 acres × 35 cwt at £24/ton	1680	—	1250*	1680
Barley	1490	60 acres × 30 cwt at £20/ton	1800	1300	800	1190

* Wheat sold for price different from the opening valuation, which is often the case in reality

Table A.5 Littledown Farm: Cash-flow budget – Years 2–4

(a) Trading cash flow

SALES AND RECEIPTS

Year 2

Item	£	£
Dairy cows, 17 at £55		935
Calves: 36 bulls at £14		644
14 heifers at £10		
Milk, 71 at 753 gal at £0·150		8032
Sheep: 33 ewes at £4	132	
1 ram at £5	5	
		137
Lambs: 170 at £7	1190	
25 at £5 store	125	
		1315
Wool		200
Sows, 8 culls at £15		120
Pigs, 320 weaners at £6		1920
Wheat		1127
Barley		651
C.D.P. wheat		276
C.D.P. barley		300
Potatoes		2430
Fertiliser subsidy		400
Sundries		20
		18507

Year 3

Item	£	£
Dairy cows, 14 at £50		700
Calves, 50 at £12 av.		600
Milk, 72 at 800 gal at £0·154		8865
Sheep: 36 ewes at £4	144	
1 ram at £5	5	
		149
Lambs: 200 at £7·50	1500	
20 at £5	100	
		1600
Wool		200
Sows, 5 culls at £15		75
Pigs, 300 weaners at £6		1800
Wheat		960
Barley		700
C.D.P. wheat and H.G.C.A. bonus as estimated in Year 2 G.M. accounts		241
C.D.P. barley and H.G.C.A. bonus as estimated in Year 2 G.M. accounts		372
Potatoes		2250
Fertiliser subsidy		420
Sundries		10
		18942

Year 4

Item	£	£
Dairy cows, 14 at £50		700
Calves, 54 at £12		648
Milk, 73·5 at 800 gal at £0·154		9055
Sheep: 35 at £4	140	
1 ram at £5	5	
		145
Lambs: 180 at £8	1440	
20 at £5	100	
		1540
Wool		170
Sows, 8 culls at £12		96
Pigs, 360 weaners at £6		2160
Wheat		1250
Barley		800
C.D.P. wheat, 52 tons at £6		312
C.D.P. barley, 65 at £5/acre		325
Potatoes		2300
Fertiliser subsidy		440
Sundries		10
		19951

Table A.5 Littledown Farm: Cash-flow budget – Years 2–4

(a) Trading cash flow—contd.

EXPENSES

	Year 2			Year 3			Year 4	
	£	£		£	£		£	£
Heifers, 3 at £130		390	Heifers		—	Heifers, 3 at £140		420
Gimmers, 40 at £10		400	Gimmers, 30 at £11		330	Gimmers, 20 at £11		220
Ram, 1		25	Ram, 1 at £25		25	Ram, 1 at £30		30
Gilts, 7 at £35		245	Gilts, 8 at £35		280	Gilts, 18 at £35		630
Boar		—	Boar		—	Boar, 1 at £60		60
Conc. feed:	£		Conc. feed:	£		Conc. feed:	£	
72 tons D. cake at £33	2376		70 tons D. cake at £32	2240		75 tons D. cake at £32	2400	
4 tons calf food at £38	152		4 tons calf food at £38	152		5 tons calf food at £38	190	
8 tons rearing mix at £32	256		8 tons rearing mix at £32	256		9 tons rearing mix at £32	288	
1·5 ton sheep mix at £38	57		1·5 tons sheep mix at £38	57		1 ton sheep mix at £36	36	
3 tons Midds at £26	78		3 tons Midds at £26	78		4 tons Midds at £26	104	
4 tons Protein sup. at £60	240		4 tons Protein sup. at £60	240		5 tons Protein sup. at £65	325	
6 tons creep feed at £45	270	3429	6 tons creep feed at £45	270	3293	8 tons creep feed at £45	360	3703
Hay, 10 tons at £12		120	Hay		120	Hay		140
Straw, 30 tons at £6		180	Straw		180	Straw		180
Seeds		991	Seeds		931	Seeds		995
Fertilisers		2405	Fertilisers		2550	Fertilisers		2600
Sprays		174	Sprays		180	Sprays		190
Wages and National Insurance		2750	Wages and National Insurance		2900	Wages and National Insurance		3000
Casual labour		95	Casual labour		100	Casual labour		110
Fuel, oil, electricity		420	Fuel, oil electricity		440	Fuel, oil, electricity		450
Mach, repairs, tax ins.		660	Mach. repairs, tax, ins.		660	Mach. repairs, tax, ins.		700
Contract		180	Contract		160	Contract		140
Repairs tenant's fixtures		45	Repairs tenant's fixtures		40	Repairs tenant's fixtures		50
Vet. and med.		705	Vet. and med.		750	Vet. and med.		800
Haulage		40	Haulage		40	Haulage		40
Water		40	Water		40	Water		40
Rent		2300	Rent		2300	Rent		2300
Rates		100	Rates		100	Rates		100
Office and gen. overheads		450	Office and gen. overheads		470	Office and gen. overheads		500
P.M.B. levy		45	P.M.B. levy		45	P.M.B. levy		45
		16189			15934			17443

(b) Capital cash flow

SALES

Column 1

1 Tractor (trade-in)	450	
Milking equipment	60	
		510

Column 2

Pick-up baler (trade-in)	320	
1st instalment: investment grant tractor purchased Year 2	50	
		370

Column 3

Combine harvester (trade-in)	420	
2nd instalment: investment grant tractor (Year 2)	50	
Grant on sow buildings (40%)	160	
		630

EXPENSES

Column 1

1 Tractor	1000	
Milking equipment	150	
		1150
		-640
Capital repayments		1000
Capital cash flow		**-1640**

Column 2

New pick-up baler	670	
New trailer	230	
New forage harvester	440	
		1340
		-970
Capital repayments		1000
Capital cash flow		**-1970**

Column 3

New combine harvester	1575	
Extension to sow buildings	400	
		1975
		-1345
Capital repayments		1000
Capital cash flow		**-2345**

(c) Personal cash flow

RECEIPTS

	Column 1	Column 2	Column 3
Less Drawings	1125	1100	1200
Taxation	170	160	180
Interest	520	490	500
Personal cash flow	-1815	-1750	-1880

(d) Net cash flow = (a) + (b) + (c).

	Column 1	Column 2	Column 3
	-1137	-712	-1717
Opening balance	-863	-2000	-2712
Cumulative balance	-2000	-2712	-4429

Table A.6   Littledown Farm: Quarterly cash flow – Year 2

(a) Trading cash flow

SALES AND RECEIPTS

	Total	January–March	April–June	July–September	October–December
	£	£	£	£	£
Dairy cows, 17 at £55 av.	935	(2) 110	(4) 220	(8) 440	(3) 165
Calves	644	180	100	164	200
Milk	8032	2016	1916	1900	2200
Sheep	137	28	—	109	—
Lambs	1315	—	—	900	415
Wool	200	—	—	200	—
Sows, 8 culls at £15	120	30	30	30	30
Pigs	1920	460	480	480	500
Wheat	1127	1127	—	—	—
Barley	651	651	—	—	—
C.D.P. wheat	276	—	276	—	—
C.D.P. barley	300	270	—	30	—
Potatoes	2430	2430	—	—	—
Fertiliser subsidy	400	170	160	35	35
Sundries	20	5	5	5	5
Total receipts	18507	7477	3187	4293	3550

EXPENSES

	Total	January–March	April–June	July–September	October–December
Heifers, 3 at £130	390	—	—	390	—
Gimmers 40 at £10	400	—	—	400	—
Ram	25	—	—	25	—
Gilts, 7 at £35	245	70	70	70	35

(a) Trading cash flow—*contd.*

		Potatoes and barley	Ley mix	W. wheat	
Concentrates:					
72 tons D. cake at £33	2376	990	132	264	990
4 tons calf food at £38	152	76	19	19	38
8 tons rearing mix at £32	256	128	—	—	128
1·5 tons sheep mix at £38	57	57	—	—	—
3 tons middings at £26	78	20	20	18	20
4 tons protein sup. at £60	240	60	60	60	60
6 tons creep feed at £45	270	67	68	67	68
Hay, 10 tons at £12	120	—	—	—	120
Straw, 30 tons at £6	180	—	—	180	—
Seeds	991	711	190	90	—
Fertilisers	2405	1000	200	205	1000
Sprays	174	—	174	—	—
Wages and Nat. Ins.	2750	660	700	730	660
Casual labour	95	—	—	45	50
Fuel, oil and electricity	420	105	105	105	105
Repairs, tax and insurance	660	165	165	165	165
Contract	180	—	—	—	180
Repairs to tenant's fixtures	45	—	—	45	—
Vet. and medicines	705	200	150	180	175
Haulage	40	10	10	10	10
Water	40	10	10	10	10
Rent	2300	—	1150	—	1150
Rates	100	—	50	—	50
Office and general overheads	450	120	110	110	110
P.M.B. levy	45	—	45	—	—
Total expenses	16189	4449	3428	3188	5124
Net cash flow	+2318	+3028	−241	+1105	−1574

Littledown Farm: Quarterly cash flow – Year 2

	Total	January–March	April–June	July–September	October–December
(b) Capital cash flow					
Sales: Tractor	450	—	—	—	—
Milking equipment	60	—	—	—	—
	510	—	—	—	—
Expenses: Tractor	1000	—	—	—	—
Milking equipment	150	—	—	—	—
	1150	—	—	—	—
Capital repayment	−640	−640	—	—	—
	−1000	—	—	—	−1000
Capital cash flow	−1640	−640	—	—	−1000
(c) Personal cash flow					
Receipts	—	—	—	—	—
Drawings	1125	250	260	340	275
Taxation	170	—	—	—	170
Interest	520	20	250	40	210
Personal cash flow	−1815	−270	−510	−380	−655
(d) Net cash flow					
(a)+(b)+(c)	−1137	+2118	−751	+725	−3229
Opening bank balance	−863	—	—	—	—
Cumulative balance	−2000	+1255	+504	+1229	−2000

Although the bank overdraft increased considerably during this period, this does not necessarily mean that the budgeted policy is any less profitable than the existing one, since before Trading Profit can be calculated, allowances must be made for:

(*a*) depreciation
(*b*) valuation changes
(*c*) capital repayments
(*d*) private drawings and taxation.

Since £1000 is repaid annually to the loan account, and since capital purchases are made during the three years, it is likely that the farmer's equity will improve in spite of his increasing bank overdraft.

The quarterly cash-flow budget for Year 2, in Table A.6, shows how the capital requirement is likely to fluctuate throughout the trading year.

There is a good positive trading cash flow in the first and third quarter, with a small negative cash flow in the second quarter, due to the combined effect of low receipts and the half-yearly rent payment and a large negative cash flow in the fourth quarter resulting from heavy autumn expenditure on feedingstuffs, seed and fertiliser for winter cereals and rent, while the current year's harvest remains unsold.

When the trading cash flow (**a**) is combined with the capital cash flow (**b**), and Personal Cash Flow (**c**), the final or Net Cash Flow (**d**) indicates how the bank balance is likely to alter during this period. A predictable pattern is thus built up which can be of great value in planning short term credit requirements.

Appendix B

Table B.1 Discount factors for calculating the present value of future (irregular) cash flows

Year	Percentage										
	5	6	7	8	9	10	12	15	20	25	40
1	0·952	0·943	0·935	0·926	0·917	0·909	0·893	0·870	0·833	0·800	0·714
2	0·907	0·890	0·873	0·857	0·842	0·826	0·797	0·756	0·694	0·640	0·510
3	0·864	0·840	0·816	0·794	0·772	0·751	0·712	0·658	0·579	0·512	0·364
4	0·823	0·792	0·763	0·735	0·708	0·683	0·636	0·572	0·482	0·410	0·260
5	0·784	0·747	0·713	0·681	0·650	0·621	0·567	0·497	0·402	0·328	0·186
6	0·746	0·705	0·666	0·630	0·596	0·564	0·507	0·432	0·335	0·262	0·133
7	0·711	0·665	0·623	0·583	0·547	0·513	0·452	0·376	0·279	0·210	0·095
8	0·677	0·627	0·582	0·540	0·502	0·467	0·404	0·327	0·233	0·168	0·068
9	0·645	0·592	0·544	0·500	0·460	0·424	0·361	0·284	0·194	0·134	0·048
10	0·614	0·558	0·508	0·463	0·422	0·386	0·322	0·247	0·162	0·107	0·035
11	0·585	0·527	0·475	0·429	0·388	0·350	0·287	0·215	0·135	0·086	0·025
12	0·557	0·497	0·444	0·397	0·356	0·319	0·257	0·187	0·112	0·069	0·018
13	0·530	0·469	0·415	0·368	0·326	0·290	0·229	0·163	0·093	0·055	0·013
14	0·505	0·442	0·388	0·340	0·299	0·263	0·205	0·141	0·078	0·044	0·009
15	0·481	0·417	0·362	0·315	0·275	0·239	0·183	0·123	0·065	0·035	0·006
20	0·377	0·312	0·258	0·215	0·178	0·149	0·104	0·061	0·026	0·012	0·001
30	0·231	0·174	0·131	0·099	0·075	0·057	0·033	0·015	0·004	0·001	—
40	0·142	0·097	0·067	0·046	0·032	0·022	0·011	0·004	0·001	—	—

Table B.2 Discount factors for calculating the present value of a future annuity (i.e. constant annual cash flow) receivable in Years 1 to n inclusive

	Percentage										
Year	5	6	7	8	9	10	12	15	20	25	40
1	0·95	0·94	0·93	0·93	0·92	0·91	0·89	0·87	0·83	0·80	0·71
2	1·85	1·83	1·80	1·78	1·76	1·74	1·69	1·63	1·53	1·44	1·22
3	2·72	2·67	2·62	2·58	2·53	2·49	2·40	2·28	2·11	1·95	1·59
4	3·54	3·46	3·38	3·31	3·24	3·17	3·04	2·85	2·59	2·36	1·85
5	4·32	4·21	4·10	3·99	3·89	3·79	3·61	3·35	2·99	2·69	2·04
6	5·07	4·91	4·76	4·62	4·49	4·36	4·11	3·78	3·33	2·95	2·17
7	5·78	5·58	5·38	5·21	5·03	4·87	4·56	4·16	3·60	3·16	2·26
8	6·46	6·20	5·97	5·75	5·53	5·33	4·97	4·49	3·84	3·33	2·33
9	7·10	6·80	6·51	6·25	6·00	5·76	5·33	4·77	4·03	3·46	2·38
10	7·72	7·36	7·02	6·71	6·42	6·14	5·65	5·02	4·19	3·57	2·41
12	8·86	8·38	7·94	7·54	7·16	6·81	6·19	5·42	4·43	3·73	2·46
15	10·38	9·71	9·11	8·56	8·06	7·61	6·81	5·85	4·68	3·86	2·48
20	12·46	11·47	10·59	9·82	9·13	8·51	7·47	6·26	4·87	3·95	2·50
30	15·37	13·76	12·41	11·26	10·27	9·43	8·06	6·57	4·98	3·99	2·50
40	17·16	15·05	13·33	11·92	10·76	9·78	8·24	6·64	5·00	4·00	2·50

Table B.3 Repayments of capital and interest – Amortisation table
Annual charge to write off £1 000

Write-off period (years)	Rate of interest (%)									
	5	6	7	8	9	10	12	15	20	25
5	231	238	244	251	258	264	278	299	334	373
6	197	204	210	216	223	230	243	265	301	339
7	173	179	186	192	199	206	219	240	278	316
8	155	161	168	174	181	188	202	223	261	301
10	130	136	142	149	156	163	177	200	239	280
12	113	119	126	133	140	147	162	185	226	269
15	96	103	110	117	124	132	147	171	214	260
20	80	87	94	102	110	117	134	160	205	253
30	65	73	81	89	97	106	124	153	202	251
40	58	66	75	84	93	102	121	150	200	250

Appendix C

Agricultural institutions

There are a number of agricultural 'institutions' which are important and a number of them are vital for anyone involved in farm management today. The scope of this book does not permit a detailed account of these but a list is given so that students can familiarise themselves with further details of these organisations:

Advisory services

    Ministry of Agriculture Experimental Husbandry Farms
    National Agricultural Advisory Service
    Private Advisory and Consultancy Firms

Marketing boards

    The British Egg Marketing Board
    The British Wool Marketing Board
    The Hops Marketing Board
    The Milk Marketing Board
    The Potato Marketing Board

Other 'institutions'

    Agricultural Central Trading (A.C.T.)
    Agricultural Market Development Executive Committee (A.M.D.E.C.)
    Agricultural Wages Board
    Buying Groups
    Co-operatives
    County Council Smallholdings
    Machinery Syndicates
    Selling Groups
    The Agriculture, Horticulture and Forestry Industry Training Board
    (A.H.F.I.T.B.)

The Central Council for Agricultural and Horticultural Co-operation (C.C.A.H.C.)

The Home Grown Cereals Authority (H.G.C.A.)

The Meat and Livestock Commission (which now incorporates the Pig Industry Development Authority – P.I.D.A., and the Beef Recording Association – B.R.A.)

Appendix D

Agricultural legislation
Those concerned with farm management should be familiar with the main provisions of legislation relating to farming.

The main post-war legislation relating to farming in England and Wales
1947 AGRICULTURE ACT

Part I Guaranteed prices and assured markets
To secure *stability* in British farming capable of producing . . . 'such part of the Nation's food and other Agricultural produce as in the National interest it is desirable to produce in the U.K.'

Part II Good estate management and good husbandry
Legislative demand for *efficiency* in management and farming . . . 'That owners of agricultural land will fulfil their responsibilities to manage the land in accordance with the *rules of good estate management* and that occupiers of agricultural land fulfil their responsibilities to farm the land in accordance with the *rules of good husbandry*'.

Part III Agricultural holdings
Deals with the terms of tenancies, rents, tenants' fixtures, notice to quit, compensation for disturbance and improvements, tenant right.

Part IV Small holdings
Provisions of County Council smallholdings.

Part V Administration
(*a*) A.L.S.　(Agricultural Land Service)
(*b*) C.A.E.S.　(County Agricultural Executive Committees)
(*c*) A.L.T.　(Agricultural Land Tribunal)

1948 AGRICULTURAL HOLDINGS ACT
This Act consolidated the Agricultural Holdings Act 1923 and Part III of the Agricultural Act, 1947. The main provisions of the Act were:
(*a*) Provision as to contracts of tenancy.
(*b*) Provisions affecting relationship of landlord and tenant.

(*c*) Extenuating circumstances.
(*d*) Provisions as to Notice to Quit.
(*e*) Compensation for Disturbance and Improvements.

1957 AGRICULTURE ACT

Part I Guaranteed prices and assured markets
Limits set on the total maximum annual decrease of guaranteed prices.

Part II Grants for farm improvements and amalgamations
Grants for long term improvements of agricultural land (F.I.S. Farm Improvement Scheme).
   Grants towards costs of amalgamation to secure the formation of economic units.

Part III Development of the pig industry
P.I.D.A. (Pig Industry Development Authority) was established to develop certain aspects of the pig industry.

1958 AGRICULTURE ACT

Covers the following:

(*a*) Repeal of supervision orders, direction to and dispossession of owners on grounds of bad estate management or bad husbandry (sections 12–20 of 1947 Act, Part II).
(*b*) Rents determined in arbitration to be at average 'market' levels.
(*c*) Powers of Agricultural Land Tribunal.
(*d*) Control of injurious weeds.

1959 AGRICULTURE (SMALL FARMERS) ACT

   Introduction of a scheme of grants for increasing the efficiency of the small farm business:

(*a*) Field husbandry grants.
(*b*) A farm business grant.

1965 THE SMALL FARM (BUSINESS MANAGEMENT) SCHEME

The 1959 scheme was modified: grants available only to small farmers who are prepared to keep farm records. The 'size' of the business qualifying for these grants was changed.

1967 AGRICULTURE ACT

Part I Livestock and Meat Marketing
Provision for the setting up of the Meat and Livestock Commission.

Part II Farm Structure and farm improvements and the promotion of agricultural investment
Includes grants for amalgamations and boundary adjustments and grants for individuals relinquishing the occupation of uncommercial units.

Part III Hill land
Grants for benefiting these areas and the provision of Rural Development Boards.

Part IV Co-operative activities
Formation of the Central Council for Agricultural and Horticultural Co-operation.

Part V Miscellaneous
Various items including financial assistance to bodies making loans, grants for keeping farm business records etc.

1970 AGRICULTURE ACT

Part I Eggs
Arrangements for marketing and subsidy payments for eggs. Provision for the establishment of an Egg Authority, and the revocation of the British Egg Marketing Board.

Part II Capital and other grants
To modernise and simplify capital grants to the industry and to give further encouragement to farm amalgamation.

Part III Smallholdings
Some amendments to Part IV of the 1947 Agriculture Act and a restatement of many of the provisions of that Act.

Part IV Fertilisers and feedingstuffs
This part modernises the law on fertilisers and feedingstuffs, replacing the fertilisers and feedingstuffs Act 1926.

Part V Flood warning system in England and Wales
    (Part VI Scotland)
Provision of grants to river authorities to establish flood warning systems.

Part VII Miscellaneous Provisions
Relating to tied cottages, the Agriculture, Horticulture and Forestry Industry Training Board and the payment of its finances through the Annual Price Review.

Appendix E

Reference books for further reading

Agriculture, Horticulture and Forestry Industry Training Board (Latest edition): Training Grants Scheme.

BLAGBURN, C. H., *Farm Planning and Management*—Longmans.

BRADFORD and JOHNSON, *Farm Management Analysis*—Chapman and Hall.

CAMAMILE, G. M. and THEOPHILUS, T. W. D., *Records for Profitable Farming*. Hutchinson.

COOPER, M. MCG., *Competitive Farming*, Crosby Lockwood and Son, Ltd.

CULPIN, CLAUDE, *Farm Mechanization Management*, Crosby Lockwood and Son, Ltd.

DEXTER, K., and BARBER, D., *Farming for Profit*.

Farmer and Stockbreeder—Guide to Farm Prices and Grants (Latest edition).

FRASER, A. K., and LUGG, G. W., *Work Study in Agriculture*, Land Books.

HARVEY, N., *Farm Workstudy*, Farmer and Stockbreeder Publications Ltd., 1958.

HAYES, GORDON, *Farm Organisation and Management*, Crosby Lockwood and Son, Ltd.

HEADY, E. O., and JENSEN, H. R., *Farm Management Economics*, Prentice Hall.

KNAPP JOSEPH G., *An Analysis of Agriculture Co-operation in England*.

Ministry of Agriculture, Fisheries and Food:

At the Farmer's Service (Latest edition)
Aids to Farm Management:
   Arable Crops
   Beef
   Dairying
   Labour and Machinery
   Pigs
   Poultry
   Sheep

NIX JOHN, *Farm Management Pocketbook*, Wye College (Latest edition).

PEARCE, D. G., *Farm Business Management*, Oliver and Boyd.

PEARCE, J., (Ed.) *Farming*, Vol. 4, Caxton Publishing Co., Ltd.
WHETHAM, E. H., *The Economic Background to Agricultural Policy*, Cambridge University Press
Wye College, *Farm Business Statistics for South-East England* (Latest edition).
WYLLIE, J., *Farm Management*, E. and F. N. Spon Ltd.

Appendix F

Conversion factors for metricated measurements

Quantity	Existing unit	Metric unit	Unit symbol	Conversion factor
Lengths	mile	kilometre	km	1 mile $= 1\cdot609$ km
	yard	metre	m	1 yd $= 0\cdot9144$ m
	foot	metre	m	1 ft $= 0\cdot3048$ m
	inch	millimetre	mm	1 in $= 25\cdot40$ mm
Area	square mile	square kilometre	km^2	1 $mile^2 = 2\cdot590$ km^2
	acre	hectare	ha	1 acre $= 0\cdot4047$ ha (10000 m^2)
	square yard	square metre	m^2	1 $yd^2 = 0\cdot8361$ m^2
	square foot	square metre	m^2	1 $ft^2 = 0\cdot0929$ m^2
	square inch	square millimetre	mm^2	1 $m^2 = 645\cdot2$ mm^2
Mass (weight)	ton	tonne	t	1 ton $= 1\cdot016$ tonne (1000 kg)
	hundredweight	kilogramme	kg	1 cwt $= 50\cdot80$ kg
	pound	kilogramme	kg	1 lb $= 0\cdot453$ kg
	ounce	gramme	g	1 oz $= 28\cdot35$ g
Volume capacity	cubic yard	cubic metre	m^3	1 $yd^3 = 0\cdot7646$ m^3
	cubic foot	cubic metre	m^3	1 $ft^3 = 0\cdot02832$ m^3
	cubic foot	litre	l	1 $ft^3 = 28\cdot32$ litre (1000 litre $= 1 m^3$)
	cubic inch	cubic millimetre	mm^3	1 $in^3 = 16390$ mm^3
	cubic inch	millilitre	ml	1 $in^3 = 0\cdot01639$ litre
	UK gallon	litre	l	1 gal $= 4\cdot546$ litre

L

Index